ate Due

THE IMPERIAL SOVIETS

Books by

HENRY C. WOLFE

THE IMPERIAL SOVIETS

THE GERMAN OCTOPUS

HUMAN DYNAMITE

THE RUSSO-GERMAN ECONOMIC TIE-UP.

HENRY C. WOLFE

THE IMPERIAL SOVIETS

DOUBLEDAY, DORAN & CO., INC.
New York *1940*

PRINTED AT THE *Country Life Press*, GARDEN CITY, N. Y., U. S. A.

DK
267
.W6

31254

To Mother

Foreword

IN SPITE OF ALL that had been written about the Soviet Union, the Nazi-Soviet deal caught the American public unawares. We had been told that such a development was "unthinkable," that it could never happen. We had failed to approach the Soviet problem realistically. And unless we approach the Soviet enigma in a spirit of realism we may be due for more shocks like the one brought on by the Hitler-Stalin pact.

In presenting the background of Soviet imperialism it is important to devote considerable attention to Russia's relations with Germany. Germany is the other side of the Russian shield.

During the years which preceded the second World War some people said to me: "Say what you will about Hitler's regimentation, persecution and the other things you don't like, you must admit that he has put an end to the danger of Communism in Europe."

Still other people said something to this effect: "Granted that Stalin has treated the kulaks harshly, granted that he has wielded dictatorial powers and granted that there are some things in Russia that we Americans don't like, you will have to concede that Stalin and his followers are our protection against the further spread of Fascism."

Many of the very people who said that a deal between the Nazis and Soviets was impossible now say that the Nazi and Soviet revolutions have "fused." There is at present no sound reason for assuming that Berlin and Moscow have "fused" their revolutions. That may come later. But it is not likely to come until one of the revolutionary regimes can take the other over.

If we wish to understand the totalitarian extravaganza that is being staged from the Rhine to Vladivostok, we must realize that ruthless *Realpolitik* is the guiding factor in both the Reich and the Soviet. Each dictatorship has its long-range objectives and each pursues opportunistic policies in order to reach these objectives.

As long as the world revolution can best be served by co-operation with Hitler, Stalin will work with the Reich against the Allies. But if the time comes when it will serve the Soviet's world revolutionary program for Stalin to help the Allies against Germany, the Russian dictator will do just that. But whether he aids one side or the other, his policy is always the same: to play his enemies against each other.

As these lines are written the Kremlin's spokesmen are denouncing the "Anglo-French incendiaries of war." Yet it should not be a shock if Stalin were to make a deal with the British. He might do this to prolong the war. He might do it to insure the destruction of the Nazi regime and speed up the Bolshevization of the Reich. In either case he will not help the Allies for their sake; he will do it to further his own program of world revolution.

Possibly not even Stalin could tell us definitely what the

Soviet's exact policies will be a few months hence. They will depend not only upon the fortunes of war but also upon the internal social and economic conditions of the belligerent countries. A great deal will depend upon the rate at which the warring nations are "ripening" for revolution. A German defeat, for example, would undoubtedly sharply accelerate the "ripening" process in the Reich. A German victory, on the other hand, would retard the "ripening." Accidents play an important role in these developments. It is Stalin's fundamental policy to be prepared to take advantage of whatever conditions may arise from the war.

H. C. W.

Contents

CONTENTS

Maps

xiii

CHAPTER I

To Moscow

By LANTERN LIGHT one night in January 1922 I boarded the Moscow train at Riga. The lantern light proved to be the single convenience afforded by our ancient coach. There was neither heat nor water. There was only cold and dirt. Ours was the one first-class carriage on the train. The other five were third-class wagons.

Through the dim corridors and into the filthy compartments the baggage-laden passengers groped and stumbled. Ordinary luggage would not be adequate for the trip. Each passenger carried blankets, packages of food, a teakettle and a primus stove. Porters added to the disorder, groaning under bags and bundles, shoving one another aside in the battle for convenient depositing places, cursing and swearing in strange tongues. Third-class passengers tried to thrust their way into the carriage.

The train crawled out into the night. We could barely see through the grimy windows. Forced to face the squalor of the decrepit wagon, one of the passengers asked a Latvian official: "Why do you use such cars as this?" The Lett shrugged his shoulders. "If we allow any of our good equipment to go into Russia," he answered, "the Bolsheviks will keep it."

Some distance out the train creaked to an unexpected stop. Why were we standing so long in this bleak expanse of snowy steppe? Our wood-burning engine had run out of steam. We could not move until enough steam was generated to get on with the journey. Before the day was over we got used to these repowering stops. It took us twenty-five hours to travel one hundred sixty miles. It was eleven o'clock at night when we passed the Latvian-Soviet frontier. At the Latvian frontier station we were put through a tedious inspection of passports and baggage. Three unfortunate passengers were hustled off the train and detained by the border guards. Slowly the train started up again, dragging along at the pace of a man's walk.

In the darkness a half mile ahead a fire was burning. We drew abreast of it. In the light of blazing logs were outlined a sentry box and five standing soldiers. On the gable-like front of their strange high caps was a red star. We had reached the first Soviet outpost. The soldiers were wearing the famous Trotzky helmets designed by Leon Trotzky, then chief of the Red Army.

In those days the Soviet Union was closed to the outside world. Famine was starving vast areas of the country and a typhus plague ravaged the population. The civil conflicts were over, but in the U.S.S.R. wartime conditions still prevailed. Russia was almost as isolated as if Clemenceau's *Cordon Sanitaire* had continued to cut it off from the rest of the world. A Soviet visa could be had only on the most pressing business approved by the Kremlin, and even at that was difficult to obtain.

What was going on behind the curtain of mystery which separated the Soviet Union from its neighbors, the border

states? Western Europe and America were both fascinated
and repelled by the extravagant stories of Soviet intrigue
and violence. In London and Paris sensational rumors
were rife of strange, terrible happenings in Russia. No tale
was too fantastic. Friends bade farewell to the man going
into Russia as if he were sentenced to an exile from which
he would never return.

When Russian officials came aboard our train the next
morning an inquisitive passenger asked them why we had
to travel in such a filthy car. A Soviet inspector replied:
"If we permitted any of our good wagons to go into Latvia,
the Letts would keep them." So this foul train was shunted
back and forth between Riga and Moscow because no one
considered it worth stealing.

As the Soviet official finished his adaptable excuse for
our miserable train I felt the gaze of a fellow passenger on
me. I looked up to meet the twinkling eyes and knowing
smile of one of the two German merchants who shared the
compartment with me. They had been in Russia before
and knew the ropes. They spoke a little Russian and a little
English. It was they who showed me how to get clean snow
to make tea, how to delouse underwear by hanging it out
in the cold and other modus operandi that made travel in
such dirty, uncomfortable quarters bearable.

The other passengers were a Soviet diplomatic courier, a
Russian journalist, four Russian actresses, a Gypsy dancer
and her partner, three nondescript Latvian men and a
Russian whom we suspected of being a secret police agent.
Of these people the Germans were most akin to the West.
It was not only that they knew a little English. In this
atmosphere of chaos and decay their sense of order and
cleanliness drew me to them.

The Germans spoke little about themselves, but occa-

sionally they said something which indicated how widely
and well they knew Russia. They were familiar with the
Russian climate, geography, history, natural resources and
economy. Once when we were looking out a doorway over
an endless expanse of snow Herr Schmidt mentioned
Napoleon's retreat from Moscow. "You can see why
General January is still the greatest Muscovite military
genius," he remarked.

We had time for long discussions of Russia and its recent
turbulent history. How much did individuals influence the
course of Russian affairs? The Germans believed that if the
Tsar had had the vision to help alleviate the food shortage
by sending supplies to Moscow and Petrograd in the early
part of 1917 the revolution could have been postponed for
years. It might even have been avoided. They speculated
on the course of affairs in Russia had someone like Germany's Noske or Hungary's Horthy been at the head of the
revolutionary government which succeeded the Romanov
regime. About the part which the German Empire had
played in bringing about the Bolshevik revolution they
had nothing to say. There was no mention of the sealed car
in which the German General Staff sent Lenin and his
disciples across Germany to Russia (April, 1917) to Bolshevize the young Russian regime that was struggling to
establish the forms of democracy.

At one of the numerous stops the Germans and I got off
and entered a third-class coach. The state of that car was
unbelievable. Animals should not have been shipped in
such quarters. Sanitary conditions were indescribable.
There was no room even for the wretched passengers to
set up primus stoves. They huddled together to keep one
another warm. The stench was so acrid, so revolting that
it seemed to penetrate my brain. Back in our dirty first-

class coach the air smelled sweet and clean in comparison with that of the reeking third class. Just before we arrived at Moscow we heard that during the trip three passengers had died in the third-class coaches and one baby had been born. I have often wondered how imperial ambitions and ideological conflicts have affected the life of that baby.

The Russian actresses had lovely rich voices. They sang beautiful sad songs whose melodies told of long sunless winters, frozen rivers and dark forests and the loneliness of the steppes. One did not need to know the story; one could feel it. This haunting music was my introduction to the Russian temperament and the Russian philosophy of life. In some subtle way its Oriental undertones evoked echoes of that distant Russia which for nearly three centuries was subject to Mongol khans. Its strains called up the cultural heritage of the children of the "Golden Horde."

Tuesday passed and Tuesday night, Wednesday and Wednesday night, Thursday and Thursday night. On Friday morning it seemed little short of a miracle to pull into a station on the outskirts of the Russian capital. Our five-hundred-mile trip was over. We had averaged about six miles an hour from Riga to Moscow. We had seen something of Russian railway transportation, ever one of the weakest links in the rusty chain of Russian economy. And we now had some idea of what winter meant in that vast cheerless country. At the station I said good-by to the two German merchants.

When I came out of Russia a year later I went to Berlin. One afternoon I was walking through the lobby of the famous old Hotel Adlon. Suddenly I came face to face with one of the German merchants of the trip to Moscow. It was

Herr Schmidt. He was not wearing the mufti of a businessman. He was smartly turned out in the uniform of a colonel
of the German Reichswehr.

"Herr Schmidt!" I called. The officer stopped and shook
hands cordially. "When did you come out of Russia?" I
inquired.

He looked puzzled. "I have never been in Russia," he
slowly replied.

It was my turn to be surprised. "But surely you recall our
trip from Riga to Moscow a year ago."

"I have never been in Russia," he insisted quietly but
firmly.

"You are Herr Schmidt, aren't you?" I persisted.

"No, I am Colonel Schlesinger. But you are Mr Wolfe."

"I am, but I am certain it was in Russia that we met."

"An understandable mistake. But we met in Munich."

It dawned on me that the colonel was trying to avoid the
subject of Russia. Munich was a subterfuge to account for
our acquaintance. I had never been in Munich. But no
matter. The colonel claimed that he had never been in
Russia. So we sat down in the Adlon lobby and had a
pleasant hour's chat over the tea table. I would have liked
to ask him what he had found in Russia and whether he
would go back. But those questions would have been embarrassing as well as fruitless. So the subject of our trip
from Riga to Moscow never came up again.

CHAPTER II

Berlin-Moscow Military Co-operation

United, Germany and Russia are invincible. They complete each other in the happiest way.—COLONEL VON NIEDERMAYER, in the German military organ, the *Militärwissenschaftliche Rundschau*.

W<small>E DO NOT WANT</small> to have to fight the Germans again." How many times Russian officers used to tell me that! "The Germans have a superlative staff; their equipment is the best; and they have an efficient industrial machine to maintain their army. Moreover, the Germans are excellent strategists. It is suicide to attack them."

Russian memories of the World War generated in the Red Army hierarchy a determination to avoid, if possible, a conflict with the Reichswehr. Russian officers dreaded the possibility of pitting their clumsy masses of troops against the small, meticulously trained legions of the Reich. Russian officers apparently felt no hatred at all for their German compeers. As a matter of fact, the Russian military attitude was characterized by admiration for German arms. From the early postwar era Russian officers hoped

7

that a close liaison would develop between the German
and Muscovite military establishments.

This feeling was reciprocated by the German officers.
When Reichswehr officers talked about the Red Army
they expressed the belief that military co-operation between Berlin and Moscow would be beneficial to both.
"There is no limit to Russian man power," German officers
have said to me. "During the war we would destroy tens of
thousands of Russian troops, but hundreds of thousands
took their places. Russians can fight on empty stomachs,
without warm clothing, without adequate supplies. Under
the right kind of leadership they would be among the best
troops in the world."

To conservative German officers of the Versailles era it
mattered little that Russia had become a Communist state,
that the Red Army was sworn to world revolution. Most of
the professional German officers looked upon Communism
as a passing experiment. Even Karl Marx, they argued,
never expected to begin the Communist conquest of the
world in a backward, sprawling Eurasiatic Russian empire.
While the Russians were orating, experimenting with fantastic political and economic doctrines, shifting party lines
and killing one another off, the Red Army could be taken
in hand by the Reichswehr and prepared for the day when
it could be used by Germany.

The German officers who burned with resentment against
the Versailles treaty saw in the enormous man power of the
Soviet Union an instrument of revenge. They would build
of it a gigantic army that could conquer Europe. For the
youth of Russia would far outnumber all the recruits from
France, the French colonies and the British Empire. It
would make no difference if the Italians sided with the
French and British. Furthermore, the rapid increase of the

myriad Russian population could provide generous replacements for the German army, even for offensives on the
scale of Verdun. What a dream for proud military men
embittered by defeat, the humiliations of the peace treaties
and the Allied occupation of the Rhineland!

As for the Bolsheviks, their attitude toward the Reich
was a mixture of fears, hopes and realism. Emerging from
the long, bloody civil wars, the Russians were obsessed
with the conviction that they would soon have to withstand
more invasions from their enemies. To be sure, they had
defeated Kolchak, Denekine, Wrangell, Yudenitch, Pet-
lura and other anti-Soviet military leaders. The White
forces had been scattered and driven off the Soviet domains. But the Bolsheviks looked for an early renewal of
the interventionist drives. This expectation was partly inherent in the Communist conviction that capitalism was
dying, that a decaying capitalist world would attempt to
stave off inevitable collapse by making war on the Socialist
fatherland.

Lenin and his followers taught that the successful evolu-
tion of a Soviet republic would spell the doom of the capitalist nations. Russia would set an example for the proletariat in other countries. This would in turn arouse the
hatred of politicians and capitalists the world over. What
would be more natural than that they should unite and
attempt to destroy the new Socialist republic?

Furthermore, Moscow claimed that during and after the
World War the capitalist powers sought to get possession of
the wealth of Soviet territory. Had not Britain tried to
take the Caucasus with its rich oil preserves? Had not
Japan tried to steal the eastern provinces of Siberia as far
as Lake Baikal? French troops occupied Odessa. The
French encouraged the Poles and Roumanians to seize

large tracts of the Ukraine. In the north, so the Bolsheviks charged, Britain waged war against the Russians and attempted to set up anti-Soviet bases in Finland and Estonia. British troops landed at Murmansk and Archangel, and British monitors operated against the Soviet naval forces in the Gulf of Finland. The terms which victorious Imperial Germany had dictated to a Soviet delegation at Brest Litovsk in 1918 were merciless.

During the meetings at Brest Litovsk Trotzky had attempted to hold out against General Hoffmann's demands. But the German general would stand for no nonsense. The Bolsheviks could accept the capitalist Kaiser's terms or take the consequences. The Soviet delegation saw no alternative to acceptance of the dictated settlement which General Hoffmann brandished in his mailed fist. Just the same the Bolsheviks kept up their fraternization with the German troops and carried on constant propaganda which they hoped would undermine the Imperial German regime and pave the way for a Communist revolution in Germany.

In November 1918 came the collapse of the Central Powers in the West. For the Soviets that did more than drive the Kaiser into exile; it tore up the Reich-Soviet Treaty of Brest Litovsk. Moscow now looked upon defeated Germany not as an enemy bent upon restoring tsarism in Russia, but as a desperately sick country ripe for social revolution. In late 1918 and during 1919 there were fights in the streets of Berlin. German Conservative fought German Communist. Rosa Luxembourg, Karl Liebknecht and many of their Red disciples fell in the fighting. Other Germans died in Communist uprisings in Munich, Hamburg and Dresden.

But in spite of bitter clashes between Communists and anti-Communists in the Reich, the military leaders of

Berlin and Moscow were beginning to draw closer together. At bottom their relation was based on *Realpolitik* (practical politics). The postwar weaknesses of both nations, their common bitterness toward the victorious Allies and their economic need for each other were powerful motivation. Again, both countries hated Poland. The territory of this reborn state had been made up at the expense of the three great prewar empires of Russia, Germany and Austria-Hungary. The prospect of a Fourth Partition of Poland appealed to both Russians and Germans, to Communists and Conservatives alike.

Anti-French feeling was another bond. German officers commiserated with the Soviet as a victim of the hated Clemenceau's *Cordon Sanitaire*. Soviet officers pointed to the fact that the Reich had been stripped of its military power by the "Tiger's" France abhorred of Russia. Ironically enough, it was the reactionary military men who were the Russophils. The pacific German Liberals were thanklessly trying to reach an understanding with their late enemies in France and Britain. It was the fighting-mad German Junkers and industrialists who wanted to tie their country to the Soviet. German Liberals desired only to reach a modus vivendi with the Western democracies. And shortsighted Western politicians, in slighting their German liberal friends, gave much unwitting comfort and support to their bitter reactionary enemies.

Thus French pressure against the Weimar Republic actually played into the hands of the extreme reactionaries, the very men who were urging a Russo-German entente against the war victors. Although French and British observers realized that military co-operation between Berlin and Moscow was beginning, few in the governing circles in Paris and London appear to have recognized the factors

that were producing the strange and dangerous fellow-
ship between German Conservatives and Russian revo-
lutionaries.

Less than two years after the Armistice of the "war to
end wars" we find these uneasy thoughts expressed in the
influential *Temps* of Paris: "In the days long ago, when the
beaten Grand Army flowed back by way of Prussia with
the great Napoleon, General Yorck signed a treaty with the
Prussians at Tauroggen. Some months later, Russians and
Prussians entered Paris as conquerers and Napoleon left
for Elba.

"This alliance may be said to have lasted until the disgrace of Bismarck and it was this alliance which permitted
Prussia to attain her greatest splendor—from which it was
hurled by the mad policy of William II. His grandfather
had a presentiment of the catastrophe. On his deathbed he
urged the future Kaiser never to quarrel with Russia."

Only a few months after the Armistice M. Pichon, the
French minister of foreign affairs, told the Chamber of
Deputies of the European menace inherent in a Russo-
German coalition. On this occasion he quoted the "prophetic words of the Russian Socialist Sairnkoff that 'if the
Entente countries advocate abstention' from intervention
in Russia, 'there will certainly be one country which will
have a Russian policy—namely, Germany. The day Russia
awakes she will be the ally of Germany.' "

Foreign Minister Pichon's friends may boast of his
startling long-range prediction of the Berlin-Moscow coalition of twenty years later. But what, we may ask, did the
France of M. Pichon do to strengthen the position of the
moderates in Germany against their (and France's) enemies, the German reactionaries and Communists? It would
seem, on the contrary, that France did everything in its

power to weaken the salutary position of the German moderates.

In the early months of the postwar period thousands of Germans were employed by the Soviets. Some of these Germans were war prisoners who sought employment; others were demobilized veterans who came to Russia from the Reich; still others were jobless engineers and skilled workers. There was a sprinkling of German officers and German Communists. It was Germans like these whom the Allied intervention campaigns gave an opportunity to strike another blow at their old French and British enemies.

After the Soviet-Polish war (1920) the military understanding between Berlin and Moscow took a more definite line. The Reichswehr chiefs now set out to organize the Red Army in order to make it a genuine threat to the Western powers. Under German tutelage the Russians were able to start a new armament industry. Moreover, in the Soviet Union the Reichswehr hierarchy saw a theater of activity against the military restrictions of the Versailles treaty. In the U.S.S.R. German officers could gain experience and training by serving as instructors for the Red Army. In circumvention of the Versailles restrictions the Reich could establish in Russia schools for heavy artillery, aviation and tank warfare. In the Berlin *Vossische Zeitung* of August 1, 1920, Vladimir Burtzeff said: "The Bolsheviki organized their army with German aid."

On February 20, 1920, the Berlin Socialist *Vorwaerts* published an interview with Comrade Kopp, the newly appointed representative of Soviet Russia in Germany. Speaking of his country's relations with the Reich, Comrade Kopp stated: "No other government that could be substituted for it (the Soviet) would be as friendly toward Germany as the present one."

In this early postwar period the Red Army was rated by some critics as "an undisciplined horde lacking equipment and arms." By its friends and some of its frightened enemies it was described as "an invincible force ready at any moment to inundate western Europe." Both these appraisals were exaggerated. The Red Army which Trotzky organized was more than an undisciplined horde. It proved itself capable of beating the Whites and Allied interventionists. But it was invincible only so long as it remained on its own territory. Western Europe at that time had far more to fear from the Soviet's diplomacy, its "ideas" and its ability to play power politics than from its army.

The one foreign military leadership which had detailed and accurate knowledge of Soviet armed strength was the German military. This was true not only in the years which immediately followed the war; it was true more than a decade later in the years which followed Hitler's rise to power.

The reactionary Germans (Pan-Germans, Junkers, militarists and industrialists) could sum up their attitude toward Russia in this doctrine: "*Ich fresse dich, oder du frisst mich!* [If I don't devour you, you'll devour me!]" The German reactionaries were confident that they could devour Russia. Just the same these men were willing to gamble on the chance that they might fail, even though failure could mean a catastrophe for the Reich. This risk-all philosophy has a direct bearing on European affairs today.

War, to these German reactionaries, is the normal state of affairs. They take literally the words of Friedrich Wilhelm Nietzsche: "War and courage have done more great things than charity." They could applaud his brutal appeal: "Is not all life robbing and slaying?" In planning to use the human and material resources of Russia as revenge weapons against the West, the German reactionaries were putting into practice Nietzsche's preachment: "Ye shall love peace as a means to new wars—and a short peace more than a long."

When it was problematical in 1918–19 whether the Soviets could win their civil war against the Whites there were German reactionaries backing both sides. General Rudiger von der Goltz and his German troops fought the Bolsheviks in Finland (1918) and the other Baltic countries. Other German reactionaries were helping the Soviet armies. Thus the German reactionaries jockeyed for position between the Reds and Whites, striving to gain a dominating position in Russia, no matter which side might eventually be the victor. Come what might, they would be ready to mount the winning Russian horse.

As for the Soviets, their attitude toward the Reich has been just as ruthlessly grounded in self-interest and stark *Realpolitik*. Lenin and his followers hoped to Bolshevize Germany. Not only did they hope to obtain military instruction from the Reichswehr for the Red Army; they expected to use the Reich as the military spearhead of world revolution. Even five years after the war the masters of the Kremlin were confidently looking to the time when the Reich would be the second great state to give up capitalism and adopt Communism.

Had not Karl Marx and Friedrich Engels taught that Communism would come to advanced industrial nations in a decaying state of capitalism? The Weimar Republic, invaded in the Ruhr by the French (1923), buried under a deluge of inflation paper marks, beset with unemployment, struggling with a dearth of foreign markets, lacking means to purchase raw materials from abroad, threatened with civil war—here, indeed, was a country ready for the social revolution that Marx and Engels had prophesied.

Those were the days when you could walk along the Unter den Linden, drop a million-mark note in a beggar's hat and have it thrown back at you. The beggar could buy nothing with so small a sum of money. A single potato then cost hundreds of millions of marks. The inflation brought hunger and despair and violence to a republican Germany desperately trying to save itself from falling into the hands of reactionaries or Communists. It seemed then that the Weimar Republic could not long continue to exist. The wonder is that it was able to survive for almost ten more years.

But in 1923 the Bolsheviks did not expect it to last that long. That was the year when the Moscow *Krassnaia Gazeta* rejoiced: "The fire is burning very well. The German mark is rushing into the precipice with admirable speed, and all the efforts of the financial past master Hilferding are doomed to failure. Unemployment is growing; factories close one after the other. The economics of the cities are shaken to the root, and the deficiencies in the municipal budgets have attained amazing proportions. The famine and the severe winter are also under way."

In August 1923 the Berlin *Vorwaerts* charged: "Russia is sending millions (to the German Communists); and the Communist Strike Committee has just received from Moscow one million gold marks. The gold meant to promote the revolution is being supplied generously. Now we know where money needed for millions of placards, pamphlets, etc., comes from."

As for the strength of the Communist party in Germany, Zinoviev, president of the Third International, stated: "At the present time it numbers 300,000 members and is one of the best organized sections of the Third International. But what really matters is the influence it has acquired among the workers."

In a manifesto issued by the German Communist party (1923) we find an appeal for "the preparation of a general strike having as its objective the overthrow of the Stresemann Government, the formation of a government of workers and peasants, the seizure of properties and the control of production, a close alliance with Soviet Russia and a liquidation of the Ruhr problem at the expense of the bourgeoisie." A concrete example of how the Stresemann Government was squeezed between the French invaders of the Ruhr on the one hand and the Soviet and its German Communist allies on the other!

A scheme was launched for making the German Communists and monarchists allies against the coalition government. Authorship of this plan was ascribed to Karl Radek, the Soviet Union's most brilliant journalist, who visited the Reich in 1923. Support for the idea came from none other than Count Reventlow, an influential German monarchist leader. An article of his published in the *Rote Fahne* (German Communist newspaper) asserted that up to a certain point Communists and monarchists could be fellow travelers.

The *Vorwaerts* published a circular letter sent out to the Communist party members declaring that it was necessary for the party to obtain the co-operation of the monarchist extremists: "As soon as we do not need them," the letter explained, "we shall be able to get rid of them." Admitting that there might be some risk in this association, the letter proceeded to explain: "The danger that the reverse may happen, that is to say, that they get rid of us, is negligible, for political leadership will in any case remain in our hands." We see here an example of the same opportunism that was to blossom forth sixteen years later in the Nazi-Soviet deal.

An article of Radek's published in 1923 in the Paris Communist *L'Humanité* throws still more light on the Soviet attitude. Said this authoritative Soviet spokesman: "Soviet Russia will find itself confronted with a new threat if Germany is colonized, dismembered, strangled and exploited by Allied capital. Ruled by the Entente, Germany will give the Allies access to our frontier, to the frontier of the republic of workmen and peasants. This will be too great a temptation to the reactionaries to impose upon Russia a bourgeois restoration and to wrest from her payment of the debts of the old regime. Gaging the proportions of this danger, Russia sees herself obliged to say that there must be a limit even to her love of peace."

Ever since the World War Russian and German military leaders alike have feared that their respective countries were being menaced by "encirclement" (*Einkreisung*). France was lining up the small countries on the borders of Germany and Russia that would isolate the Reich and the Soviet from politico-economic support and military aid. At times the Russians feared that the Germans were being drawn into the "encirclement of the Socialist fatherland." At times the Germans suspected that the Western powers were about to draw the Soviet Union into the iron band of encirclement about the Reich.

But despite mutual fear, distrust and ill will on the part of the two outcast powers, we must not lose sight of the fact that from the early postwar era to the beginning of the second World War the entente between the German Army and the Red Army never died. There were times when it languished, but it was never extinguished. It lived on in spite of government changes in Germany and purges in Russia. If the military leaders of the Reich and the Soviet could have had their way, the co-operation would undoubtedly have been close and uninterrupted. But even in spite of interference from political bosses, the army men never allowed the old sympathy to die.

CHAPTER III

Russo-German Complementary Economies

THE MILITARY ENTENTE between Russia and Germany was antedated by the traditional economic bonds of the two countries. Six centuries ago the merchants of the famed Hanseatic League of northern European cities were pushing their commerce eastward into the hinterland of the Baltic and the Gulf of Finland. Hansa traders from Hamburg, Lubeck, Danzig and other German towns were reaching out for business into lands to the east that were inhabited by Slavic peoples. From Riga, Tallinn and other cities along the Baltic and the Gulf of Finland they traded with Russian communities. The Russian city of Novgorod on the river Volchor became one of their thriving commercial centers and a member of the Hanseatic League.

From western and central Europe the Hansa merchants carried manufactured articles and luxury goods to the Russians; in return they bought Russian furs, metals, honey, wax and other products of Muscovy. It was an exchange which benefited both parties economically and helped carry the culture of the West into the still primitive lands of the Russian tribes.

Long after the Hanseatic League had been dissolved enterprising German merchants continued to ply their trade in the Baltic area and in Russia. Some of the cities of Imperial Russia were dominated commercially by the German part of the population; German was as common a language in Riga and Tallinn as was Russian. Throughout the Tsar's empire French was the language of the Russian aristocracy, but German was the language of the commercial people.

When Russians saw a foreigner they were likely to assume that he was a German. Indeed, among many uneducated Russians the term for German (*nemetski*) came to be applied to all foreigners. By reason of their long commercial relations with Russia and the fact that a considerable German minority lived in the great Slavic empire, the Germans came to know Russia far better than did Englishmen, Frenchmen or Italians.

In 1913, according to an official German communiqué of February 12, 1940, the Reich took one third of Russia's exports and furnished approximately half of Russia's imports, "showing the natural way in which the German and Russian economies supplement each other." This was the trade balance the year before the World War.

At the end of the World War, let us not forget, Russia and Germany were prostrate economically. Both governments were bankrupt; both countries were blockaded; both nations faced starvation, unemployment and civil wars. The Reich had the problem of trying to restore order in a chaotic economic situation at home and of enlisting help from abroad. So did the Soviet.

In this state of affairs many citizens in each country looked to the other for help. Why not, they argued, since Germany and Russia have complementary economies? In-

dustrial Germany needed Russia's raw materials and agricultural Russia needed the Reich's manufactured goods,
especially machinery and medicines. To many students
of the situation nature seemed to have planned Russo-
German economy as an indivisible entity.

There is no way by which German soil can grow enough
food to feed Germany's close-packed population. Not even
the unsurpassed legerdemain of the German chemists and
the wizardry of the German agriculturalists have succeeded
in inventing an *Ersatz* to solve this problem. The Germans
must bring some food in from the outside. In order to pay
for the food imports the Reich must sell goods abroad.
Therefore she must have foreign markets. But unless Germany can buy raw materials and food abroad, fabricate
some of her imports into finished goods and sell them
abroad, she has no means of purchasing food to eke out
what she raises at home. Thanks to her foreign markets,
Imperial Germany had fed her subjects well.

After the war the Weimar Republic found itself confronted by economic bafflement. More than four years of
conflict had destroyed the foreign trade which Imperial
Germany enjoyed in July 1914. German industry and railroads were badly depreciated from war service and lack of
repairs. But replacements and goods for export were held up
for lack of raw materials. A vicious circle was in operation.

And the French fear of an economically powerful Reich
determined to gain revenge on France was a factor of prime
importance. The postwar blockade of Germany (1918–19)
was excused by its sponsors on the ground that it was "war
waged by other means." Moreover, the Treaty of Versailles
saddled defeated Germany with a fantastic reparations
load, a burden that could be carried even in part only
through the medium of German export trade.

Just what was the nature of postwar Germany's raw materials problem? Post-Versailles Germany lacked sufficient quantities of every mineral except potash and coal. She had about half the zinc required for her own needs but produced within her borders only small and inadequate amounts of copper, iron ore, lead, petroleum, wool and sulphur. There was no domestic supply of nickel, tin, manganese, rubber, bauxite, chromium, tungsten, antimony, mercury or mica. There was no cotton crop. Vegetable oils and fats represented urgent needs, especially for the fat-starved German citizenry.

In striking contrast to the raw materials poverty of Germany the Soviet Union ranks next to the United States in the extent of its self-sufficiency. It has an ample supply of two of the main essentials of manufacturing: coal and iron ore. Chromium, petroleum and manganese afford an export surplus. Although the Russian supplies of cotton, wool, mercury and phosphates may not be adequate for home consumption, they are considerable. And the U.S.S.R. has vast timber reserves, a fur trade and a gold-mining industry.

But here is where the Soviet Union presented an extremely weak side. Her transportation system was archaic. Her production methods were primitive. Her marketing system was poor. Her raw materials resources were undeveloped. Her industry was inadequate. She had few technical experts and skilled workers.

In German technical aid the Soviet leadership saw the means of rehabilitating Russian industry from the effects of the war and the civil conflicts, of starting the wheels of transportation rolling once more and preparing the Soviet Union for national defense. German machinery and instructors could help transform backward Russia into the first successful Communist state in the world. It was a prospect to intrigue the messianic Soviets.

The German industrialists thought of Russia in terms of exploitation. Properly managed, Russian natural resources and man power could provide German plants with raw materials and foreign markets. From the Polish frontier to the Pacific this gigantic land could become a vast *Absatz-gebiet* (raw materials reserve) and a market for the finished products of German assembly lines, looms and lathes. Here, indeed, would be the Reich's opportunity to win back the economic ground lost in the destruction of pre-war foreign markets and the forfeiture of colonies, the opportunity to win that back and more.

German Liberals and Conservatives together favored this economic integration with the Soviet. For the Liberals it offered a chance that the German unemployment problem might be solved; it offered the way for improving the lot of the masses and strengthening the economic life line of the fledgling German democracy. For the Conservatives, of course, it meant the eventual return of the old order. This Russo-German economic entente would accomplish what Imperial Germany had vainly tried to do after the ill-starred Treaty of Brest-Litovsk.

For the two "outcast" nations economic co-operation would help break the wall of Franco-British "encirclement" built up by the *Cordon Sanitaire*, the "hunger blockade," the intervention in Russia, the Allied occupation of the Rhineland, French invasion of the Ruhr and the power of French and British capital. It was an exciting outlook for more than one commissar in Moscow, for more than one industrialist in Berlin. Indeed, the promise of economic collaboration was the leitmotif of both capitals at the beginning of the year 1922.

CHAPTER IV

The First Rapallo

In APRIL 1922 the Reich and the Soviet threw their first joint bombshell. Together they exploded a politico-economic bomb which wrecked the Genoa conference. The bombshell took the form of the Rapallo treaty, named from the picturesque little Mediterranean town where the representatives of Berlin and Moscow reached their sensational agreement.

The preceding January, during the meeting of the Supreme Council of the Allies at Cannes, Prime Minister David Lloyd George of Great Britain suggested that an international conference be called. This conference would attempt to restore to Europe some measure of economic and financial order. It would try to untangle some of the skein of debts, reparations and loans which had tangled European international finance into a state of near-chaos. To this end it was deemed wise to invite to the conference not only the victorious powers and their associates, but the defeated nations and the Soviet Union as well. Invitations were sent, therefore, to Germany, Austria, Hungary, Bulgaria and the U.S.S.R. Altogether thirty-four nations would take part.

It should be pointed out that the debts and reparations problems were growing increasingly unmanageable. The Reich and the Soviet, the two chief debtors, were deluged by their own printing-press money. A dollar's worth of marks or a pound's worth of rubles skyrocketed into an astronomical amount of paper currency. The total external indebtedness of the Soviet Union was estimated to be something more than eight billion dollars. The creditors wanted the Soviets to acknowledge the Russian indebtedness. Moscow was paying nothing on this debt; every demand of the creditors was met by a Kremlin suggestion that the creditors loan more money to the U.S.S.R. As for Germany, she had been assessed a punitive reparations total of nearly thirty-three billion dollars. It was a fantastically unrealistic sum. It had been set by the war victors because the Reich and its allies had been guilty of "causing all the loss and damage to which the Allied and Associated Governments and their nations" had been compelled to suffer by the war.

Lloyd George believed, therefore, that the time had come to do something about this situation. At this meeting the Russian and German representatives would be called in on the carpet and have their problems examined. They would retire while the Allies and their friends pondered the solution and found a way to collect from Moscow and Berlin. The French and British did not, of course, intend to receive the Russians and Germans as equals at Genoa. The Reich and the Soviet were still "outcasts."

In Moscow, however, there was no intention of playing the game according to London-Paris rules. Karl Radek charged that the forthcoming Genoa conference was nothing less than "the weapon of international capital against Russia." Nevertheless, the Bolsheviks saw in the conference the first recognition on the part of their enemies that the Soviet Union counted in the economic and political structure of Europe. The Moscow *Pravda* (Truth), official organ of the Communist party, described the approaching meeting as "a peace conference about to take place after three years' war between the capitalist states of Europe on the one hand, and Soviet Russia on the other."

When the personnel of the Soviet delegation to Genoa was announced one fact stood out: Lenin was sending his shrewdest traders and dialecticians to the meeting. Among them were Foreign Commissar George Tchicherin, Maxim Litvinov and Christian Rakovsky. The latter had a varied reputation. Communist officials in Russia assured me that Rakovsky was a former wealthy Ukrainian landowner who had voluntarily given his great estates to the peasants and joined the Bolsheviks. But this was not the story told of him in Paris. There *Le Temps* had him down as a former Bulgarian agitator in Roumania who had been a German agent during the war. Be that as it may, Comrade Rakovsky had a statement to give out on the eve of the Genoa meeting. According to *Le Temps* Rakovsky said that the Red Army consisted of 1,450,000 men. This piece of news hardly seemed intended to create a spirit of mutual confidence and good will when capitalists and Communists met in conference.

Meanwhile in Russia a great propaganda drive was being made to acquaint the Russian people with the Soviet viewpoint about the Genoa meeting. From Moscow down to the small village Soviets people were talking about this event. The name of the wily Tchicherin was on every party member's lips. Wherever I went in the Soviet Union the Genoa meeting was the chief topic of discussion. Tchicherin, so I was told by countless Russians, would out-

maneuver the capitalist nations. The British and French,
I was assured, had no diplomats who could stand up to this
astute man with the Vandyke beard. All this talk about the
forthcoming Genoa conference helped take Russian minds
off the current catastrophe in their own country, the most
terrible famine in modern European history.

When the conference of thirty-four nations convened in
Italy on April tenth it was attended by all Russia's creditors except the United States. The French and British
started it off along the lines of previous meetings, taking
the lead in directing the program. The Russians and Germans, like poor relations, were permitted to attend, were
tolerated on a strictly inferior footing.

But while the Allies and their friends deliberated the
Germans and Russians were holding a meeting of their
own. At the near-by town of Rapallo the "outcast" representatives met and worked out an agreement. There was no
by-your-leave about it. The pact was signed on Easter
Sunday. Dr Walter Rathenau affixed his signature for the
Reich; Tchicherin wrote his name for the Soviet.

By the Rapallo treaty Germany accorded de jure recognition to the Soviet Government and both parties renounced all reciprocal war claims and prewar indebtedness.
Furthermore, "the two governments undertake to give
each other mutual assistance for the alleviation of their
economic difficulties in the most benevolent spirit." In
itself this treaty was not sensational. If any other two nations had made the same kind of an agreement it would
hardly have rippled the surface of international waters.
But a Reich-Soviet pact under the conditions was of alarm-
ing importance.

The Allied politicians at Genoa were stunned. The Russians and Germans had defied the rest of Europe. To the

French in particular the Rapallo treaty seemed to forecast an "alliance of the vanquished." With prophetic vision Edwin L. James cabled from Genoa to the New York *Times:* "The possibilities of Russo-German co-operation are unlimited; they stretch from Vladivostok to the Rhine." The New York *Tribune* called it a "brotherhood of outlawry," an "alliance of hatreds."

General Ricciotti Garibaldi, the only surviving son of the Italian patriot, made this analysis of the situation: "Anyone who has followed European politics knew the Russians and Germans always work hand in glove, and this treaty (Rapallo) is merely tangible proof of their partnership."

Back in Germany there was understandable rejoicing among the Communists. But the Communist newspaper *Rote Fahne* asserted that the "treaty of trade and amity" written at Rapallo was not enough. This newspaper wanted an out-and-out alliance. Pan-German enemies of the German Communists agreed with their Bolshevik opponents that the Rapallo pact was a step in the right direction. For Pan-Germans and Communists alike saw in the Rapallo treaty an omen of a more important union, a Second Rapallo that would go much farther than the first.

When the Genoa delegates packed up their bags and started for home few of the economic problems which had been on the agenda of the meeting were any nearer solution than before. The conference had given the Allies another opportunity to attack these problems; it had also given them another chance to play power politics against one another. And this was grist for the Soviet mill. But what seemed to weigh most heavily on the minds of the Genoa delegates was the fact that they had given the cynical Tchicherin a chance to cock a grandiose snook at the capitalistic world and its blundering diplomats.

For the next seventeen years the specter of a Second Rapallo was to hover over all European conferences and the conduct of governments and peoples. It was to account for the inconsistent course of many a foreign policy. Never could this ghost be laid. Seldom discussed openly, it was none the less real because it hid in the back of men's minds. It was to throw its shadow across council tables at which Western statesmen deliberated the fate of the Old World. It was to hover high above Lake Leman when the League of Nations meetings were holding the center of the world stage. It was to show its power in mounting armament burdens. It could be invoked on any occasion that demanded an international skeleton in the closet to frighten people.

The specter was destined to inspire its greatest fears in the small countries of the *Zwischenland* (in-between land) between the Reich and the Soviet. Here it would never cease to cause apprehension and uncertainty until the Second Rapallo should break on a startled and incredulous Europe. For in the Baltic countries, Poland, Roumania, Hungary and Scandinavia there were some informed observers who were not to be fooled by the gigantic propaganda enmity staged by Berlin and Moscow. The shrewd observers in the *Zwischenland* feared that the First Rapallo was but the seed of a Second Rapallo.

Russo-German relations after the Rapallo treaty tended to follow the original pattern of the secret postwar military entente. With the passing of time, however, Berlin and Moscow seemed to become less cautious.

In December 1926 the *Manchester Guardian* published some startling revelations concerning the extent of Russo-German military activities. "These activities," said the

Guardian, "began at least five years ago, but have been going on ever since. To make the necessary arrangements officers of the Reichswehr have travelled to and from Russia with false papers, visaed by Russian authorities. General von Seeckt, until recently Commander-in-Chief of the Reichswehr, was on the best of terms with the Russians, particularly with officers of high rank in the Soviet army."

In the same issue of the *Guardian* the following disclosures appeared: "A rather disconcerting fact is that in November this year several ships arrived in Stettin from Russia. There were, I believe, six in all, though some of them were small sailing vessels. One of them foundered on the way. Their cargoes consisted of arms and ammunition, apparently for the Reichswehr.

"The question is, to what extent can the German Government be held responsible? These things went on with the connivance of officers of the Reichswehr and some high officials, at least, of the Ministry of War. They are in keeping with the policy begun by the Germans at Rapallo, but inconsistent with the policy of the present Foreign Minister, Dr Stresemann, who is anything but Russophil."

CHAPTER V

Soviet Education and Propaganda

In ORDER to understand the Russia of 1922 and of succeeding years it is imperative to know something of the fundamentals of Sovietism. Without this knowledge the reader may misconstrue Soviet motivation and miss the point of the Soviet's aims and methods.

A basic and egregious error made by many people in the Western world is to judge the Russian Bolsheviks by our standards and to try to interpret Russian affairs by Western norms. There is no point in trying to predict what Russians may do under certain conditions because we think that under those conditions Westerners would do a certain thing or react a certain way. The reasoning of Soviet Russians and that of people in Western democratic countries are worlds apart. And we must approach the Soviet enigma with that difference always in mind.

In the autumn of 1939 Americans frequently asked the question: "What will the Russian people think of the Soviet invasion of Finland?" The man who asked that question probably assumed that the Russians are in the habit of thinking things over and discussing them as we do

32

in America. He does not understand, in all probability, that the Russian populace was indoctrinated with the idea that the Finns were the aggressors in the recent Russo-Finnish war. In any case, if a Russian "thinks" out loud in contradiction to the current Soviet policy he is guilty of counterrevolutionary activity. And there is no more serious crime in the Soviet Union than that.

It is worth repeating: there is no free speech, no free press, no free assembly and no freedom of religion in the U.S.S.R., all the talk about the "Soviet democracy" and the "most democratic constitution in the world" notwithstanding. No intelligent Communist in any country believes that freedom and the present form of government in the Soviet Union are compatible. Stalin's regime is an out-and-out dictatorship. As a matter of fact, the U.S.S.R. is the oldest of the major dictatorships.

Even as late as August 1939 it was the fashion in certain circles to speak of Germany and Italy as "the dictatorships." The Soviet was held free from the stigmatization of this term. Whoever included the U.S.S.R. among the dictatorships displeased these circles. The Nazi-Soviet deal accomplished one constructive result. It put an end to much of the nonsense of classifying the Soviet Union as a democracy, in contradistinction to the Fascist dictatorships. Even many disillusioned American Communists agreed with President Roosevelt when he characterized the Soviet Union as "a dictatorship as absolute as any other dictatorship in the world."

Although for years many idealists in the Western world deceived themselves about the methods and purposes of the Soviet Union, the men who live and work in the Kremlin have never been anything but hard-boiled realists. Astute in their political calculations, these Bolsheviks know what they want to do and how they intend to accomplish their ends. When they can use people in capitalistic states they freely exploit them. But at heart the Communist strategists despise any but their own kind. They know that there is a dividing line which separates the two worlds, the Communist world and the capitalist world.

Lenin, who was a clear thinker and a man of exceptional intellectual attainments, did not delude himself or confuse his followers about the inevitability of a struggle between these two worlds. In the early days of the Soviet state he declared: "The existence of the Soviet Republic side by side with imperialist governments for any considerable length of time is unthinkable." Lenin gave a clear warning of the inescapable conflict ahead.

Every true disciple of Marx, Engels and Lenin looked upon this "other world" of capitalism as the Carthage which must be destroyed. There was the "fundamental antagonism" between the bourgeois society of the capitalistic world and the "classless society" of the Soviet Union. The "exploiting classes" must be wiped out. Wherever the "toiling masses" are they can look to the U.S.S.R. for deliverance from their masters. The young Soviet Union had its money engraved in seven languages with the battle cry of the world proletariat: "Workers of the world unite!"

Education in the Soviet Union means the teaching of the Communist politico-economic creed. No other than the Communist viewpoint would be tolerated. The teacher must not only follow the party line but the current party line. And woe betide any instructor who fails to keep up with that party line! For that party line changes; it zigzags; it occasionally contradicts itself.

A few years ago, for example, Nikolai Bukharin was writing the party line. To deviate in the slightest from the line as it was marked out by Bukharin made the citizen guilty of counterrevolution. Faithful Communists and Russians who wished to continue enjoying the breath of life followed Bukharin's writings scrupulously. It was an excellent form of life insurance. Teachers studied what Bukharin said in order to pass it along to their pupils. And foreign observers read Bukharin's works in order to understand the Kremlin's policies.

Yet the day came when Bukharin fell into disgrace. His teachings suddenly became "counterrevolutionary." This Soviet leader who had been making the party line now found himself accused by Stalin of "wrecking," of "plotting," of "counterrevolutionary activities." Bukharin was "purged," and good Bolsheviks had to master the newest party line.

There are many peoples who live in the Soviet Union. There are the Great Russians, Little Russians (Ukrainians), White Russians and Jews. There are tens of millions of other Soviet citizens belonging to such tribes as the Tartars, Bashkirs, Kirghiz, Mordvas, Chuvashes, Samoyedes, Kalmuks, Georgians, Armenians and scores and scores of others. Under the Imperial Government efforts were made to Russify many of the non-Slavic citizens of the empire. That the tsars had no great success in this work is a matter of history.

Now the Soviet attitude toward these minority peoples differs from that of the tsars. In the matter of education the Soviet authorities have actually encouraged these non-Russian peoples to speak their own languages and retain their own cultures so far as is consistent with Communism. Stalin is a non-Russian. He comes from Georgia, in the Caucasus, near the boundary of Middle Asia, and speaks Russian with a noticeable Georgian accent.

But no matter how tolerant the Soviet dictator may be toward the languages and cultures of the minorities, these peoples must have only one political loyalty, only one economic point of view. And these must faithfully follow the current Kremlin teachings. A Bashkir from Ufa who deviates from the current party line can expect no more mercy than the Great Russian who lives in Moscow. The non-Communist heresy of the Samoyede along the frozen coast of the Arctic is just as much a manifestation of "Trotzky-Bukharinist wrecking" as an expression of political independence from the Ukrainian living in Kiev.

In Soviet schoolrooms from the plains of newly conquered Poland to the Pacific children are taught to think and act as young citizens of the Communist state. Reading is a means of teaching them the party principles and the party outlook. Young boys and girls studying their Soviet primers learn that they must hate and destroy that "other world" of capitalism. From reciting their Soviet catechism they learn that they will some day help free the "toiling masses" of the world from the "exploiting classes." They are "building a new world."

Education under the Soviets is propaganda for the Communist party. Soviet officials used to tell me: "We don't care about the old people. Let them keep their religion and superstition. Before long these old people will die off and be replaced by today's children. We shall make these children Communists, and when they grow up we shall have an entire generation of young Communist men and women. Later on, all our people will be good Communists."

In their school propaganda for Communism the Soviet rulers have had considerable success. Children have supplied multitudes of recruits for Communism—in its modern form, Stalinism. And there have been many examples of these youthful Communist fanatics who have turned against their own parents. There was a notable case a few years ago that was heavily publicized by the Kremlin. The boy involved became a world hero of Communist youth. He had discovered that his father was breaking some government order about hoarding food. The boy denounced his father and had the parent thrown into jail. A relative of the father took revenge by killing the child. The Soviet made the dead boy a martyr because the young zealot had not hesitated to denounce his own father in order to promote the interests of the Soviet state.

In schoolrooms all over the Soviet Union children are being turned into Stalinists. This not only serves the purpose of building a solid population of Communists in the U.S.S.R.; it helps prepare the psychological approach to world revolution. For the children are taught that one day they must take their places in the death struggle with that "other world." They must go out and do battle for the "toiling masses." They must carry the victory of Communism to the "exploited" men and women in other lands. And they are given political training that will prepare them for Red Army service. We repeat, then, education in the U.S.S.R. is propaganda for Stalinism.

From the cradle to the grave the citizen of the Soviet Union is nourished on propaganda. Whether he is a child in school, a recruit in the Red Army, a factory worker, a laborer on a collective farm or in some other category, he is constantly fed by the Kremlin's never-ceasing stream of propaganda. If he reads a newspaper, if he listens to a radio program, if he goes to a cinema, if he sees a play, if he walks along a street where there are amplifiers, if he rides on a railroad train, he is certain to receive only the official version of news and views. In this connection it is interesting to note that reading statistics released in Moscow on May 5, 1940, bring out the fact that in the U.S.S.R. almost 274,500,000 copies of Stalin's works have been circulated as against 127,500,000 of Lenin's.

The Bolsheviks do not understand the use of the theater and the moving picture as vehicles for entertainment. The newspaper *Kino*, for instance, criticizes the film *Gone with the Wind* as "a eulogy of slavery, lynching and race chauvinism and as the most reactionary film since David Wark Griffith's *The Birth of a Nation*." The Soviets judge the theater and the cinema by their social and political implications.

Stage and screen must be vehicles of propaganda. The American screen play *Grapes of Wrath* is said to have been approved as acceptable entertainment for the Soviet public because it shows the unhappy lot of the workers in a capitalist country. Soviet cinema patrons are thus made to feel grateful to their Socialist fatherland for providing a "workers' paradise."

Even comedy must play up the citizen's satisfaction in his Soviet way of life. The Leningrad studios announced for production in early 1940 a comedy film featuring an American "billionaire" by the name of Spiegelglass. His pockets bulging with bank bills, he tries to lure one after another of the girl workers on a collective farm to run away to the wicked capitalistic world as his wife. It goes without saying that all the virtuous Soviet heroines spurn Mr Spiegelglass.

Special propaganda trains go wherever there are railroad tracks in the U.S.S.R. When the train stops peasants and townspeople enter it and see still and moving pictures of the revolution, of the vast Soviet plans afoot, of the achievements of Communism and of the sufferings in capitalist lands. There are propaganda trains devoted to the war against religion. Propaganda trucks drive into country districts and visit isolated villages. Orators go along who can address the non-Russian peoples in their own languages.

In the summer of 1922 I witnessed a large mock trial of the executed Admiral Kolchak staged at the town of Melekes, Samara Gubernia. It was propaganda par excellence. Needless to say, the case against the unfortunate admiral was damning; his defense was preposterously incriminating. The audience was encouraged to howl down the cringing attorney for the accused. At times the spectators became so aroused against the doomed Kolchak and his supporters that they threatened to get out of hand and rush the stage. This was, of course, the kind of atmosphere the political directors and actors were trying to create. It was effective melodrama, and the Melekes populace reacted to it wholeheartedly. Little boys on the streets shouted "Kolchak!" in derision at their enemies. Elderly peasants who could not read spat when the admiral's name was mentioned.

But the Kremlin does not reserve its propaganda only for its own subjects. "Communism," Soviet leaders have maintained all along, "is not for export." Actually, Soviet propaganda has been from the beginning one of the important exports of the U.S.S.R. As the New York *Times* remarked in an editorial on December 30, 1939: "Propaganda, indeed, has been Soviet Russia's principal export."

"What frank propaganda for imperialism, militarism and enslavement of colonies!" exclaims *Izvestia*, government newspaper, on the hundredth anniversary of the issuance of the first postage stamp. "How many kings, emperors, dukes and princes! What a preponderance of saints of all churches!" Soviet stamps, on the contrary, "reflect the flourishing science and art of our country, and the construction of industrial giants. Our stamps arouse the hatred of foreign enemies and the enthusiasm of our friends in all countries."

The Soviet Union not only sends abroad its own propaganda; it carries on what the Communists call counterpropaganda work in the U.S.S.R. Censorship is one phase of this program. The Russian masses must be saved from the contamination of bourgeois ideas. The traveler entering the country has his foreign newspapers confiscated at the frontier. When he leaves the Soviet Union he may find that Russian newspapers, posters, even postage stamps are taken away from him at the border. A propaganda medium that is in high favor inside the U.S.S.R. might not, in the opinion of the Soviet propaganda chiefs, work to the advantage of Communism in other lands. So it is confiscated.

But the traveler probably does not come into contact with Soviet censorship. That is left to the foreign correspondents working in Moscow. For almost two decades after foreign journalists were admitted to the U.S.S.R. the Soviet censorship worked through the bureaucrat's blue pencil. Sentences and paragraphs might be deleted. The sense of the dispatch might be altered; the dispatch might be eliminated entirely.

In May 1939 the censorship on outgoing dispatches was lifted. The resident foreign journalists in Moscow were informed that they would work under a personal censorship. Each correspondent would act as his own censor. At first glance this seemed like a welcome change. But was it? In the old days a dispatch might be chopped to pieces, but if it went through at all, as much of it as went through was passed by the government. There was not likely to be a flareback later on that might cause the correspondent to be expelled. The censor was, to some extent, a protection to the journalist. But the personal censorship put all the responsibility on the correspondent. If the dispatch displeased the Kremlin, its sender might be summarily expelled from the Soviet Union. In the summer of 1939 foreign correspondents in Moscow complained that they worked under the danger that some seemingly harmless and unimportant statement might cause them to be expelled.

Rigid censorship was imposed again in December 1939. This turned out to be anything but good news for the foreign journalists in the Soviet capital. A summary of the new censorship conditions explains the reason. In the past, *Tass*, the official Soviet news agency, usually released its important news announcements about three in the morning. Owing to the difference of time between Moscow and New York, these dispatches arrived in time to appear in the morning editions of American newspapers. But coincident with the reimposition of the censorship it was announced that the bureaucrat with the blue pencil would be on duty only until one in the morning. He would not come on duty again for seven hours. The correspondents could not, accordingly, cable any news they obtained between one and ten A.M. This gave all the breaks to *Tass*. It meant in practice that the correspondents' dispatches talked about events that had been discussed hours earlier by *Tass*. Furthermore, it meant that the Soviet Government's version of the news reached the American reader hours ahead of the dispatch of the foreign journalist. It is axiomatic that a correction never catches up with the original misstatement, a publicity truism not lost on the propaganda chiefs of the U.S.S.R. According to an editorial in the New York *Times*, May 4, 1940: "Dispatches are sometimes slashed by the Russian censor until only the signature remains."

But Soviet censorship goes much farther than mere interference with newspaper dispatches. It is a campaign of insulation waged against the entire population. Unwillingly the Russians have been cut off from all intercourse not only with the outside world but also with foreigners inside the Soviet Union. Only a few years ago the foreign visitor easily made friends among the Muscovites. He found the Russians friendly and engaging companions. More than one foreign correspondent, engineer or businessman married a Russian wife. Russians and foreigners enjoyed normal social relations, dined together and shared entertainment. All that has changed.

In order to insulate Russians from any manner of un-Soviet thinking and "dangerous ideas," the Kremlin instituted a campaign of drastic segregation. A veritable Chinese Wall was erected around the Russians to prevent their contacts with that "other world." Gone now were the times when foreigners and Russians could associate with one another. Thousands of Russians were dragooned by the OGPU on the charge that they had engaged in espionage with foreign secret agents. Some spectacular public trials were held, but in most cases the victim merely disappeared. His family never heard a word about him again. Nor did anyone dare to ask questions. The unfortunate accused simply dropped from sight.

Before long the foreign legations and embassies in Moscow were cut off from almost every contact with Russians except the most routine business. No more could the young secretaries of these missions take charming

Muscovites out to dinner or invite them to legation parties. Nor could the foreign missions have any but the strictest diplomatic relations with Soviet government officials. Even high functionaries of the U.S.S.R. were unwilling to take any chance that some enemy might denounce them to the OGPU as accessory to foreign intelligence services.

A well-known foreign correspondent tells of the trouble he had finding a garage in Moscow. Garage managers, it seems, are afraid to risk even the slight contact entailed in sheltering a foreigner's automobile.

The upshot of this situation was that the foreign missions were thrown upon their own social and business resources. Not only did they associate entirely with their own kind, but it was largely from one another that they gleaned their information about Russia for their respective governments. Pooling information became, therefore, a common practice among the foreign missions. One legation secretary described the process to me as "picking each others' brains." The member of an embassy staff told me that it reminded him of Mark Twain's darkies: "Here in Moscow we just take in each others' washing."

The late Count Brockdorf-Rantzau, German ambassador in Moscow, was reported to have made this sharp observation about the Communists: "Parvenus are sensitive!" That may or may not be correct. But, if true, it had nothing to do with the segregation of the foreigners in the U.S.S.R. The Bolsheviks are not so sensitive as that. They created a kind of social *cordon sanitaire* around the foreign residents for practical reasons. It was really an act of war. For it was preparation for the inevitable conflict with that "other world" which the Kremlin leadership believed could not be postponed for many more years.

Stalin knew that it would be a much more difficult

problem to mold the opinion of people who had foreign friends. He realized that these foreign contacts could sabotage his own internal propaganda campaign. If thousands of Russians daily talked with foreigners, it would be infinitely more difficult to cover up scandals, internecine party brawls and other happenings which it would be inexpedient for the Russian public to know about. Further, it would be a far more arduous task to spread the Stalinist version of conditions in the outside world.

How much more difficult, for example, it would be for the Soviet propaganda machine to convince the Russian masses that starving Americans were being shot down in thousands by brutal police if Russians talked with American friends in Russia. How much harder it would be for Stalin to convince his people that the "other world" was preparing an imperialist war against the Socialist fatherland if his Russian subjects were allowed to make friends among that "other world's" representatives in Russia.

From the propagandists' viewpoint religion is not dangerous because it is the "opiate of the people," but because it would afford the Russian believers bonds with people in other nations. It would nullify the insulationist policy of the Soviet propagandists.

Atheism has been, of course, one of the cardinal tenets of Communism. One of the reasons for the Stalinist war on the "religious front" is that religion would teach ethics which conflict with Bolshevik materialism. Most important of all, religion would act as a brake on the regimentation of the Russian masses which is essential to Soviet imperialism. Like the Kremlin's propaganda offensive, its collectivization campaign, its program of industrialization, its purge of all political and economic dissenters, its liquidation of dissident national minorities, the war on religion has a definite place in Stalin's "long-sight" plans to bring about a new world order. Just as religion played a part in Tsarist imperialism, so in reverse does antireligion play a role in Red imperialism.

When Stalin decides upon a party policy there are no halfway measures about it. He goes the whole distance. When he decreed that Russians should have no contact with foreigners in the U.S.S.R. all the power of the OGPU was mobilized to enforce that ukase. So effectively was this program carried out that a sick member of the American Embassy staff could not obtain treatment from a Russian physician. Every Muscovite doctor feared that if he visited an ailing American he might be thrown into the dreaded Lubianka prison charged with espionage against the Soviet Union. So he refused to answer the calls from sick members of foreign missions. To meet this situation an American physician was brought from Washington to the American Embassy in Moscow to treat its staff and visiting American citizens.

All of this repression, censorship, segregation and terrorism was the prelude for the events of late 1939. Education and censorship prepared the right state of mind for the acceptance of Stalin's sudden and sensational shift from his anti-Nazi attitude to the position of quasi-partnership with the hated Hitlerites. And it made possible the loudly voiced claims that the Finns were invading the Soviet Union. Education and propaganda in the U.S.S.R. go hand in hand. They are part of the war being constantly waged, by one means or another, against that "other world." They are indispensable to Soviet imperialism.

CHAPTER VI

The Third International

IT WOULD BE DIFFICULT to conceive of a Soviet imperialism without the Third International (Comintern). The Third (Communist) International is a vital auxiliary of Soviet imperialism. It enables the Soviet Government to practice the most colossal duplicity, a duplicity important to the progress of Soviet imperialism. It enables the Kremlin to carry on warfare against a nominally friendly government within that government's borders without running the risk that would ordinarily beset any such alien agency. When the injured government protests Moscow blandly avoids responsibility by protesting that the hostile activities were the work of the Third International. Everyone sees through this subterfuge, but up to the beginning of the second World War little had been done about it.

When Gregory Zinoviev was president of the Third International he made this proclamation: "The task of the Communist (Third) International is not only to prepare for the victory and to lead the working classes during the period of seizure of power—it is also its task to direct the entire activity of the working classes after the conquest of power."

Perhaps a brief historical background of the International will help us better to understand this organization and what it stands for. Let us go back to London in the year 1864. Here met representatives of the working men of all nations who formed the (First) International, also called the International Working Men's Association. Karl Marx helped form it. It was a labor society embracing a membership somewhat on the order of an international trades union. But it was also a kind of clearing house for labor problems, a medium for the protection of labor's rights, a forum for the discussion of the laboring man's aspirations and ideals.

In 1889, fifteen years after the dissolution of the First International, the Second (Socialist) International came into existence. Its early years were largely devoted to debates about the tactics and methods of the various Socialist organizations which composed its membership. Jean Jaurès, the French Socialist leader, was one of the moving spirits of the Second International. At the end of the first decade of this century the increasing danger of war overshadowed all its deliberations and influenced its policies. Jaurès and his collaborators strove to head off the approaching cataclysm. They prepared to hold the tenth congress in Vienna during August 1914. But the war intervened. And on the evening of July 31st Jaurès was assassinated as he sat by an open window of a Paris restaurant facing the Rue Montmartre. A short time later the Second International collapsed.

The demise of the pacifistic Second International suited the plans of Lenin. He and his Communist followers had never been in sympathy with the evolutionary Socialism of the Second International. Their sympathies were devoted to the defunct First International, inasmuch as they believed that body to be a suitable instrument of active revolution.

The outbreak of the World War was welcome news to Lenin. To him it meant an opportunity for world revolution. Out of the ruins of "dying capitalism" would emerge Communism. Not without reason he believed that this international struggle would accelerate the revolutionary cause by decades. Lenin's strategy toward this conflict can be summarized in the statement that he struggled to "transform the imperialist war into a civil war."

It is not without a certain ironic significance that it was the German General Staff which in early April 1917 made it possible for Lenin to reach Russia. They wanted the revolutionary leader to hasten the national disintegration of the month-old democratic Russia and to take the confused new state out of the World War. In six months Lenin had replaced the democratic government with his Bolshevik regime. The program of world revolution had found a home.

In 1919 the Third (Communist) International came into existence. It was founded as the international organization of the Communist parties in the countries all over the world. It was bold enough to state that it was ready to support the Socialist parties only so far as "the hangman's rope supports the convict." The seat of the Third International would be Moscow.

The First Congress of the Comintern was convoked by the Central Committee of the Communist party. It was attended by such important Communist hierarchs as Lenin, Trotzky, Stalin, Zinoviev, Bukharin and Tchicherin. Blustering Gregory Zinoviev, president of the Leningrad Soviet, was the first president of the Third International. He was to hold this post until 1926, when he was succeeded by Bukharin. Later on, both were to be purged by their old friend and fellow worker, Comrade Stalin.

From the first days of the Comintern there was friction among the various factions regarding the policies and strategy of this organization of world revolution. Fire-eaters like Trotzky, Zinoviev and Bukharin wanted to get on with the world revolution. After all, that was the purpose of the Comintern. And Lenin was making it clear that Communism and capitalism could not indefinitely live side by side. So on with the world revolution!

But Bolsheviks like Tchicherin and Krassin thought otherwise. No less than the fire-eaters these men wanted to further the world Communist movement, but they believed that it must first be made strong in Russia. They reasoned that a weak U.S.S.R. would be a poor opening wedge for a world-wide revolutionary crusade. After all, they argued, the capitalist world held many of the things which the Soviet Union needed and would need for many a day. Why not turn the resources of that "other world" to the advantage of the U.S.S.R.? Time was working on the side of Bolshevism; time was working against the "decaying" capitalist empires.

Time was also working against the Trotzky-Zinoviev-Bukharin group. After the death of Lenin (1924) the star of Stalin began to rise, slowly but steadily. Ominously, too, for the intellectuals of the party who had opposed the taciturn Georgian. For this wily master of machine politics not only set to work to eliminate his enemies and all whom he considered even potential opponents; he began to direct with a sure and ruthless hand the policies of the Comintern. No longer was it the battleground of conflicting cliques inside the Communist hierarchy. Having liquidated all dissenters, actual, potential and suspect, the Red tsar used the Comintern as his exclusive tool. From now on it was the instrument of his foreign policies, the servant of his imperialism.

"The world-wide nature of our program is not mere talk but an all-embracing and blood-soaked reality," declares *Pravda* (September 9, 1928). . . . . "Our ultimate aim is World Communism, our fighting preparations are for World Revolution, for the conquest of power on a world-wide scale and the establishment of a World Proletarian Dictatorship."

The Seventh Congress of the Comintern, convened in July 1935, afforded an example of the devious ways of Stalin's *Realpolitik*. The international situation was developing increasingly dangerous symptoms. Italy was about to invade Ethiopia. Hitler's Third Reich had but recently declared that it was instituting conscription. Britain and France showed few signs of determination or the ability to make a decision about the deteriorating economic and political situation in Europe. The new international technique of streamlined aggression had worked in Manchuria; it seemed destined to succeed in other areas. Always plagued by the fear that the "other world" would attack the Soviet Union, Stalin had the previous year taken the Soviet Union into the League of Nations. But that sharp move was not enough. He needed other safeguards against an attack by a combination of his capitalist enemies.

Here is where the Comintern came into the picture. It could be used to advantage in just such a situation. But its methods would have to be camouflaged; its strategy would have to be carefully disguised. On the opening day of the Congress *Pravda* announced the new direction of the Comintern policy. The Third International would be instructed to abandon for the time being its program of world revolution. Its new task would be the job of organizing the Liberal parties of all countries in a grand crusade against Fascism. Into this situation was injected the "Trojan Horse" tactics of the United Front. Bolshevism's old enemy, capitalism, would now be enlisted in the fight against the new ideological opponent which aped the methods of Communism.

Pravda announced: "Communists must fight with complete unselfishness to save the remnants of bourgeois democracy." The remnants of bourgeois democracy were being saved, of course, in order to pit them against Fascism. The "Popular Front" movement was now an important instrument of Soviet foreign policy. The quasi-alliance with capitalism would prove a valuable gesture in the *reculer pour mieux sauter* (retreat the better to advance) strategy against capitalism.

At the Seventh Congress of the Comintern Earl Browder, American Communist leader, brought the Kremlin the cheerful news that Communism was making important headway in the U.S.A. The membership in the United States, he stated, was thirty thousand. To the average American that was a negligible number; to the Moscow hierarchs it meant thirty thousand trained party workers, actually the nucleus of a potentially much larger force of Communists.

Now let us move on more than four years to the evening of November 6, 1939. The scene is Moscow's great Bolshoi Theatre, home of the state ballet, the setting of many important gatherings since the Bolsheviks came to power. The Soviet capital is thronged with visitors for the celebration of the twenty-second anniversary of the November revolution. Inside the crowded Bolshoi the tiers of boxes

seat the diplomats who are here to see the political spectacle. Revolutionary slogans are featured on great banners.
The American and British ambassadors and the French
chargé d'affaires are present.

The featured orator of the evening is the Soviet's premier
and foreign minister, Comrade Vyacheslav M. Molotov.
The stage from which he speaks is decorated with scarlet
draperies, a mound of flowers, a bust of Lenin and an
enormous portrait of Stalin. Molotov's speech is a ringing
call to arms against "dying" capitalism. He denounces
"imperialist" expansion. He lauds the Soviet Union's
"tested policy of peace." And he pledges his government
to "unswerving" pursuance of this peace program "which
has already brought us no mean successes." Stalin looks
on approvingly. By his side sits the Bulgarian, George
Dimitrov, secretary-general of the Third International.

On the same day as the Molotov speech the November
seventh announcement of the Comintern is read. Here we
find the charge that Britain, France and the United States
hold "in subjection more than half of mankind." The
inference is not thinly veiled that the Comintern and the
Soviet Union mean to do something about that. The
Comintern's new "Popular Front" is to be a general front
of all workers and exploited peoples against imperialism
and capitalism.

"Exploitation of toilers," says the Comintern manifesto,
"and exploitation of oppressed colonial peoples are covered
with the hypocritical flag of democracy in order more easily
to deceive the masses." And in another place: "Three of
the richest states—Britain, France and the United States—
dominate the most important world routes and markets of
raw materials." Once more the inference is that the
Soviets mean to do something to remedy this situation.

Other excerpts from the manifesto continue the attack on the democracies: "The Soviet Union has waged a tireless struggle for the preservation of peace for more than a score of years . . . But the war provocateurs sought something else. They sought to use negotiations to lull the vigilance of the masses and to rid themselves of the responsibility for a war that had already been prepared by them.

"They instigated Poland against the land of the Soviets. While conducting negotiations with the U.S.S.R. they (Britain and France) sought on the sly to goad Germany against the Soviet Union.

"By concluding a nonaggression treaty with Germany the Soviet Union disrupted the crafty plans of the provocateurs of an anti-Soviet war.

"By its appeals for cessation of the war and by its treaty of friendship and border delimitation with Germany, the Soviet Union introduces a new element into the cause of peace."

These are the words of the Comintern headed by the Nazi-hating Bulgarian, Dimitrov. This is the message of a manifesto composed to justify the Nazi-Soviet deal to the Russian masses at home and to the Communist party organizations abroad. The voice indeed is the voice of the world's Communist party organizations, but the hands are the hands of Stalin.

CHAPTER VII

Collectivization and *Pyatiletka*

Old Russia was continually beaten because of backwardness.
It was beaten by the Mongol khans. It was beaten by Turkish
beys. It was beaten by Swedish feudal landlords . . . It was
beaten because of military backwardness, cultural backwardness, industrial backwardness, agricultural backwardness. That
is why we cannot be backward any more.—JOSEPH STALIN.

AT THE TIME of the Treaty of Rapallo Russia was an
economic anachronism. The projected "workers' paradise" was even less utopian than Imperial Russia.

Imperial Russia was a vast land of undeveloped natural resources, primitive industrialization, a backward
peasantry and, at the top, a deadly bureaucracy. Its railroad system was weak and it had few good roads. Its water
power potential had hardly been tapped. Famines peri-
odically swept over a farming country which should never
have experienced a serious food shortage. When the World
War broke out in 1914 Russia was adequately equipped
only in man power. Her industrial mobilization was utterly
inadequate to meet the needs of modern warfare. Her
agriculture was not well organized. Her bureaucracy was

inefficient and lacking in initiative. The wonder was that under these conditions the Russian Empire did as well as it did in the first two and a half years of a major war.

The revolutions and civil wars further disrupted Russian economy. There was widespread destruction of property. The war with Poland in 1920 continued the economic deterioration of the country. By 1921 it was estimated that some of the basic industries were reduced to a production level as low as that of a century previous. During 1920–21 the industrial production of Russia was estimated to be only fifteen to eighteen per cent of the prewar average. And the agricultural output was reputed to be about half of the normal prewar yield. This was the broken-down industrial and agricultural system that the Bolsheviks had to work with when they finally found themselves victorious over their domestic and foreign enemies.

All the intelligent Soviet leaders realized that this state of affairs was not only a bad advertisement for Communism abroad; it was actually an acute military weakness which endangered the Union's safety. How could so primitive a war economy hope to withstand the attacks of highly industrialized states? And every true Bolshevik believed that it would be only a matter of time until the imperialist powers renewed their struggle to destroy the Socialist fatherland. The Soviets could not, therefore, hope to perpetuate their state unless they could build a strong industrial and agricultural economy as a backing for the army in the field.

But when Lenin and his collaborators set out to improve the national economy they found out that in some respects they were even more hampered by a shortage of directing personnel than the imperial regime had been. Thousands of executives, engineers and other technical men had been killed in the series of wars, and many others had been driven into exile. Moreover, Lenin dared not put too much faith in the members of the former regime who still remained in Russia. The U.S.S.R. would have to depend primarily on Soviet party members and the aid of technical advisers and teachers from abroad. The economic climb from the low level of 1920–21 was, therefore, a slow process. For the following seven years the Soviet Union painfully struggled to regain lost ground and to make some headway.

In October 1928 was announced the first Five Year Plan (*Pyatiletka*). It was heralded by an enormous propaganda campaign. The resources of the U.S.S.R., human and material, were mobilized to make it succeed. Grandiose promises were made for it. In five years, so some enthusiastic Communists asserted, the Soviet Union would reach the industrial level of the western European countries and America. Socialist planning and dynamism would soon make the U.S.S.R. the foremost industrial nation in the world.

Whether Stalin and his immediate collaborators believed the fabulous predictions made for the Five Year Plan is a matter of conjecture. But we can be certain that the rulers of the Kremlin felt sure that the plan would be a long step toward making the Soviet Union impregnable to attack and would hasten the day when the Russian experiment's success would encourage revolution in the capitalist countries. *Pyatiletka* was, accordingly, a basis for defense and offense. It was another step toward the fulfillment of the dream of Soviet world power.

The first Five Year Plan was put into operation at approximately the time when the Russian national economy reached the prewar level. The debris from the revolutions and wars had been cleared away. Years of Bolshevik education and propaganda had prepared the psychological background for it. The party members were enthusiastically mobilized as the first-line troops in this new offensive. And Communist organizations were schooled in their role as shock troops of *Pyatiletka*.

From the Polish border to Kamchatka the Russian masses were told that they must labor and undergo sacrifices for the plan that was to bring them material benefits. Toil and sacrifice now, they were assured, would raise the standard of living for the people of the U.S.S.R. Indeed, in a few years the plan would give the Russians the highest standard of living on the globe. But they must throw every ounce of their energy into the struggle. They were building a new world. Socialist construction would build on the ruins of the capitalist world. Their rallying cry was: "We must master technique!"

Pyatiletka soon brought striking changes to the U.S.S.R. In every direction there was building in progress. Roads, waterways and rail lines were under construction; dams were being built; new coal mines were being opened. In former wastelands industrial projects sprang into life. In the Urals, in Siberia, in the Donetz, great colonies of workers were being mobilized to erect factories and build new cities. Vast industrial centers were created hundreds of miles east of Moscow, where it would be difficult for enemy bombers to penetrate. The emphasis was on heavy industry. The industries to make consumers' goods would have to wait. Visitors who had known old Russia were powerfully impressed by the portentous changes, by the tempo of the work, by the enthusiasm of the young Communists.

Engineers, executives and skilled workers were brought

to the U.S.S.R. from abroad. These foreigners were employed to teach Russia's unskilled and technically backward millions. Americans, Englishmen, Germans and others helped introduce large-scale industry. Long before the first Five Year Plan had run its course and the second Five Year Plan had started, conveyors were working day and night; assembly lines were turning out great numbers of machines. Stalin and his collaborators could point triumphantly to the advances scored by the plan.

In some respects *Pyatiletka* was a young peoples' crusade. The Communist youth responded to the propaganda, the slogans, the excitement, the pep meetings. And it may be worth mentioning that here youth had its day. At this time in the "other world" thousands of young men and women with degrees in medicine, law, engineering, journalism and other professions found that there was no employment for them. They remained jobless. In Germany many of them were drifting into the ranks of Communism or Nazism. In Austria, in England, in France and other capitalistic countries these youthful graduates drifted into a condition of hopelessness. There appeared to be no place for them in capitalistic society. Some of their elders realized the dangers inherent in this state of affairs; others did not.

In the U.S.S.R., on the other hand, every young man and woman believed that he or she had a future. They became ardent Communists. There was no lack of jobs; there was, on the contrary, a shortage of qualified people to fill them. Young people labored by day and studied by night. Everyone, it seemed, wanted to be an engineer. But skilled workers could not be turned out in a day, especially in an agricultural country. It would be necessary for Russia to grind through years of patient work in order to create a sufficient body of trained executives and workers.

And there was another side to this picture. Youthful enthusiasm sometimes destroyed more than it created. It was easier to build plants than to operate them efficiently. Machines were not infrequently wrecked beyond repair by youthful operators who were exuberantly trying to meet or exceed the factory quota. The toll from mistakes and poor workmanship was enormous. And it had to be paid for in terms of a lowered standard of living. More money went into circulation, but it bought less. The purchasing power of the ruble was dropping. There were many necessities of life that it could not purchase.

Apropos of the lowered value of the ruble in terms of everything the Russian had to buy, William Henry Chamberlin passes on a quip of that period: "Who are the wealthiest people in the world? The Russians, of course. And why is that true? Because the Russians don't know how to spend all their rubles."

In order to throw the economic strength of the Soviet Union behind the industrial offensive Stalin was compelled to sacrifice agriculture. The peasant was taxed all that could be forced out of him in order that steel mills, tractor factories, power plants, mines and munitions works might be set up as part of the military system of the U.S.S.R.

But Stalin's economic mobilization of the Soviet Union did not stop on the industrial front. He set out to Bolshevize agriculture. This proved to be an even more arduous task than building a vast industrial system. In the industrial field he met little opposition; he was helped by enthusiastic Russians, Communists and non-Communists too. But out in the villages there were millions of Russians who did not approve of his plans for a collectivized rural economy. They remained individualists.

The Russian peasant has long been land hungry. For

centuries he has desperately wanted to own soil. Throughout the serfdom of Tsarist days he developed this longing
to own his bit of the earth. Ownership meant life and
hope to him. When the March revolution came in 1917
the peasant believed that his shackles were being broken.
But he soon learned that he could not have the land of
the great estates all at once. There would be land reform,
yes, but it would take time. The peasant was disappointed.

Then came the Bolsheviks with their appeal to the
hungry proletariat of the cities, to the peasants and to the
soldiers tired of war. "Bread! Land! And peace!" Lenin
shouted. His slogan was taken up by his followers. "Bread!
Land! And peace!"

After the November revolution the peasants seized lands
belonging to large estates. At last, thought the peasant,
my dreams have come true. I own land. Although I do
not approve of the Bolsheviks' attitude toward religion,
I do approve of their land policy. And the peasants were
pleased.

But the peasants had little time in which to enjoy their
new property. The civil wars brought them new troubles.
Both the Red and White armies pillaged them. Their food
reserves were confiscated. When winter came they had
little for themselves. In the great Volga region the drought
cut down their crops. Then came bands of Communists
from the cities to confiscate what grain they still had. It
would be fed to hungry workers in the cities. The ruthless
"iron broom" of these requisitioning bands of Bolsheviks
swept clean villages which already were on starvation
rations. I have talked with scores of peasants in this region
whose meager food reserve was swept away by the Communist "iron broom."

Yet all the time the great black plains of the Volga

should have supplied food reserves to carry the peasants through more than one season of drought.

Even after the Volga famine had been brought under control, thanks to the food supplied by Herbert Hoover's American Relief Administration, the peasant's troubles did not end. He had to accept whatever he could get for the things he raised for market; he had to pay high prices for all the articles he was compelled to buy. Trotzky said that the peasant was caught between the "scissors" of low prices for his sales and high prices for his purchases.

In 1923 J. Yakovlev, an investigator for the Communist party sent out to make a report on the peasantry, made this entry in one of his records: "The peasant is like a sheep. Whoever needs wool fleeces it. It was fleeced by the Tsar, the landlords, Denikine's army and the comrades. They ought to have pity on it, otherwise it will be skinned altogether and there will be no wool to fleece."

But the Bolsheviks had no pity for the peasant. On the contrary, the Kremlin set out to break the power of the peasantry. Stalin could not hope to have absolute control of the U.S.S.R. if a landowning peasantry gradually improved its economic position. That would threaten his plan for complete control of every phase of the economic, social and political life of the Soviet Union. Every peasant was a potential capitalist. Stalin would have to smash these peasants and bring them to heel. As a step toward obtaining the absolutism he wanted he set out to transform the peasants into state serfs.

Not all the Communist party leaders agreed with Stalin. Even some of those who supported his plans for collectivization advocated that it be undertaken by a slow, gradual process. Stalin retorted that they were *Mensheviks*. (*Mensheviks* split with Bolsheviks before the war. The former preferred an evolutionary, less drastic kind of Socialism.) He would not listen to their counsels. Later on, most of those who had dared to plead for caution in the collectivization program were purged.

In order to carry through his plan to regiment Russian agriculture Stalin set out to "liquidate the kulaks." "Kulak" means "big fist." The Bolsheviks charged that the kulaks exploited their less fortunate neighbors. Actually, the kulak was what we in America would call a poor farmer. The average kulak owned a few acres, perhaps a cow, a horse, a pig and some chickens. His house might be thatched. He lived in humble circumstances. But the point was that he worked harder than some of his neighbors, he planned his work better and he saved. Often the poor neighbor whom the Communists championed against the kulak was lazy, inefficient and stupid.

I have eaten and slept in dozens of kulak homes. I have known hundreds of these poor people. They were little interested in ideological questions; they were deeply concerned with weather and crop conditions, the health of their animals, the plagues of locusts and grasshoppers, and market prices. Perhaps the kulak could neither read nor write, but he hoped that his children might have these advantages. His wife's kitchen and bedrooms were likely to be clean, and her windowsills were nearly always gay with potted flowers. Not expensive blossoms, but colorful, living plants that, during the long winter months when snow was piled high beneath the windows and the landscape was a great vista of white and crystal, would remind them of gardens and verdant fields.

The most cruel and diabolical thing that has happened in our generation was the "liquidation of the kulaks." Millions of these decent, self-respecting people were uprooted from their homes and scattered. Families were broken up; children were sent to orphanages; many of the parents died or were killed; and tens of thousands of the men and women were sent to forced labor camps in the wastes of the Arctic region, Siberia or Central Asia. The most virile blood on the Russian land was wasted. The progress made by generations who struggled against exploitation, against the elements and against adversity was wiped out. In place of personalized kulak initiative was substituted the drab uniformity of collectivized farming. The land was completely dekulakized.

Stalin was right about the kulaks' potential threat to his personal dictatorship and Soviet imperialism. They represented the beginning of a middle class in Russia. In another generation this middle class would undoubtedly have become a force to reckon with, and the Bolshevik experiment might have been pushed off the land and confined to the urban centers. The independent spirit of kulak initiative conflicted with Stalin's fundamental philosophy of one-man rule. The kulaks had to go.

But the kulak did not go down without a struggle. True, he had no arms. He could fight the Kremlin's army and the OGPU with little more than passive resistance. When the collective farms were being organized the kulaks killed and ate millions of their animals. Better to enjoy this food yourself than to turn it over to the enemies who were despoiling you. The government estimated the loss of farm animals in this peasant sabotage as sixty millions. So serious was this kulak slaughter of pigs and cattle that the Soviet Union has not even yet recovered from the effects.

In a few cases desperate kulaks fought with axes, clubs and bare fists against soldiers and police who came to seize their property and scatter their families. But kulak resistance was usually passive. The farmers could not produce when they were being driven off their property. They could not work well when they were virtually outlawed. History repeated itself; famine once more ravaged Russia.

William Henry Chamberlin, who personally investigated this famine, told me he estimated that about four million people died during the worst of this disaster in 1932–33. It brought suffering and death to many communities, especially in the Ukraine and the North Caucasus. Mr Chamberlin describes it ably in *Russia's Iron Age*.

Although the collectivization program put a tremendous strain on the Soviet's economy, created dissension within the Communist hierarchy and caused some unrest among the peasant recruits in the Red Army, Stalin carried the day. The kulaks were liquidated. Russian agriculture was placed directly under the power of the Kremlin, and what little independence had formerly existed on the farms and in the villages was exterminated.

Stalin had succeeded in carrying out his "leveling" process among the Russian peasantry. And the Soviet "classless" system levels down, not up.

The three Five Year Plans and the collectivization of agriculture have been long steps in the preparation of the U.S.S.R. for its program of imperialistic conquest. By 1939 every phase of Russian industry and agriculture had come under the direction of Stalin's myrmidons in the various commissariats. Let the obviously inevitable "second imperialist war" come. The Soviet Union would be ready to profit by it in the manner dictated by Stalin's opportunism.

CHAPTER VIII

Kremlin Asks Total Disarmament

THE KREMLIN LEADERSHIP has rarely been unrealistic
in its foreign policies. It is hardly an exaggeration to say
that for the past two decades it has been the most realistic
leadership in Europe. It has been given to far less wishful
thinking than the Western democracies and guilty of
infinitely less bombast than the Fascist states. It has not
built diplomatic card houses such as the pact of the Little
Entente (Czecho-Slovakia, Roumania and Yugoslavia).
The Soviet hierarchy has nearly always been clearheaded
in its appraisal of foreign governments, their aims, their
psychology and their weaknesses.

We must not lose track of the fact that the U.S.S.R
leadership believes that the day will come when most of
that "other world" is pitted against it in war. Against that
day the Kremlin has formulated its diplomatic strategy.
One way to forestall a coalition against you is to confuse
your enemies. To cause them to regard one another with
suspicion is an achievement of political genius. If you can
turn them against one another on the battlefield, so much
the better. To these strategic ends Moscow has followed

an opportunistic foreign policy planned to take advantage of its enemies' mistakes.

By 1927 the capitalistic world was talking a great deal about the armament burden. Liberal economists warned that the old order could not indefinitely stand the burden of vast armies and navies. Armaments, they admonished, were unproductive. They were luxuries that nations could not afford. Every dollar that went into the financing of armies and navies was spent at the expense of the state's social needs. Taxes to carry this armament burden came out of every man's income; it hit the poor with special vengeance. The cost of battleships, bombers, tanks and other essentials of "national defense" lowered the standard of living.

Many Conservatives realized the soundness of these arguments against the armaments burden. Yet the war to end war had not abolished the armament evil. It had merely reduced the armies and navies of one group—the defeated nations. The promises of the Allies to put into effect a general arms reduction had been flouted when the victors set out to enforce the peace treaties. France, the world's most powerfully armed nation, self-righteously pleaded for "security." But security for one country often spells insecurity for another. France's neighbors also wanted security.

The Soviet Union, still a backward agricultural country with only the beginnings of a modern industry, naturally feared the vast armaments of her enemies, actual and potential. Moreover, in the opposition to vast armaments the Kremlin leadership saw a propaganda weapon of immense value to the Soviet Union.

When the Preparatory Disarmament Commission of the League of Nations assembled at Geneva early in 1928 the U.S.S.R. was represented by its brilliant diplomatic ace, assistant commissar of foreign affairs, Maxim Litvinov. Experienced, astute, cynical, Litvinov knew the ways of the diplomatic world. Unlike most of his fellow Bolsheviks, he was entirely at home in the bourgeois atmosphere of the Swiss city on Lake Leman.

Litvinov's diplomacy had a "take it or leave it" finality. A skillful oratorical fencer, he loved to find the weak spot in his opponent's armor and drive his weapon into that spot. Above all, the Kremlin's representative loved to embarrass his opponents; he enjoyed exposing sham. He was feared also because he followed the rules of diplomatic etiquette only when those rules served his purpose.

Litvinov knew that the fine expressions of devotion to peace and disarmament poured out by the politicians assembled at Geneva were not free from cant. He realized that the League spellbinders were speaking for the record. In the background, he knew, moved the sinister and powerful representatives of the great armament interests. Some of the delegates to the disarmament conference had heavy financial stakes in these companies which manufacture arms, naval vessels and munitions.

Litvinov knew well the records of the De Wendels, the Zaharoffs, the Krupps and others in the armament business. Too, the hard-boiled commissar suspected that at Geneva there would be only shadowboxing with the armament evil. There would be many strong verbal blows struck against armaments, but nothing would happen to reduce the profits flowing into the pockets of the munitions kings. The Liberals who came as interested visitors would be allowed to have their say. Afterward the politicians would get down to business and see that nothing was done to interfere with the traffic of the salesmen of death.

Versed in the ways and psychology of bourgeois politicians, Litvinov knew that any forthright proposals to
choke the armament dragon would embarrass the other
chief delegates. It would be considered extremely bad man-
ners. It would not be playing the game. But a forthright
proposal was just what the Bolshevik prepared to make.

On March nineteenth (1928) the Soviet representative
stood before the conference and demanded action. "It
seems to me that there has been more than enough discussion of disarmament," he shouted. "I venture to furnish
the members of this Commission with a few data from
which it will be seen that in addition to the General
Assemblies of the League of Nations and the Council meetings, thirty-eight sessions of which occupied themselves
with the question of disarmament, not fewer than fourteen
different commissions have devoted over 120 sessions—not
sittings, mark you, but sessions—to this same question on
which 111 resolutions have been passed by the General
Assemblies and Council alone."

The disarmament delegates were uncomfortable as the
enfant terrible from Moscow continued: "Turning to the
results of this vast quantity of work, the documentation
of which has taken reams of paper, we are forced to the
conclusion that not a single real step has been taken
toward the realization of disarmament. The Soviet delegation considers that an end should be put to a situation
which may discredit every idea of disarmament."

Litvinov's audience was aghast. No one could challenge
the truth of what he said. What threw the meeting into a
near panic was the fact that anyone had the bad taste to
come right out in public and air these truths before the
world. Every man in the hall knew that the wily Bolshevik was addressing a far larger audience than those who

sat uneasily in front of him. He was broadcasting his message to the world's proletariat.

Litvinov continued: "The Soviet Government has not sent its delegation to Geneva for this sort of work. The Soviet Government declares it is ready to abolish all military forces in accordance with its draft convention as soon as a similar decision is passed and simultaneously carried out by other states. The Soviet Government asks the other governments represented here if they are also ready."

Here was a clear, unequivocal proposal to disarm. After all, this was a disarmament conference. But it is safe to say that no delegate to the meeting had expected to make or hear any such proposal. And it was all the more embarrassing that the Communist representative should be the first to propose disarmament to a disarmament conference.

Without pausing for his audience to recover from their chagrin Litvinov pounded on: "The Soviet Government expects a reply to this question at the present session of the Preparatory Disarmament Commission, at which all the bigger states are represented. No subcommissions, nobody of lesser authority, can give the answer. The proposals formulated by myself are so clear as neither to demand nor admit of preliminary diplomatic negotiations between the different countries."

Litvinov was leaving no loophole. He was not proposing a general debate on an academic question. He was demanding action on a specific proposal.

"I repeat the two main questions," he cried. "First, does this Commission agree to base its further labors on the principle of complete disarmament during the period proposed by us? Second, is it prepared to carry out disarmament so as to make the conduct of war, if not an absolute impossibility, of extreme difficulty in a year's time?"

When the meeting was over worried delegates hurried to their hotels to dictate long cables to their respective governments. What should they do? How should they meet this unexpected challenge from the Bolshevik representative?

No practical politician at Geneva believed for a moment that the conference would adopt the Soviet proposal for immediate and total disarmament. A few idealists, strangers to the ways of power politics, might take this proposition seriously. But none of the delegates expected anything to come of it. Least of all did the Soviet delegation. Litvinov was far too intelligent, too well informed, too sophisticated, to expect the great powers to follow his suggestion. His purpose was to embarrass them and expose the hypocrisy of the disarmament show. In this he was completely successful. He was also successful in stirring peace hopes in common people all over the world. Until late August 1939 governments were to be nagged on many occasions by visionaries who took literally the Litvinov proposals for general disarmament.

The day after the Litvinov speech the other delegates had recovered somewhat from their surprise. Lord Cushendon of the British delegation replied to the Soviet disarmament challenge. In a bitter vein he charged that for seven years the League had been laboring to establish peace in the world, but in all that time it had never received help or encouragement from the Soviet Government. "Not only so," he exclaimed, "but the Soviet thought it right to lose no opportunity to revile the League and overwhelm it with derision!" The British diplomat's words were all too true.

Lord Cushendon then went on to express his suspicion of so sudden a change of view at Moscow. To bolster his argument he quoted from *Izvestia*, official organ of the Soviet Government, which predicted that the Geneva meeting would be futile. Litvinov, he reminded his audience, had expressed virtually the same conclusion the previous day. The Soviet delegate had not come to Geneva, he charged, to help disarmament but actually to block any serious attempt toward progress in the solution of the arms problem.

Referring again to *Izvestia*, the British representative continued his attack: "This article adds its scorn and is shared by the Soviet delegates. This is significant. It tells us that their purpose of coming here is to unmask the capitalistic states and—notice the words—to disclose sabotage of the Soviet proposals for disarmament." He charged that there was an "ulterior motive."

And what about the matter of police forces? If all armies were abolished, the police force of each country would, Lord Cushendon contended, be a kind of standing army. The country with a large police force would, accordingly, have a great armed superiority over the peaceful nation with few police. In this situation the Soviet Union would have the largest armed organization in the world.

Reaching his climax, the Briton asserted: "It is a fair question to ask whether the Soviet Government sets its face against civil war as resolutely as against international war ... because speaking about things that are notorious to the world—for years past the whole basis for the Soviet world policy has been to produce armed insurrection amounting to civil war in every country where they can exercise influence ... We ought to be told whether the Soviets now have decided no longer to interfere in the affairs of other nations."

The delegates from London and Moscow had shot it

out at the disarmament conference. Each had scored direct
hits on the other. But neither had contributed to the solution of the problem for which the conference was called,
the reduction of armaments.

Litvinov pressed on with his argument: "The U.S.S.R.
already has a smaller army, not to mention its navy, than
any other state in proportion to its population and the
extent of its frontiers, while if we consider individual
security—the favorite theme of this assembly—it must be
admitted that Soviet Russia is in a less favorable position
than any other state."

Less favorable than Poland or Czecho-Slovakia, Comrade Litvinov?

The Soviet delegate kept returning to his complaint:
"It (the U.S.S.R.) has almost the whole of the world
against it, in unconcealed hostility to the new state."
Against this assertion other delegates brought up Lord
Cushendon's charge that the Soviet Union was covertly
carrying on war against all capitalistic nations by means
of its Communist party organizations inside these states
and its incitements to civil war.

The disarmament conference dragged out its futile
course for months. The arguments wound on. Litvinov
often held the center of the stage, arguing with his usual
brilliance, always looking beyond his immediate audience
to that vast invisible audience of millions inside the
countries represented at the disarmament conference. He
was carrying out his purpose. He was confusing his opponents; he was causing international ill feeling. He was
killing any possible chance that the meeting might have
had to make a start toward the reduction of the world's
crushing armament burden.

Above all, at Geneva Litvinov had spoken for the

record. Henceforth whenever anybody took exception to the rapidly increasing militarization of the Soviet Union he could retort that the U.S.S.R. had vainly proposed immediate and total disarmament. The capitalistic nations had turned it down. The men who play power politics recognized the insincerity of the Soviet attitude toward disarmament, but millions of people who pay taxes and make sacrifices to support the armament burden did not. To many of them the Soviet Union was their hope for relief from the arms burden and Litvinov the high priest of the temple of disarmament.

CHAPTER IX

Litvinov Returns to Geneva

There are people who think that it is possible for us to conduct a revolutionary foreign policy and have the bourgeoisie of Western Europe kiss our hand for it. Such people can have nothing in common with our party.—JOSEPH STALIN.

THE SOVIET UNION'S RECORD in the League of Nations is one of the important dossiers of Stalin's diplomacy. It exemplifies the windings, the contradictions and the hypocrisy of the Kremlin's *Realpolitik*.

Why did the U.S.S.R. join the League? All true Communists condemned the Society of Geneva as a cabal of rapacious aggressors, an alliance of heartless imperialists. Did not the Soviet press take delight in exposing the "interested motives" of the League nations? Was not the Communist press throughout the world busily engaged in sowing suspicion and enmity toward the League? Had not Lenin himself referred to the League of Nations as a "gang of thieves"?

True. But by 1934 European events were moving fast. And the Kremlin found itself compelled to keep its diplomacy abreast of the times. There was no change in the Soviet leadership's fundamental hostility to the League, but much had happened to force Stalin into adopting new forms of diplomatic strategy. In the alchemy of power politics even Communism and Fascism must sometimes blend.

During the previous year, 1933, Hitler had come to power in the Reich. What the Bolsheviks had called the "pseudodemocratic German Government" had been swept away. In its place was now a militant National Socialist Third Reich.

For years the Nazis had made enmity to Communism one of the planks of their political platform. Thousands of German Reds were now incarcerated in National Socialist prison camps. Hitler shouted tirades of hatred against the U.S.S.R. Stalin and the Soviet leadership were the "bloodstained scum of humanity."

In spite of his anti-Bolshevik crusade, however, the Fuehrer made no move to break the secret liaison between the Reichswehr and the Red Army. Stalin knew that his staff officers were maintaining their co-operation with Hitler's military. He realized that it would be impossible for the Reichswehr hierarchy to keep up this relationship with the Soviet high command without Hitler's approval. It seems likely, therefore, that Stalin took Hitler's threats against the U.S.S.R. at somewhat less than their face value. Certainly he took them less seriously than did many people in France, Britain and America.

Just the same, Stalin could not afford to overlook the possibility that a little later on, when the German Army would have become a powerful fighting machine, Hitler might attack the Soviet Union. Too, Stalin knew that Hitler was carrying on a strong campaign in France and Britain to obtain Western support for a Nazi attack on the

U.S.S.R. Stalin apparently decided that it was no longer prudent for Moscow to play a lone-wolf role.

Besides, the Kremlin had to think not only in terms of Europe but also of Asia. For in the Far East an aggressive Japan was already entrenched in Manchuria. Moreover, Nipponese army circles were known to covet Vladivostok and the Soviet's maritime provinces. The Soviet leadership knew, too, that certain influential people in England looked without disfavor upon Japan's march northwestward toward the Soviet's Siberian life line. Japan's troops were now within striking distance of the trans-Siberian railway. Every mile Nippon advanced in this direction deflected her troops that much farther from the Yangtze, where Britain's Chinese investments and interests were concentrated.

How was Moscow to head off a twofold invasion of her territory, from the West and East simultaneously? Stalin could not afford to ignore the possible threat of a combined attack from the Germans, Poles and Japanese, backed by the British and French.

France at this time was growing increasingly uneasy about Hitler. No longer was the man with the *Charlot* mustache a boulevardier's joke. No longer could the Quai d'Orsay talk down to a Social Democratic German government. Paris, moreover, was never quite comfortable about the menace of a Second Rapallo. The French Government, therefore, urged the U.S.S.R. to enter the League of Nations. It was power politics and not the spirit of brotherhood, then, that brought the anticapitalist Soviet into that "gang of thieves" which Lenin had denounced.

When the League delegates assembled in September 1934 Maxim Litvinov was there to represent the Soviet

Union. He had given such a good account of himself at the disarmament conference that Stalin sent him back to Geneva as the League representative of the U.S.S.R. But let us not make the mistake of thinking that Comrade Litvinov formulated Moscow's foreign policies; he only carried out those policies as they were laid down for him by the master of the Kremlin.

For it must be kept constantly in mind that although Litvinov was a loyal Bolshevik, whose ability was respected by the Kremlin, he was never a dominant figure within Moscow's innermost circle. He was never a member of the all-powerful Politburo. He enjoyed no free hand to bind the U.S.S.R. to any policy which might conflict with Stalin's long-range imperialism. The sharp-tongued diplomat was almost indispensable for certain foreign missions. He was to serve his purpose as Stalin's front. As soon as no such front was needed he was to be unceremoniously dropped.

Stalin's League representative was in some respects a man of two worlds. As one of the Old Bolsheviks, he had been a disciple of Lenin long before the revolution. And he was one of the few Soviet leaders who understood the psychology of the Western world. In this respect Litvinov held an enormous advantage over all the other Russian Communist leaders, Tchicherin included, who came into contact with representatives of the capitalistic nations.

Born in 1876 at Byalystok, then a town of Russian Poland, he attended a gymnasium and served in the army. When he was only twenty-two he ran afoul of the Tsar's secret police, was arrested, charged with revolutionary activities and sentenced to five years in Siberia. Soon afterward he escaped from his prison and fled Russia. For the next two decades he was to pursue an active and hazardous existence as a revolutionary, part of the time in Russia but most of the time in western Europe. He was once arrested in Paris as he was trying to cash some Russian rubles, the numbers of which proved that they had been stolen in a bold holdup in the Caucasus. Stalin and his group are credited with having engineered this act of banditry. The French promptly expelled Litvinov. He went over to England.

From each country that he visited he learned more about the ways of bourgeois society. In appearance this enemy of the bourgeoisie came to look like a middle-class businessman. He wore correct clothes, carried himself conventionally and played his bourgeois part well. It is a tribute to his sagacity, savoir faire and nimble wits that during the war years he was able to go from country to country with little trouble. At that time travel was extremely hard even for people who had bonafide business. At one period during the war Litvinov seems to have been a language teacher in Amsterdam; at another time he met with Lenin and Bukharin at a revolutionary conference in Zurich. When the revolution broke in Russia, strange to say, he appears to have been on the staff of a Tsarist purchasing commission in London.

When Litvinov chose a wife the lady was Ivy Low, member of a family of good standing in England. When he joined his fellow Bolsheviks in Russia she voluntarily left England to take her place beside him in that land of hardship and mystery then cut off by the Allied blockade and the *Cordon Sanitaire*. She was to help her husband entertain bourgeois diplomats in the former Sugar King's Palace which faces the Kremlin.

A man of extraordinary energy and tenacity, Litvinov could outhaggle nearly every man who had to negotiate with him. Rarely was he at a loss for an answer or a move. In August 1921, when he met Herbert Hoover's representatives at Riga, he made himself obnoxious by his suspicion and obstructionism. In exasperation one of the Hoover men finally exclaimed: "After all, Mr Litvinov, all we are trying to do is send food in to your starving people!" Litvinov shot back: "But food is a weapon!"

In almost every case this stratagem of tireless haggling wore down the resistance of his opponent. But in the foreign missions at Moscow they used to tell the story of the one occasion when Litvinov was outhaggled. It was at a session with the Japanese ambassador to the U.S.S.R. The Japanese diplomat, trained in Far Eastern diplomatic dueling, could more than hold his own with Litvinov. Outmaneuvered at his own Oriental game of having the final word, the Soviet's champion negotiator was said to have complained: "These Japanese seem to have no conception of time whatever!"

Litvinov's opponents could always expect the unexpected. On one occasion the representative of a capitalistic nation suggested that an "impartial" chairman should be appointed to preside over a meeting called to discuss the Soviet Union's indebtedness. Litvinov sneered: "Only an angel could be an impartial chairman. There are two worlds, capitalist and Soviet. There is said to be a third world in the skies—the only one where angels live. I do not think that any of its inhabitants are present at this conference."

When Litvinov took his seat as a delegate to the League of Nations his keynote resounded: "Peace is indivisible!" War, or the threat of war, anywhere was everybody's business. The peace-loving nations ought to form a coalition against the aggressor nations. Moscow, so Moscow's man maintained, was the champion of collective security. He righteously denounced the Japanese aggression in China. On every occasion he attacked the policies of National Socialism. He was critical of Poland's diplomatic adventures in both camps, the German and French.

In the spring of 1935 Maxim Maximovitch Litvinov began his campaign to bring the Western democracies into his proposed "Eastern Locarno." By this ingenious plan he hoped to draw Britain, France, the Little Entente and the Soviet Union into a powerful alliance to preserve the status quo of eastern Europe. This coalition would nail down the current frontiers against German and Polish aggressors. Moreover, it would give the Soviet some freedom of action in the Far East to deal with the Japanese menace to Siberia. The Eastern Locarno received no little encouragement from the French. The Quai d'Orsay saw immediately that if this pact could be put over, Hitler's *Drang nach Osten* (drive to the East) would be stopped before it really could get started. And if the Fuehrer moved against the West, France would have the support of the nations to the east of the Reich.

The Czechs liked the Eastern Locarno idea immensely. It promised to guarantee their frontiers, boundaries which enclosed a German minority of more than three millions, a Magyar minority of three quarters of a million, a half-million Ukrainians, about one hundred thousand Poles and many dissident Slovaks. Such an alliance would assure the Czechs of overwhelming support in the event that the safety of their republic was threatened.

Elsewhere the Eastern Locarno did not arouse a great deal of enthusiasm. British Conservatives were unwilling to guarantee the borders of central Europe. Many Englishmen felt that some of these frontiers had been drawn in contravention of justice, economics, self-determination and common sense. They foresaw the day when the territorial settlements which emerged from the postwar peace conferences would be challenged. Britain hoped to escape commitments to fight again on the Continent. To boot, tricky Comrade Litvinov did not inspire a great deal of confidence in the ranks of British Conservatives. And it was the Conservatives who were in power in Britain.

In Hungary the Eastern Locarno was violently denounced as an effort to encircle and enslave the Magyars permanently. Hungarians blamed the Russians and Czechs with equal bitterness, seeing in the proposed pact an attempt to perpetuate the "crime of Trianon," by which Hungary had lost about two thirds of her prewar territory. Hungarian diplomacy looked hopefully to Berlin, Rome, Warsaw and Sofia for friends who would help Budapest achieve territorial adjustments at the expense of the hated Little Entente countries.

The Poles were hardly less hostile to Litvinov's Eastern Locarno. For Poland, though holding vast tracts of land inhabited by non-Poles, had her own expansionist ambitions. There were "Poland from sea to sea" Poles who dreamed of bringing back a great Polish empire that would stretch from the Baltic to the Black Sea. But there were more realistic Poles who were thinking first in terms of Teschen, a small border district held by the Czechs but claimed by the Poles. If the Eastern Locarno became a reality, the Poles would have to give up any idea of seizing Teschen at an opportune moment. And it did the Eastern Locarno cause no service in Warsaw when the Quai d'Orsay tried to promote the cause over Colonel Beck's head. For the Colonel held an old grudge against France, an ancient grudge that had lasted since he was the Polish military attaché in Paris. And the French had no love for the Colonel.

As the spring months passed the Eastern Locarno project made no headway. Does that mean that Litvinov's diplomacy was not successful? On the contrary, it was succeeding very well. For part of his strategy was to confuse and divide—a basic feature of Stalinist foreign policy. As long as his opponents were quarreling with one another they were not likely to unite against him. Litvinov was using French and Czech support of the Eastern Locarno scheme to further Stalin's plans against the Germans and Poles.

While the League members were still arguing hotly about a collective security pact for eastern Europe, there were disquieting developments in another quarter. Italy was making preliminary gestures of attack against Ethiopia. The Duce was threatening action to stop alleged Ethiopian aggressions against Italian territory in East Africa. Encouraged undoubtedly by the ease with which the Japanese had, with tacit British approval, successfully defied the League, Mussolini was preparing to extend the boundaries of his budding Roman empire. Here was a clean-cut challenge to the League. If one member could attack another member with impunity, what would happen to Geneva's prestige?

The Russian implications of the situation were not lost upon diplomat Litvinov. It was at once a threat to the Soviet and an opportunity for his diplomacy to shine at Geneva. And diplomatic shining was no hard work for Maxim Maximovitch. Throughout the summer of 1935 he watched Mussolini's preparations to invade the land of the Negus. And with equal interest he observed Britain's preparations to bluff the Duce out of his African conquest.

When the League assembled for an extraordinarily important meeting at the beginning of September Litvinov was on hand to play a stellar role. As the champion of collective security, the opponent of war, the friend of small nations, the eternal enemy of imperialism, the last-ditch antagonist of Fascism, the Soviet Union saw its chance to make a grand stage play. And without taking undue risks.

On September fourteenth Litvinov held the center of the Geneva forum. The world spotlight was turned on him. He could rest assured that his words would be translated into languages read by hundreds of millions of people. He was speaking not only to the world's proletariat; he was working to win the support of millions of moderates all over the globe who hated war and unilateral treaty breaking. His was an impassioned speech. He furiously challenged the opponents of peace.

"The Soviet Government," he shouted, "is opposed to the system of colonies, to spheres of influence and imperialism.

"For the Soviet Government there is only one question: of defending the Covenant as an instrument of peace.

"The Soviet Government will be second to none in loyally discharging its obligations."

He went on to demand a permanent peace conference to warn "an aggressor that there is an organ permanently keeping watch on the maintenance of peace."

Litvinov's eloquence drew applause from the world press. Here, at long last, was a man willing to speak out against wrong. In the U.S.S.R. the peace-loving peoples of the world had a protector. The Litvinov speech made splendid newspaper copy. It provided material for innumerable editorials, sermons, lectures and articles praising the Soviet stand against Fascist aggression.

For all Litvinov's lofty condemnation of the Duce, however, the Soviet was supplying the Italian Army with large quantities of oil and other war materials. Stalin's commercial relations with the Duce were on a most co-operative basis. The Red dictator could be reasonably sure that a master politician like the Duce would recognize Litvinov's oratory as super-stage play.

But the Soviet was not the only inconsistent member of the League. Even while Britain's representatives at Geneva were trying to line up the world against the Duce, British oil was flowing into Italian tankers to supply fuel for Italy's motorized divisions and bombing planes in East Africa. If Britain denounced the Soviet for helping Mussolini, Litvinov would point an accusing finger at John Bull and make the welkin ring with charges of Albion's perfidy. So Britain's representatives did not bear down too hard on the U.S.S.R. to stop arming the aggressor for an assault on a fellow member of the Society of Nations.

But now that Britain's life line was threatened by Italy, John Bull took no such tolerant view of the aggression as he had done when Nippon invaded Manchuria. When Britain dispatched her fleet to the Mediterranean in late August it looked as if the Empire meant business. The hostility of the U.S.S.R. toward Britain began to undergo a slight change. The Soviet press even praised Britain for her efforts to "reinforce the interests of peace and strengthen the authority of the League of Nations."

Then came Sir Samuel Hoare's sturdy declaration at Geneva that Britain was devoted "to the League Covenant in its entirety." London's spokesman went even farther when he declared that his government stood in "solid opposition" to all cases of aggression. This is the Sir Samuel Hoare who a few months later worked out with Pierre

Laval the ill-starred Hoare-Laval Plan which allocated a large part of Ethiopia to the Duce.

Sir Samuel's forthright words at Geneva in defense of peace and the League gave Litvinov an opening to bring up once more his project of an Eastern Locarno. If the British opposed aggression in the interior of far-off Africa, argued Maxim Maximovitch, why should they not be concerned with threats to peace in the heart of Europe? Should not charity begin fairly near home? John Bull was asking other nations to help him stop the Duce, who was not threatening their interests but Britain's. Very well, then, why should not John Bull be willing to help stop aggression when it did not immediately threaten the Empire's holdings? These questions were all the more embarrassing because they were to the point. Still London refused to commit Britannia to defense of the status quo in eastern Europe.

One of the sideshows of Litvinov's antiaggression speech was staged by the Polish delegation. The Soviet spokesman took the opportunity to denounce the nonaggression pact which binds two nations not to make war on each other. Such a pact leaves each signatory free to attack a third party. Colonel Beck, head of the Polish delegation, assumed immediately that the Bolshevik delegate was referring to the German-Polish pact. He was probably correct in this assumption. Beck made a vigorous speech attacking the Soviet representative and impugning his motives. When Litvinov got up to reply the entire Polish delegation ostentatiously marched out of the hall.

Not of great importance in itself, the Beck-Litvinov clash high-lighted the situation in eastern Europe. And it corroborated the French, Russian and Czech belief that Poland and Germany were playing a close game of diplomatic co-operation. Superficially, it gave them the impression that the Nazis and Poles were allies. Beck's gesture in walking out on Litvinov probably strengthened the Soviet delegate's diplomatic position, especially in his relations with France and Czecho-Slovakia.

Now Litvinov did not approve of Mussolini's invasion of Ethiopia. Undoubtedly he opposed it wholeheartedly. For that matter, Stalin probably disapproved of it. But Soviet opposition to the Duce was not based on concern for the Negus and his primitive landlocked kingdom. It was motivated by the Kremlin's fear that if the Duce swept to an easy victory in East Africa, the Japanese militarists and the German Nazis would be tempted to try similar aggressions at the expense of the U.S.S.R. If the Italians could be stopped, their defeat would be a warning to the ambitious militarists in Tokio and Berlin. Meantime the Communist dictator could be doing business with the Fascist dictator.

The September session of the League of Nations also gave orator Litvinov an opportunity to return to his old love, the campaign for total disarmament. Almost apoplectic in his appeals that the great powers disarm, he indignantly repudiated the argument that total disarmament was utopian.

"I maintain, on the contrary," he shouted, "that the utmost difficulty is presented by partial, and the least difficulty by total, disarmament.

"If and when it seems that the feasible has proved utopian let us try whether what seems to be utopian will not prove feasible." It was tremendously effective propaganda for the Kremlin. Litvinov knew the art of making it sound sincere, especially for the proletariat the world over.

By 1937 the member states of the League of Nations had taken a fatalistic attitude toward armaments. All the great powers were feverishly gathering reserves of raw materials, strengthening their industrial machines, adding to their armies, navies and air forces and accumulating vast hoards of munitions. The Soviet Union was appropriating almost fabulous amounts of rubles for its armaments. Already it claimed the largest air armada in the world. And it maintained that its army in the Far East was now on its own, entirely equipped and supplied by the collective farms and factories of Siberia.

It would be a slur on Litvinov's intelligence to suggest that he believed that there was any longer a chance to stop the headlong armament race. The competition between the rival coalitions, the competing blocs and the hostile ideologies was too bitter and powerful. And Stalin must have realized that the trend toward autarchic national economies was in itself creating increasing unemployment, trade stagnation and the seeds of war. The Soviet leadership obviously meant their reiterated warnings that Europe was heading for a major conflict.

Maxim Maximovitch Litvinov, as president of the Council of the League of Nations, occupied a reserved seat at Europe's ringside. He continued to make careful preparations for whatever turn events might take. Undoubtedly he personally would have preferred to carry through an alliance between the U.S.S.R. and the Western democracies. We can be certain that the non-Aryan diplomat was never friendly to the Nazis. We can be sure that he tried to forestall any situation that would promote a Nazi-Soviet deal. Blocked, however, by the British Conservatives, his Eastern Locarno project was dead. And France was still unwilling to implement with a military alliance the rather indefinite entente which had been formed between Paris and Moscow. The British and French feared a Second Rapallo, it is true, but they were even more afraid of the Frankenstein which the Soviet Union might prove to be as an ally.

CHAPTER X

"If You Know Your Dostoyevsky . . ."

ON DECEMBER 1, 1934, there was a shooting in Leningrad. Now a violent death more or less in the Red dictatorship is as the fall of a sparrow. But this was shaggy-haired Sergei Kirov, Bolshevik party boss of that region and close friend of Stalin, and he was assassinated by Comrade Leonid Nikolaev. The shooting took place in historic Smolny Institute, an aristocratic girls' school in Tsarist days and Lenin's headquarters during the Soviet revolution. In every European capital the chancelleries watched for the aftermath. A mysterious political murder in the Soviet high places would undoubtedly prove of more than local significance.

When the news of the Kirov murder was flashed to the Kremlin Stalin hurried off to Leningrad to supervise the investigation. Accompanied by Genrikh Yagoda, chief of the OGPU, and picked operatives of the secret police, the Soviet dictator arrived on a bitterly cold winter morning. Within a few hours the Soviet authorities announced the arrest of seventy-seven alleged "White Guardists." Before a week had passed sixty-six victims of

Stalin's man hunt had been put to death. They were charged with conspiring against the Soviet Government.

The Kirov murder, according to the OGPU, was part of a gigantic plot against the Soviet leadership organized by the followers of Trotzky, Kamenev and Zinoviev. The conspirators were accused of attempting to interfere with the Soviet's relations with other countries. Most damning of all was the accusation that these so-called Trotzkyites advocated "permanent revolution." Before the end of December at least fifty more victims of the Stalin dragnet had been executed. The former Leningrad Soviet chief, Yevdokimov, was placed under arrest.

Resolutions from village soviets, collective farms, factories, mines, theatrical companies and other groups poured into Moscow. "We will give blow for blow to our enemy!" read a typical resolution. "Death to the enemies of the working class!"

Pravda displayed little editorial reticence in the matter. "The bloody capitalist beast, which is weakening and is mad in its resistance, will be exterminated!" warned the official organ of the Communist party.

Premier Molotov thundered his vengeance against the foe. "We swear to carry on a merciless fight against every enemy of our revolution!"

Resolutions from every corner of the U.S.S.R. continued to pour in. The Kremlin blandly publicized them. Denunciation of the Kirov crime was not held incompatible with pep-meeting zeal. "We shock-brigade workers of the Neva hydroelectric station," read one such message, "pledge ourselves to complete it ahead of time as our answer to the dastardly assassination of Comrade Kirov!"

Throughout this propaganda tirade against the murderers of Stalin's "dear friend Sergei" the Zinoviev faction seems to be confused with capitalism. Thus the reader would be led to believe that Zinoviev, an Old Bolshevik, a former president of the Leningrad Soviet and president of the Third International was a champion of capitalism. Judging from some of the resolutions and editorial broadsides, he might have been president of the Bank of England. This confusion is exemplified in a statement of the Moscow Soviet: "The abominable cunning agents of the class enemies, the coward scum of the former Zinoviev anti-Party group, have torn Comrade Kirov from our ranks. We will stamp out every one of the vile counter-revolutionary followers of the anti-Party."

While this post-Kirov cleanup was in progress Kamenev and Zinoviev were arrested. These two were former members of the Soviet hierarchy. Both had been members of the all-powerful Politburo of the Central Committee of the Communist party. Kamenev had enjoyed the distinction of being president of the Moscow Soviet. Here were no helpless kulaks, but Old Bolsheviks, close associates of Lenin, men who had been prominent in Soviet affairs when Stalin was almost unknown even in the U.S.S.R. Now they lay in the cells of the OGPU, charged with conspiracy against Joseph Vissarionovitch Djugashvili, now become the "man of steel"—Joseph Stalin.

Even five years after the Kirov murder the foreign intelligence services operating inside the Soviet Union were not in agreement as to the reasons underlying the assassination. Did Trotzky's friends in Russia actually attempt to strike at Stalin through the person of Kirov? Or did Stalin himself arrange this murder to have a pretext for the party bloodletting that he had planned? Who could say for certain? But the second question gave the measure of Stalin's reputation among the best-informed foreign observers.

It seems safe to conclude that in any event Stalin took instant advantage of the situation to liquidate his intra-party enemies and gain undisputed control of the Communist party and the Soviet Government. The purge was to go on until every man who might have ideas that conflicted with Stalin's would go down before a firing squad or die miserably in the cork-lined cellars of the OGPU. In this demoniac annihilation of Old Bolsheviks sardonic melodrama was to be staged in Soviet courtrooms. And the consequences were to influence Russian affairs, in war and in peace, for years to come.

As part of Stalin's campaign against the intraparty opposition his propaganda machine went to work to build him up as the loyal disciple and aide-de-camp who always stood at the right hand of Lenin. The Red tsar could afford to give Lenin unstinted praise because Lenin was dead and could not be a rival. In the offensive to eradicate Trotzky's name from Russian books, his face from Russian pictures and his body from Russian statues, Stalin's minions performed a thorough job. Russian school children are now brought up in the belief that it was Lenin and Stalin who carried through the revolution and civil wars to their triumphant conclusion. Not only Trotzky but nearly all the Old Bolsheviks were propagandized into historic oblivion by Stalin.

As the months passed the purges went on. Men and women were expelled from the party by thousands. The OGPU arrested numberless victims, at all hours of day and night. Few of these people went on public trial; most of them simply dropped out of sight. And no friend or relative ever risked asking the fate of an OGPU captive.

The Stalin purge took the line of uprooting the Trotzky "enemies of the people" who were charged with "wrecking" the industry and agriculture of the U.S.S.R. These alleged followers of Trotzky were accused of causing thirty-five hundred railroad wrecks in the two years from 1935 to 1937. Unbiased foreign observers in Moscow suspected that the "Trotzkyist wreckers" were the Kremlin's scapegoats for the widespread inefficiency and bad technology of unskilled industrial workers and the resistance of an unsympathetic peasantry. It was a simpler matter for Stalin to charge his failures to Trotzky than to acknowledge that many of his industrial plans were impracticable and that his henchmen lacked the experience and technical knowledge to make them succeed.

But the Russian public was given no opportunity to suspect that Soviet industrialization was not rapidly overtaking that of the western European nations and America. The badly clothed, underfed and overworked Russian citizen was told day in and day out that the Socialist fatherland was the target of attacks by envious capitalist states and their Trotzkyist agents. In order to expose these evil machinations, the Kremlin explained, it was necessary to make an example of the "wreckers" before the Soviet public. Hence the theatrical and highly publicized treason trials.

To repeat, the men on trial for "wrecking" and "treason" against the U.S.S.R. were not the remnants of the old bourgeoisie; they were not monarchists or former Tsarist officers. In many cases they were Old Bolsheviks, the comrades of Lenin, the men who had made the Bolshevik revolution possible, the men who had fought for the new Soviet republic in the civil wars.

The treason trials followed a formula. The victim signed a written confession recounting his plots against the U.S.S.R. He confirmed this confession, and perhaps even added to it, in open court before microphones and newsreel men. He did not merely admit, he positively proclaimed, that he was a member of the Trotzky-Bukharin-Zinoviev conspiracy. It was a Red revival of the auto-da-fé.

On August 19, 1936, Kamenev, Zinoviev and fourteen others were brought to trial in Moscow. "Revolution," said some observers, "once more is devouring its own children." The Soviet press outdid itself in heaping abuse on these Old Bolsheviks. No name was too vile for them; no charge too fantastic. Specifically, the court charge against the victims was an alleged plot to murder Stalin. They were, of course, charged with being associates of Trotzky. Four days later the trial was over. All were condemned to death. Ignominiously in the OGPU cellars Kamenev and Zinoviev were done to death, two of the leaders of the November revolution.

The next treason trial came in January 1937. The chief victims were Gregory Sokolnikov, formerly vice-chairman of the Commissariat of Foreign Affairs and onetime ambassador to Great Britain, Karl Radek, the brilliant Soviet journalist, and G. L. Piatikov, a former vice-chairman of heavy industry. The fundamental accusation was the same as that of their predecessors, a conspiracy to murder Stalin. The variation on the theme was the charge that these victims had been in touch not only with Trotzky but also with Adolf Hitler.

According to the prosecution Trotzky had met Rudolph Hess, one of Hitler's keymen, in Oslo. There he and the men on trial had arranged to instigate a war between the Reich and the Soviet, assassinate Stalin, wreck the Russian armament program and bring about a German-Japanese victory. The object: the Reich was to have the Ukraine; Japan was to have a sizable area of eastern Siberia.

At one point in the trial Radek proclaimed: "I am guilty of all the charges of all the terrorist plots—even those I didn't know about." At another point the prosecutor shook his fist in Radek's face, shouting: "You prince of two-faced scoundrels!"

Radek and Sokolnikov were given long prison sentences; thirteen others were condemned to death.

The next month the purge moved from Moscow to Paris. Comrade Navachine, formerly in the service of the Soviet Government, had broken with the Kremlin and threatened to deliver a lecture exposing the treason trials. This would have been extremely embarrassing to Stalin, inasmuch as he counted on continued support from Blum, Herriot and other French Left leaders. As Navachine was walking in a Paris park a man fired at him and fled. Navachine would never give the anti-Stalin lecture.

During the following April sensation was piled on sensation by the arrest of Genrikh Yagoda, for ten years chief of the dreaded OGPU and for a time commissar of internal affairs. He was succeeded by Nikolai Yezhof. Ironically enough Yagoda, who had sent so many thousands of people to their doom, now found himself caught in the lethal net he had spread for others.

The purge was speeding onward at a dizzy rate. It was disclosed, for example, that fifty-three per cent of the Communist party members at Minsk, capital of White Russia, had been expelled. They were charged with Trotzkyist activities.

Apace with the purge inside the party, proceeded liquidation of "enemy agents." In Svobodny, a hamlet in eastern Siberia, forty-four Russians, men and women, were shot at one time on the charge that they were in the service of the Japanese intelligence service.

At the end of May Marshal I. B. Gamarnik, an Old Bolshevik and vice-commissar for defense, committed suicide (according to the government).

In June the Red terror took a new turn. For some time there had been rumors of dissension within the leadership of the Soviet military establishment. Stalin, ever suspicious of anyone in authority, decided to reinstitute the system of army commissars. This system diminished the authority of the army officers, because the officer could execute a command only if the commissar countersigned it. No army officer in the world would like such a system. Such a divided command hamstrings the officer and works against authority and efficiency. Marshal Tukhachevsky, considered by many foreign observers the most brilliant officer in the Red Army, opposed the commissar system. Some concluded, therefore, that it was for that reason that Stalin decided to liquidate him.

But that was not the reason ascribed by the intelligence agents of certain Baltic countries. They reported to their respective governments that a bitter feud had developed between Tukhachevsky and Marshal Klementi Voroshilov. This quarrel between rival leaders in the Red Army hierarchy placed Stalin in the same position that was Hitler's three years previously. At that time (1934) in Germany the notorious Captain Roehm was demanding that his Storm Troops and the Reichswehr be consolidated. Naturally the German army chiefs objected. The Roehm-Reichswehr dispute finally reached the point where Hitler had to make an irrevocable choice between the two. He was compelled to make a "totalitarian decision." He sided with the Reichswehr and had Roehm and his confederates shot.

Stalin, the Baltic governments were informed, was compelled to choose between his two rival military leaders. Voroshilov was amenable to machine policies. Tukhachevsky was more independent. In a democracy Marshal Tukhachevsky would probably have been publicly thanked, ceremoniously decorated and painlessly retired. But Asiatic Stalin had his own way of retiring an officer.

Marshal Tukhachevsky and seven generals (Kork, Putna, Yakir, Eideman, Uborevitch, Feldman and Primakov) were brought to trial simultaneously. The charge was treason against the Soviet Union. They were apparently not accused of Trotzkyism. According to the prosecutor they had been in contact with a foreign government. Although it seems that no name was mentioned (at least publicly), everyone understood that the foreign government was the Third Reich of Adolf Hitler.

One of the eight accused, General Putna, had served at various times as the Soviet military attaché in London, Berlin and Tokio. But that is hardly a damning fact. If a government cannot trust its military attachés it is in a bad way indeed. As for Tukhachevsky, he had made a brilliant record and was highly respected abroad as a military strategist. It was sadistic irony for Stalin to charge that the marshal had been in touch with the Reichswehr. Of course he had.

The governments of Lithuania, Latvia, Estonia, Finland and probably several other countries knew that the Reichswehr-Red Army relationship had never been broken. The entente could be maintained only with Stalin's approval. Had Stalin suddenly changed his mind about the co-operation? And might he not change his mind again just as suddenly? In the small states of the borderland these questions caused no little anxiety at foreign ministries and general staff headquarters.

The intelligence services of the Baltic countries stood by their reports that the purge in the Red Army did not involve a change of Soviet foreign policy; it was Stalin's way of gaining absolute control of the U.S.S.R. by the mass elimination of opponents, actual and potential.

Meanwhile the trial was coming to an end. In his verdict Judge Ulrich asserted: "The Court has established that the defendants were employed by the military secret service of a foreign government conducting an unfriendly policy toward the Soviet Union."

The eight victims were condemned to die before a firing squad. *Pravda* exploded: "Dogs die like dogs! There is no place for such murderers in the Soviet scheme of things!"

These killings moved the New York *Times* to speak of "Stalin's new five-year plan to eradicate the entire population of Russia."

Additional light was thrown on Stalin's motives and methods in the Tukhachevsky case by Alexandre Barmine, former Soviet chargé d'affaires at Athens and once a brigadier general in the Red Army. Mr Barmine, by the way, seems to have narrowly escaped being returned to Russia and purged. In a letter to the New York *Times*, dated March 25, 1940, Mr Barmine asserted that "the OGPU and Gestapo jointly manufactured 'proof' of Tukhachevsky & Co.'s pro-Germanism and the legend that they carried on secret negotiations."

These fabrications were supplied to Stalin by agents working simultaneously for the Soviet OGPU and the Nazi Gestapo. "Then he (Stalin) used these forgeries to convince the Czecho-Slovak leaders, and through them the French and English, of Tukhachevsky's guilt, which created the proper camouflage to enable Stalin to continue playing his game of duplicity."

The reverberations from the Tukhachevsky affair lasted a long time. Perhaps more than anything else that Stalin could have done it lowered the prestige of the Red Army. Either the Soviet army was permeated with treason, observers reasoned, or Stalin had framed his best military men. The Red tsar had, it is true, strengthened his tyranny over the army. But he was winning this victory at the cost of a rapidly deteriorating military leadership. Two and a half years later in Finland the world was to see the results of Stalin's Red Army purges.

The following December (1937) Leo Karakhan, a former Soviet diplomat of the first rank, and several others were executed for alleged conspiracies with the Japanese. Again observers pointed out that treason in the Soviet Government must be on a gigantic scale or that men were being convicted on bogus charges. In either event the prestige of the U.S.S.R. could hardly be said to have increased.

By this time the Soviet populace should have been shockproof. But the most sensational of all the public Soviet inquisitions was yet to be staged. In early March 1938 Alexei Rykov, Nikolai Bukharin, Genrikh Yagoda, Gregory Grinko, Nikolai Krestinsky and more than a dozen others were brought to trial. Rykov, former premier, and Bukharin, whose writings had charted the official party line, had been members of the all-powerful Politburo. Yagoda was chief of the OGPU. Now they were "enemies of the people."

At this trial Rykov and Bukharin were the targets of special vengeance from their Stalinist enemies. It seemed as if all the comrades not actually under arrest were vying with one another to vilify the accused. This was, of course, a form of life insurance. Not an infallible one, however, because not infrequently the judge and prosecutor of one trial would be the accused in a subsequent showing of Stalin's Grand Guignol.

Undoubtedly Valery I. Mezlauk, commissar of heavy industry, was speaking for the record when he said: "It is hard to imagine a more atrocious spectacle than Bukharin and Rykov, who have betrayed the interests of the working class and of their country."

And Comrade Stalin added this condemnation of his enemies: "It is a rotten theory to say that Trotzkyists do not have reserves in the Soviet Union among the remnants of the exploiting classes and among foreign traitors."

At the close of the trial Rykov, Bukharin, Krestinsky, Yagoda, Grinko and thirteen other purge victims were killed, adding eighteen more names to the long list of Old Bolsheviks liquidated by party boss Stalin.

Word from Paris that Leon Trotzky had set up a committee of his Fourth International in the French capital undoubtedly spurred Stalin and his satraps to even greater activity against all those in the U.S.S.R. who might fall under the suspicion of the OGPU. Neutral observers in Moscow discounted the charges of widespread Trotzkyist activities in the Soviet Union. In the face of the ubiquitous OGPU it was unthinkable that even so clever a conspirator as the former chief of the Red Army could set up a formidable organization in a land ruled by absolutist Stalin and his secret police.

In America Professor John Dewey did not mince matters: "If Trotzky is guilty no condemnation can be too severe, and if he is innocent there is no way in which the existing regime in Soviet Russia can be acquitted of deliberate, systematic persecution and falsification."

But if these trials were colossal frame-ups, how was it possible for the government to induce the damning confessions made by the accused? Why did these men, especially the Old Bolsheviks, stand up in court and describe in detail their plots against the state, against their fellow workers, against Soviet property, against the life of Stalin? How explain such macabre self-accusations?

"If you know your Dostoyevsky," explained one well-known foreign correspondent in Moscow, "then these trials make sense."

But many who know their Dostoyevsky were unable to attribute to the purge victims anything of the famous novelist's morbid psychology. Foreign observers of long residence in Moscow could find nothing in the Russian character to account for the almost psychopathic behavior of the men on trial. Neither Russian fatalism nor the Slavic love of grand-scale tragedy made any clearer the strange fact that men who had spent their lives working for a cause should suddenly announce that they had been sabotaging their lifework. The Dostoyevsky theory hardly solved the mystery.

Those who took a more practical view of the situation had explanations that might have been taken from a volume of Poe. They believed that the victims were subjected to OGPU torture to wring the desired confessions. Those who were obdurate found that their relatives were being persecuted. In order to save a wife, a mother or a child they made the confessions supplied by the OGPU. In certain cases, so it was believed, prisoners were shown men who had disappeared and were supposed to be dead. The latter, the OGPU were said to have told the new prisoners, had confessed and saved themselves. Some purge victims undoubtedly played their weird parts in the courtrooms on the promise that their lives would be spared. How many of them were rewarded by prolonged imprisonment, instead of immediate death, in return for their confessions only the OGPU records could tell us.

We do know that the vast majority of Old Bolshevik leaders were liquidated in one way or another. Of the seven men who comprised the Politburo in 1924, when Lenin died and Stalin began to take over, only Stalin remained. Trotzky was driven into exile. Tomsky, evidently expecting to be purged, committed suicide. Zinoviev, Kamenev, Rykov and Bukharin were shot. Their comrade Stalin, sole survivor, now dominated the powerful board on which they had formerly been members. In *The Inside Story* Eugene Lyons calls the purge of Old Bolsheviks "Stalin's counterrevolution."

There was one person from the outside world who bluntly questioned Stalin about the purges and received just as blunt a reply. This happened when Lady Astor and George Bernard Shaw went on their sight-seeing junket to Moscow. Lady Astor asked the Soviet dictator: "When are you going to stop killing people?" Stalin replied: "When it is no longer necessary."

In the light of the Berlin-Moscow pact of August 1939 we have an interpretation of the purges which began almost five years before. Stalin was not only eliminating the men who might oppose his internal policies; he was ridding himself of the Old Bolsheviks who might be expected to veto an entente with Nazi Germany. For most of these Communist veterans supported the policies charted by Lenin. They had, it is true, approved the military relations with the pre-Hitler Reichswehr. That was only a means to an end. But many of the Old Bolsheviks were last-ditch opponents of Hitler. This was especially true of Jewish Communists like Zinoviev, Kamenev, Radek and Rosengolts.

And why was Litvinov spared by Stalin? Until the pact with Hitler was assured, Litvinov was needed to represent the U.S.S.R. at Geneva. Stalin needed him to encourage the United Front of anti-Fascist groups in the democracies and to negotiate with the British and French governments. It was Litvinov's job to prevent the formation of an anti-Soviet coalition. No one could do this work so well. But Litvinov's days as commissar of foreign affairs were numbered. His exit would be the signal of a drastic change in Stalin's diplomatic tactics. That is why my contacts in the Baltic States during the latter part of 1938 and early 1939 kept advising me: "Keep your eyes on Litvinov!"

CHAPTER XI

Moscow's *Realpolitik*

IT WAS THE SOVIETS who originated the streamlined technique of undeclared war which Hitler brought to perfection in his program of expansion. Yet for years before the outbreak of the second World War, as we have seen, the U.S.S.R. posed as the world's foremost champion of the rights of small nations. Maxim Litvinov had taken the leading role in the attempt to tie Europe up into one vast network of nonaggression and mutual-assistance pacts. Many people in the Western democracies and America believed the Kremlin's vaunt that the Soviet Union had always respected the territorial integrity of other countries. But was this true?

The democratic world quickly forgot certain events that took place in eastern Europe in the latter months of the World War and in the years immediately following that conflict. Little is said these days about the Bolshevik depredations toward the small Baltic countries. There is an impression current that the Soviet invasion of Finland in late 1939 was the first recorded instance of aggression by the U.S.S.R. But what of the Soviet's attack on Finland in 1918?

Let us cite an unbiased authority. In his Report for the Foreign Policy Association, dated May 27, 1931, Professor Malbone W. Graham says: "Because of her position in adjacence to the group of northern neutrals, Finland was felt to form an excellent base from which revolution could spread westward into Europe. To convert the former Grand Duchy into a Soviet Republic became, accordingly, one of the initial missionary enterprises of the Communist faith. But the efforts to spread Communism by fire and sword among a basically democratic people, steeled in defense of their native institutions by the excesses of czarism, proved a distinct failure."

In January 1940, on the sixteenth anniversary of Lenin's death, *Pravda* stated that the 1939 invasion of Finland followed the line charted by Lenin. This mouthpiece of Communism justified the invasion of Finland on the ground that Lenin "as far back as the spring of 1918 raised the question of the defense of the approaches to the Soviet border." Finland is one of those approaches.

The 1939 invasion of Finland did not, therefore, mark a sudden reversal of policy; it was of a piece with the strategy of aggression initiated by Lenin and carried forward by Stalin. We have *Pravda's* word for that.

The 1918 defeat in Finland did not halt the immediate course of Soviet imperialism. In other places the expansionist tactics were more successful. Non-Bolshevik governments in Georgia, the Ukraine and Daghestan were overthrown. That these were not democratic governments does not affect the issue. Invasion is invasion regardless of what form of government the invaded territory may be robbed. No matter how benighted the invaded state may seem to the invader, its independence is its inalienable right and its most precious treasure.

A significant instance of Soviet streamlined aggression proceeded all but unnoticed in 1921 and 1922. This time it was in the Far East. Dreary, almost inaccessible Outer Mongolia became the victim of the Soviet urge to empire. People in the democracies who waxed extremely indignant a decade later when Japan invaded Manchuria paid no attention to this victory of Russian imperialism. Yet it remains a noteworthy chapter in the political philosophy of the postwar era. And it set an important precedent for Nippon's aggression against China.

Mongolia formerly belonged to China. In the period of anarchy which swept large areas of Asia at the end of the World War, Outer Mongolia was the scene of savage fighting between Chinese and Mongols, White Russians and Red Russians and various factions of Mongols. The White Russian leader, the "Mad Baron" Ungern-Sternberg, set up a lawless government there. When he was killed and his forces scattered by the Reds a Soviet government was established. It was a Red puppet regime. Moscow staffed it with "advisers" and tied it up in close economic, political and military bonds with the U.S.S.R. The Soviet adhered to the fiction that Outer Mongolia was an independent nation. By 1934 Moscow negotiated a mutual-assistance pact with the so-called Soviet Republic of Outer Mongolia. At the same time the Soviet social and economic systems were transplanted to the Mongolian territory under Red control.

Now no one will claim that the Soviet destroyed a democratic government in Outer Mongolia. Not at all. The country had a most backward political satrapy of lamas. In Western eyes it may have been a benighted country. But the Russians had no more right to take it over and establish their regime there than did the Nippon-

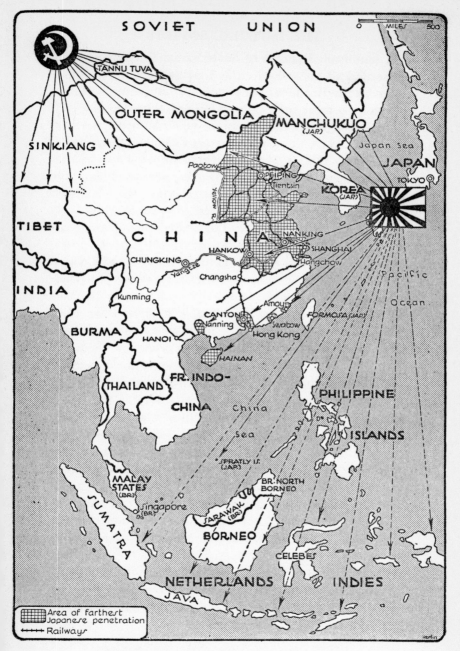

CROSSROADS OF EMPIRE IN THE FAR EAST.

ese when they put Henry Pu Yi on the puppet throne of Manchukuo.

Any reference to Soviet imperialism in Outer Mongolia evokes the same self-righteous protest from Moscow that mention of Japanese imperialism in Manchuria calls forth in Tokio. The same people who defended the Russian conquest of Outer Mongolia protested violently against the Japanese seizure of neighboring territory. And the Japanese and their friends who claimed that Nippon's army was merely on a "civilizing" mission to Manchuria were highly indignant over the Soviet's smoother acquisition of Outer Mongolia.

Mussolini in Ethiopia and Hitler in Austria and Czecho-Slovakia are usually acclaimed as the inventors of streamlined aggression. This form of strategy is the Soviet's contribution to the mechanics of empire building. The Fascist dictators took over a technique initiated by the Soviet and improved upon by Japan. Although the details of the original pattern have been considerably refined, the Soviet technique of 1921 and 1922 has hardly been surpassed. It must not be forgotten that it was Stalin who said: "Wars are not declared, nowadays. They simply start."

In 1929 the Chinese, attempting to gain some measure of control of the Chinese Eastern Railway in Manchuria, came into conflict with Soviet troops. The fighting did not last long. The Chinese resistance collapsed, leaving the Red Army victorious. The American secretary of state, Colonel Henry Stimson, sent a note to the Soviet Government reminding it of the Kellogg Pact, by which the U.S.S.R. renounced war as an instrument of national policy. The Kremlin hierarchy was furious. Litvinov denounced the Stimson note as "unjustifiable pressure."

The inevitable mass meetings were held all over the Soviet Union, excoriating capitalistic America for its amazing affront to the republic of workers and peasants.

It may not be amiss, by the way, to point out that all China may yet fall to the Soviet. Despite her colossal expenditures of blood and money, Japan may be driven from the Asiatic mainland and experience social revolution at home. Stalin may yet be the sole winner of the Far Eastern imperial sweepstakes.

And now back to the subject of Russia and Europe. From the beginning of the Soviet experiment many people in the Western democracies and America were misled about the alleged lack of progress in the U.S.S.R. Stories of failure were carried abroad by foreign engineers and technical men. Russian automobiles could not run; tractors were good for only a few hundred miles; inefficiency was rampant; the average technical worker was only a crude mechanic. These reports created the impression that the Soviet Union was getting nowhere. The West refused to take seriously the possibility of Bolshevist aggression.

Granted that Soviet industrialization was advancing slowly, laboriously and expensively. What the Soviet lacked in an advanced industry trained reserves of workers and an efficient transportation system, it more than made up for in its ability to play superlative power politics. The "man of steel" is astute. He it is who has made the foreign policies of the Soviet Union for more than a decade. Be the spokesman Litvinov or Molotov, the policies were Stalin's. His diplomatic canniness has all along been underestimated, especially by his adversaries.

Stalin has made blunders, of course. But on the whole his diplomacy has been outstandingly successful. It is rooted in the simple principle that you cannot lose if you play your enemies against one another. At this game Stalin has shown himself a genius.

But while Stalin was proceeding with his program to divide Europe into mutually hostile coalitions which he could manipulate against each other, the Kremlin's old bogey of an anti-Soviet alliance rose again. This time Benito Mussolini gave it life. The Duce had a grandiose plan which he claimed would provide a solution for Europe's pressing problems, a solution in keeping with the "master directives" of Fascist philosophy. Italy received a hint of this plan as early as October 1932, when Mussolini made a speech at Turin. But he did not follow up the hint for another five months.

On March 18, 1933, he laid the plan before Mr Ramsay MacDonald and Sir John Simon in the course of their visit to Rome during an interlude of the Disarmament Conference. What the plan proposed was a four-power pact of Britain, France, Italy and Germany. Such a quadruple entente would give Italy a permanent place with three other great powers and assure the Duce an equal voice in all the important deliberations of Europe. It would form a veritable Directory of the Old World. In many respects it would resemble the Quadruple Alliance that was founded in 1815 by England, Prussia, Austria and Russia.

What inspired the Duce to propose the four-power pact was the increasing clamor of the "have-not" nations for treaty revision. These "starving" nations must have justice from the "satiated" powers, so the argument went, or there would be war. It would be to the advantage of the Western democracies, therefore, if Germany's campaign for treaty revision could be deflected eastward. Poland would be a scapegoat. No doubt Mussolini had in mind the fact that the more deeply Herr Hitler became involved along the Baltic the less danger there would be that the Nazis would invade Austria, the Brenner Pass—and Italy.

Stalin immediately took alarm at the pact as a scheme that would isolate the Soviet Union. The Soviet would be excluded from the deliberations of the great powers, the only major power in Europe not represented at meetings. An anti-Russian coalition in the making! Litvinov went into action. But the U.S.S.R. was not to battle alone against the four-power menace. Poland denounced the pact; the permanent council of the Little Entente attacked it; members of the British Parliament assailed it; France announced that it could not be considered in its original form. Under this barrage of criticism the plan formulated by the Duce was radically changed. Stalin saw the danger pass by.

But the Soviet, too, had some ideas on isolation. Its ideas were concentrated on the Reich. Stalin had two main reasons for his attempts to isolate the Reich: to protect himself from attack by Germany, and to drive a wedge between the Reich and other powers. The more isolated the Germans the more dependent they would be on Russia. The more probable, therefore, a deal between Hitler and Stalin! When this was pointed out to certain political leaders in the democracies it seemed an extravagance of some overactive imagination. In fact, Stalin's (and Hitler's) *Realpolitik* often appears to belong to the world of imagination.

As a move in the strategy to isolate the Reich, Stalin began in 1934 to draw closer to France. The French foreign minister, Louis Barthou, was championing the Eastern Locarno. Mussolini's four-power pact had set Poland against France, thereby inclining her somewhat in the direction of Germany. France, therefore, strove harder

to bring the Soviet into line against the Reich, thus
compensating herself for the loss of Poland's unequivocal
support. And now that Poland and France were no longer
on cordial terms, the U.S.S.R. was readier to consider
French overtures. Moreover, as the rearmament of Germany proceeded, Stalin realized that he ran the risk of
being caught between a Reich-Japanese nutcracker. It
was only ordinary prudence, therefore, to take an ally
which could exert pressure on the western flank of Germany. France fitted the Kremlin's specifications.

But France had long been a bitter foe of the U.S.S.R.
French bankers and bondholders had suffered at the hands
of the Russian Reds who boldly repudiated Tsarist loans
from French investors. France had waged war against
the Bolsheviks in South Russia; she had supported Admiral
Kolchak; she had given de facto recognition to the White
regime of General Wrangell; she had sent General Weygand
to help the beleaguered Poles in 1920. Moreover, thousands
of White Russian refugees had been admitted to France.
Anti-Soviet intrigues by the Whites had long been permitted on French soil. And the Kremlin had given France
blow for anti-Bolshevist blow.

Now France has long been at home in the ways of
Realpolitik. When French political leaders began to talk
seriously of an alliance with the once-hated Soviet Union,
French writers were quick to find historical precedent and
justification for such a move. Had not the Christian Francis I allied himself with Moslem Turkey against most of
Christendom? Had not he done this to promote the special
interests of France? Could not the Third Republic do
what Francis I had done, if such a move added to the
security of France? The Soviet's internal policies were the
Soviet's business. But Frenchmen might have done well

to study a little more carefully the fundamentals and direction of Stalin's foreign policies.

Certain steps toward a Franco-Soviet rapprochement had already been taken. A nonaggression pact between France and the U.S.S.R. had been signed on November 29, 1932. Litvinov had visited Paris; Herriot had visited Moscow. Each had received what was considered a friendly reception. In September 1933 Air Minister Pierre Cot had gone to the Soviet Union as the head of a French aviation mission. None of these events signified anything that could be called friendship, but they were integrated with the gradual alignment of Paris and Moscow against Berlin.

Further preparation for the Franco-Soviet entente was the Russian entry into the League of Nations, September 1934. Moscow was given a permanent place on the League Council. Litvinov assured his French and British League colleagues that the Third International had been relegated to the background. Had not Paris and Moscow agreed in their nonaggression pact to prevent any political action in their respective territories against the other member of the pact? This was generally regarded as a pledge by the French to squelch White Russian anti-Soviet activities in France and a promise by Moscow to forbid Communist intrigues in France and her colonies.

By 1935 the stage was set for closer Franco-Soviet relations, a mutual-assistance pact. It was supposed to be tied up with the League of Nations obligations of both parties, and there was a great deal of pother about the pact's being "in the spirit of the League." On May second it was signed by Foreign Minister Pierre Laval and by Vladimir Petrovitch Potemkin, chess-loving Soviet ambassador to France and Litvinov's right-hand man. The pact was to run for five years.

Here, indeed, was a first-rate diplomatic triumph for
Joseph Stalin. With the Franco-Soviet agreement in his
possession he could congratulate himself on the steady
progress he had made in pursuing his foreign policies.
A far cry this from the days of the *Cordon Sanitaire!* But
the Red tsar knew that he could not rest on his oars. The
work of isolating Hitler must be carried much farther.

French spokesmen were quick to point out that the pact
with Moscow was not an exclusive arrangement. Other
nations would be welcomed to membership. Germany
would be accepted, provided Berlin met the conditions.
But Stalin was under no apprehension that his diplomatic
game would be spoiled by a request from Hitler that the
Franco-Soviet pact be made a three-party document.
True, the Kremlin made no headway in its efforts to
implement the Franco-Soviet pact with military con-
ventions. But the fact that Stalin had been able to draw
once hostile France into a rather vague political entente
was reason for satisfaction in Moscow.

Two weeks after Potemkin signed the Franco-Soviet pact
Stalin supplemented it with a treaty of mutual assistance
with Czecho-Slovakia. But there was a provision in this
treaty which robbed it of real effectiveness. Moscow made
the stipulation that the Soviet need go to the aid of Czecho-
Slovakia only if France helped the victim. This provision
was to be of vital importance three years later.

Meanwhile the Reich was protesting vigorously that the
Franco-Soviet pact was a direct breach of the Locarno
treaties. Berlin argued that France was pledging military
support to a non-Locarno power (Russia) against her
Locarno treaty partner (Germany). There were not a few
people in Britain who supported the German thesis that
France had violated the spirit, if not the letter, of the

Locarno pacts. Some Britons agreed that the Reich was justified in its claim that it was "ringed with enemies" —the old cry of "encirclement."

J. L. Garvin in the *Sunday Observer* bitterly assailed the Soviet-Czech relationship. In his view Czecho-Slovakia was a "geographic, racial, political and economic monstrosity." He denounced what he termed the "suicidal statecraft of Dr Beneš." According to him Prague had become the "door-opener" for Moscow. He spoke for other Englishmen when he attacked the danger inherent in the pact of mutual assistance between the Soviets and Czechs which gave Stalin powerful influence on the affairs of central Europe.

Mr Garvin wrote: "Czecho-Slovakia, for instance, has had the suicidal folly to make itself a corridor six hundred miles long through which the air forces of Soviet Russia might strike into the Reich."

Meanwhile Stalin, his pacts with the French and the Czechs safely locked in the Kremlin's vaults, could afford a satirical smile. His game was proceeding merrily enough. Not only was he protecting the diplomatic approaches to the U.S.S.R.; he was isolating Hitler and he was spreading confusion and suspicion among his Western enemies (mutual-assistance allies and Nazi foes alike).

But Stalin's entire strategy was based on a long-range plan. It looked farther ahead than the immediate victories against his political opponents in France, Britain, Poland and other countries. He was infinitely more interested in the fundamentals than in the superficial bickerings and intrigues at Geneva and at the capitals where his agents carried on their Kremlin-directed roles.

Stalin understands, as many of his capitalist contemporaries do not, that war speeds up social change. International conflict, he knew, would result from the political and economic lunacies of the so-called civilized nations. Since war would come, Stalin would be prepared for it. And not merely in the military sphere. He would be ready to capitalize on it in the revolutionary realm. All his preparations were to that end.

In the Kremlin view the plight of France and Germany was growing more serious. France, according to the Soviet viewpoint, is dying. It is rotten inside. The decreased birth rate is only a symptom of its fatal disease. The parliamentary chaos in France, the bloody Stavisky riots, the increasing Communist membership, the warfare between Right and Left—these were some of the indications that a doomed France was fast moving toward social convulsions. War would, in the Soviet view, hasten the disintegration already in progress in France. And before the end of the conflict it was reasonable to believe that France would fall victim to Communism.

As for Germany, Stalin believed that here, too, was a prize that would eventually fall into the waiting hands of Sovietism. Hitler would only accelerate the natural process of social upheaval. The German people had lived through one great war since the turn of the century without surrendering to Communism. But another major conflict, with its attendant hardships for a blockaded Germany, would almost certainly plant the red flag on Berlin's public buildings. In fact, a major war might bring France and Germany into the Union of Socialist Soviet Republics.

Britain might hold out a little longer. But the disintegration of the Empire was well under way. And the condition of the island's working class was unlikely to improve under the present system. War would raise taxes, lower the standard of living, further weaken the middle class and prepare the way for a social and economic collapse. So reasoned the Kremlinites.

But Britons, Frenchmen, Germans, Czechs, Poles and other non-Soviet peoples were thinking in terms of the immediate political developments. By 1936, when Hitler was spouting anti-Soviet philippics, London was growing suspicious of Nazi attempts to create an anti-Bolshevik coalition of nations.

Said *The Times* of London: "The German leaders will quite misjudge the temper of the British people if they suppose that—to adapt the famous quip of Charles II—this country would be ready to help cut off the head of communism in order to make fascism king in Europe."

But Stalin would have turned that English statement around. His purpose was to enlist all his enemies—democratic and Fascist—to cut off the heads of both their ideologies in order to make Communism (more accurately Stalinism) king in Europe. For the Kremlin's *Realpolitik* envisaged nothing less than the spectacle of non-Soviet Europe willingly committing suicide to make way for the Soviet empire.

CHAPTER XII

Soviet Nationalism

A prudent ruler ought not to keep faith when by so doing it would be against his interest, and when the reasons which made him bind himself no longer exist.—MACHIAVELLI.

WESTERN EUROPE was much relieved when Stalin repudiated the program of world revolution and announced his intention of "building Socialism in one country." Trotzky, the firebrand, the advocate of "permanent revolution," was stripped of his power in the U.S.S.R. and exiled. The series of five-year plans got under way. Communist agitation in France, Britain and other non-Soviet countries seemed to be dying down. Western writers explained that the Russians were intent on the task of making Communism work in their own country as an example to the capitalistic states. Western politicians complacently dismissed the Soviet as a threat to the present world order. Russia, they asserted, had all the work at home that she could do for the next century. Moscow would be too busy to disturb the peace of the other nations. And by and by there would no longer be any Communism in Russia, just an evolutionary form of mild Socialism that would merge with the capitalism of the West. It was a pleasant myth.

Those who found the slightest cause for alarm in the longer range Soviet picture were "scaremongers." Or perhaps Fascist agents. It was a simple matter to explain that anyone who was concerned about the trend of the Soviet experiment was an alarmist. This was, of course, the state of mind Stalin was trying to create. It served his purpose to lull the world into indifference toward what was taking place inside the U.S.S.R. And what the Kremlin's agents were doing abroad.

But western Europe's diagnosis of the Russian situation was hardly accurate. True, Stalin had shelved the early program of organizing civil wars and rash uprisings in other countries. The attempts to establish Red regimes in Germany, Hungary, Estonia, Latvia, Finland and Poland had failed. Western observers felt justified in their assumption that Stalin's plans and methods were different from those advocated by Lenin, Trotzky and other Old Bolsheviks.

It seemed, too, that a new nationalism which was developing in the U.S.S.R. was a further source of relief to the Western politicians. In London and Paris this was welcomed as a trend away from dangerous internationalism toward a safe form of nationalism. For if Russia became nationalist, was it not reasonable to assume that the Soviet would cease to be interested in overthrowing other governments? It was a comforting thought, but it was none too well grounded.

The new nationalism in Russia is entirely different from that which the West knows. It is even more intolerant than Western chauvinism. It seeks to spread its own particular form—the Soviet nationalism—into other lands. For this Soviet type of nationalism is as fanatical as any warlike creed of the past. It might be compared with the messianic fervor of the Moslem Turks or the Saracens. Because it is nationalism it is none the less a threat to other countries. For that reason it may be far more perilous to other countries than the internationalism of Lenin and Trotzky.

Let us take one field of the new nationalism, the Red Army. The old oath administered to all recruits began with these words: "I, son of the toiling people . . ." and included a pledge to "direct my every act and thought toward the great aim of emancipation of the toilers." The Red soldier was the champion of the downtrodden of the world. His duty might take him anywhere. He might have to go to the aid of downtrodden workers in Finland, in Egypt, in North America, in French Indo-China. He was not in the service of a country, but of a cause. "Toilers" everywhere were his brothers. Propaganda directed to foster and sustain this solidarity of the "toilers" was dinned into him constantly. His marching songs were revolutionary. His life was devoted to the furtherance of his oath to emancipate the "toilers" in other countries.

In January 1939 a new oath was announced for the Red Army. Its keynote was patriotism. The old internationalism was dropped. This is the way the new oath starts: "I, a citizen of the Union of Soviet Socialist Republics . . ." It proceeds to bind the Red soldier and sailor to shed the last drop of blood for "my people, my Soviet Fatherland and the workers' and peasants' government."

In the border states between the Reich and the Soviet it was noted that during the Nazi persecution of Jews in Germany the Soviet refused to open its doors to these unfortunate people driven from their homeland into exile. Yet the Soviet Union has been badly in need of engineers, scientific research workers, economists, physicians, dentists and other professional people who could have been recruited from the ranks of the refugees. Some observers have regarded this Soviet attitude toward the Jewish refugees from the Reich as a manifestation of anti-Semitism. By nearly everybody in the border nations it has been considered a symptom of the new Soviet nationalism.

The worship of Lenin now has an air of nationalism. Any American who has stood in the Red Square and watched thousands of Russians voluntarily wait in line for hours under a broiling sun or in the bitter cold of a Moscow winter, to pass into the tomb and gaze at Lenin's body, must have been impressed. The line winds back and forth in an almost endless queue. It moves slowly and seems to advance but little. Yet the Russians wait patiently to enter the tomb, move down half-lighted stairs and pass through a sepulcher that has the *mise-en-scène* of a superlative theater setting. Inside the tomb the weird lighting, the statuelike guards, the yellow Tartar features of Lenin and the hushed awe of the spectators create an extraordinary effect. It is all subtle and resourceful stagecraft. To these Russians Lenin was not only the leader of the crusade to free the "toiling masses of the world." He was a Russian. He was one of them. Stalin encourages this worship of Lenin; it suits his purpose.

Even the theater has been profoundly affected by the new Soviet patriotism. In one instance a favorite satiric poet who had formerly been honored for his work suddenly fell from grace. The reason: he had not shifted his writing direction to harmonize with the increasing Stalinist nationalism. In his comic libretto *Bogatyr* he had made the mistake of casting aspersions upon the religion of early Muscovy. He had poked fun at the conversion to Christianity of the eleventh-century rulers of Kiev, "the mother of

Russian cities." But the Russian priests and rulers of those days did more than uphold religion; they fought for Russia against her enemies, the nomad marauders of the steppes. In ridiculing these early Russians the poet made a grave error and was called to task for maligning Russia's glorious past. His old-fashioned ideas conflicted with Stalin's new nationalism. The unfortunate librettist did not know that Stalin was now following in Tsarist imperial footsteps.

Early in 1939, when the first performance of the revised version of Glinka's opera *Life for the Tsar* was given in Moscow, Joseph Stalin applauded. The rest of the audience quickly took the cue and applauded too. Foreign observers in the theater instantly grasped the significance of the incident. Here was another manifestation of the Soviet nationalism that is built on Russian patriotism. The subject of the opera was the revolt of the Muscovites—noblemen, merchants and toiling workers—against the Poles. The action took place 326 years before (1613) when large areas of Russia were under Polish control. The Muscovites were striking a blow to win independence from the alien ruler. And a new dynasty, the Romanovs, was coming into being. That dynasty was to rule Russia for 304 years, until the year that the Bolsheviks would come to power.

A change has been made in the final chorus of the opera. No longer do the singers chant: "Glory, glory to the Tsar!" In the new version, which Stalin applauded, the cast sings: "Glory, glory to the Fatherland!"

Perhaps an even more striking example of the propaganda for the new nationalism was provided by the Russian film *Alexander Nevsky*, directed by Sergei Eisenstein. The action took place seven centuries ago when the Russians were battling against the invading Teutonic Knights. This warfare was waged in the neighborhood of

Lake Peipus, now on the border between Estonia and the U.S.S.R. The theme of the film was the struggle carried on by the Russians, under Alexander Nevsky, against the foreign armies. The redoubtable Alexander had defeated a force of Swedes, then among the foremost soldiers in the world. Next came the powerful army of Teutonic Knights, highly trained and disciplined, their mounted knights in heavy armor, their foot soldiers swarming behind.

Against the Germanic invader Alexander Nevsky had only an inferior force of poorly armed Russians. But the Russian knights were supported by a vast army of determined peasants. When the epic battle took place Russians (nobles and mouzhiks) stood shoulder to shoulder. The Russian victory over the invader was the triumph of all the Russian participants. The film ends with Alexander's declaration that anyone who comes to Russia with a sword will perish by the sword. It was not only an outstanding example of cinema art; it was excellent propaganda for the new Soviet nationalism.

In Soviet textbooks the new nationalism is revaluing Russian history. For example, as late as 1930, Minin, leader of the 1613 revolt against the Poles, was portrayed as a stalwart of the bourgeoisie. In the reinterpretation that has been initiated by Stalin, Minin is a national hero, a Russian empire builder.

During the past few years there has been a subtle change in the Kremlin's attitude toward the tsars and their imperialism. In the time of Lenin it was the official line to portray the tsars as rapacious imperialists who waged war against the toiling masses of the world. Stalin has changed all that. It is now the Kremlin's policy to portray the tsars as rulers who strove to further the interests of Russia.

Their wars of aggression were waged in a good cause, the expansion of the Russian fatherland. When the tsars thrust southwestward toward Constantinople, when they pushed into Central Asia, when they drove eastward to the Pacific, when they occupied Finland, when they partitioned Poland, they were serving the Russian homeland. In fact, Tsarist imperialism acquired for the Soviet Union its vast territory, its rich natural resources and its geographical security. And when imperialist Joseph Stalin follows in Tsarist footsteps he, too, is wisely seeking to protect the "approaches" to the beloved Russian fatherland.

Into the ring of the new nationalism humor has lately cast its hat. World revolution was once a pretty grim business, collectivization nothing to smile over, and the five-year plans incompatible with bourgeois laughter. Dictators know all too well that jests can sabotage.

But Stalinism has apparently weathered the stormy stage where a joke can tip the ship of state. In a March 1940 issue of *Izvestia* Comrade I. Bachelis denounced the shortage of humor in the U.S.S.R. Six new comedies had just been released, it seems, by the Soviet film studios. All except one, the Comrade laments, lacked originality and humor. Speaking of the script writers, he says, "They run from laughter as from a cannon shot." He further charges that the scenarists are afraid to transfer to the screen the amusing incidents of daily life. That the grim Soviet press champions collective laughter would seem to augur a vital new trend in the social pattern of Soviet nationalism.

A curious side light on this new Russian nationalism is the changing attitude of some White Russians toward the Soviet Union. These refugees from the Bolsheviks have not come to love Stalin, it is true. Yet it is surprising how much their viewpoint has changed in recent months. No longer do some of these Whites look upon the Kremlinites as foreign agents bent upon the destruction of Russia. Few of them like Lenin and Trotzky any better than they did twenty years ago. But they appear to feel somewhat differently about Stalin. He is, of course, their enemy, but at the same time he is maintaining Russia in her position as a world power. And for that not a few of them feel a strange sense of loyalty toward even the Soviet fatherland. As this White Russian attitude toward the U.S.S.R. evolves into a definite feeling the conviction grows among some of these people that Stalin is actually following a policy that was initiated by Tsarist rulers centuries ago. They do not like his methods, but they believe that any catastrophe which might happen to his government would retard the fortunes of the post-Stalin Russia that will come into existence some day.

Another manifestation of Stalin's nationalism and Pan-Soviet ambitions is apparent in the steady climb of Russia's military expenditures. These are no longer justified on the ground that the Red Army must be put at the disposal of the world's proletariat. The Red Army will, of course, fight for the toiling masses of the world, but it is primarily for the defense of the Soviet fatherland. That is the Kremlin's justification for the enormous amounts of rubles which have been poured into the armament coffers. "What is needed for a real victory?" asks Stalin. "For this three things are needed: first, we need arms; second, arms; third, again and again, arms."

In May 1939 it was announced in Moscow that the Red Army and Navy would receive sixty-six per cent more than during the previous year. *Pravda* could boast: "The defense industry has forged an imperishable shield for Soviet land." On the last day of March 1940 the largest budget in the history of the U.S.S.R. was presented to the Supreme Soviet. The sum allocated for military expenditures amounted to fifty-seven billion rubles, an advance of thirty-eight per cent over the previous year.

One of the late developments of the trend to nationalism is the abolition of political commissars in the Soviet army and navy. After the Finnish war the authority of command, hitherto shared with the commissars, reverted entirely to the military and naval officers. Moreover the officers' titles have been changed. Formerly military officers were known as commanders, of the first, second, or third grade, depending on whether they were in charge of battalions, divisions or corps. Now, as in other countries, they are designated as Marshal, Army General, Colonel General, Lieutenant General and Major General. And the Red Navy has adopted the usual titles of Admiral, Vice-Admiral and Rear Admiral.

What is even more significant is the antifraternization rebuke carried in the *Red Fleet* of May 6, 1940. The Soviet navy newspaper condemns "familiarity and false democratization" between officers and men as "foreign to the spirit of our navy." The rebuke calls for a "merciless" campaign against a camaraderie which would lessen the fighting strength of the fleet. It urges a discipline not unlike that which prevails in capitalist navies and which is the antithesis of the old *tovarisch* (comrade) spirit between officers and men.

Ardor for Russian industry and military power engenders patriotic scorn in a *Pravda* editorial: "The stupid chattering of the hired scribblers of the foreign press about the failures of our industry is worth exactly the same as their fantastic ravings about the successes of the White-Finnish bandits."

But the high note of nationalistic fervor was struck by Defense Commissar Klementi E. Voroshilov in a May Day speech about the Red Army. Shouted the Soviet military chief: "Whoever dares to step on the thresholds of our home will be destroyed. We not only know how to fight, we love to fight!"

CHAPTER XIII

Moscow and the Czech Crisis

... as the generality of mankind are wicked, and ever ready
to break their words, a prince should not pique himself in
keeping his more scrupulously, especially as it is always easy to
justify a breach of faith on his part.—MACHIAVELLI.

IF YOU FRENCHMEN and we Germans are ever so idiotic as
to go to war with each other, the Russian Bolsheviks will
come in and take us all. And we shall deserve it." Marshal
Goering was whispering to Foreign Minister Pierre Laval.

It was May 1935 in Krakow. A great state funeral was
being held for the late Marshal Pilsudski, dictator of
Poland. Distinguished mourners were assembled in the
ancient Polish capital to pay their respects to the man who
had molded the destinies of the reborn Polish nation.
Cabinet ministers, ambassadors, generals and high political leaders came to represent most of the important countries of the world. Foreign Minister Pierre Laval was there
to express the sorrow of the French Government. Ponderous, bemedaled Marshal Goering came to represent Adolf
Hitler and the Third Reich.

Such an occasion always presents an opportunity for

political discussions. Mourners take advantage of the gathering to get together and compare notes. The Pilsudski mourners held many a tête-à-tête. Goering sought out Pierre Laval for a little parley, in the course of which he delivered himself of the Russian warning.

The words whispered to Laval at Krakow were to influence decisions in European affairs for years to come. They were to play their part in the Munich settlement. They would have a bearing on the attitude of France toward both Germany and the Soviet Union.

In justice to Pierre Laval it must be kept in mind that he was never an admirer of the U.S.S.R. He had, it is true, negotiated the Franco-Soviet pact. But he had done this for practical reasons. Unlike Premier Herriot, who was friendly toward the Soviet, Laval distrusted the Kremlin and all its works. But he was too realistic a man to allow personal feelings to influence his foreign policy. Laval was uneasy over the possibility of a Second Rapallo. He feared that eventually Berlin and Moscow would unite against the West. It was as a measure of defense against a Nazi-Soviet coalition that Laval favored the Franco-Soviet pact.

Laval never accepted the theory that the Soviet Union had turned its back upon world revolution, that it was the champion of peace and the rights of small countries, the defender of the League of Nations and the supporter of collective security against Fascist aggression. But Laval hoped that if the U.S.S.R. could be drawn into the Franco-British alignment the Reich would be isolated—encircled—to the benefit of peace.

During the latter part of 1935 France and Britain were divided by a serious conflict of interests. Each was thinking primarily of its own security. France, facing Germany across the Rhine, let no other preoccupations divert her attention from her hostile vis-à-vis. Britain, disturbed by the Duce's invasion of Ethiopia, saw in Italian aggression a threat to her dominion in the Mediterranean and Red Sea. The British wanted French and League support to curb the belligerent Duce. Adolf Hitler seemed to the British less of a menace than Mussolini. For the Italian dictator was thinking in terms of a new Roman empire that would jeopardize the interests of the British Empire.

But Downing Street was not able to rally the Quai d'Orsay for the crusade that she was crying up against the Duce. Paris was unwilling to make any sortie into the Middle Sea that would weaken French strength in Middle Europe. But just as Britain could not stir up French fears of Mussolini, France could not arouse British fears of Hitler. This was the stalemate that gave the democracies pause on the evening of March 6, 1936.

The following morning was Saturday. It was then that Adolf Hitler staged one of the most spectacular *coups de théâtre* in modern history. He sprang one of those "Saturday surprise" demonstrations of Nazi ruthlessness that Europe was learning to dread. At thirteen minutes after nine German war planes roared over Cologne in the demilitarized Rhineland. Thousands of wondering Germans poured into the streets to see what the swastikaed planes portended. A little later German army cyclists rode into the city square. Behind them goose-stepped nineteen battalions of infantry, and behind these clattered thirteen battalions of artillery. These were Hitler's "symbolic" battalions sent into the Rhineland to tear up the Treaty of Versailles and the Pact of Locarno.

Before his brown-shirted Reichstag in Berlin the Fuehrer was justifying this act of treaty breaking. The "fathomless" tragedy of the Franco-Soviet pact left the Reich no alternative. The Nazis were compelled, he declared, to seek peace and security by occupying and remilitarizing the Reich's Rhineland provinces. "Men of the German Reichstag," he shouted, "when in the gray November days of 1918 the curtain was lowered on the bloody tragedy of the Great War . . ."

German remilitarization of the Rhineland had Europe aghast. French military leaders realized the staggering significance of Hitler's Rhineland *fait accompli*. France wanted to move against the Germans and drive them out of the Rhine provinces. But Britain, occupied with the Ethiopian crisis, held out against any French action that might precipitate war in western Europe. France threatened to act alone, carried out a partial mobilization, but in the end made no military move against Hitler.

The Fuehrer was left in possession of the Rhineland. His engineers were now free to begin fortifying the Reich's western border. The West Wall was started. Europe's next war was just over the wall. Reoccupation of the Rhineland was unquestionably the most far-reaching event since the days of the peace conference.

Once Hitler had fortified his western frontier, he would be able to turn toward the East. His back would be protected from French intervention when he invaded his neighbors in central Europe. He would recover the freedom of action that had been lost when the Versailles and Locarno pacts provided for permanent demilitarization of the Rhineland. The remilitarization appeared to be an immediate threat to France. Actually it was only an oblique threat to the French; it was an immediate menace to Austria, Czecho-Slovakia and other countries in central Europe.

Not a move of the Nazi Rhineland program was lost on

the Kremlin. Nazi prestige went up; French and British prestige went down. What would be the best tack to take in the sudden shift of the diplomatic winds? Stalin and his henchmen realized full well that when Hitler remilitarized the Rhineland the Franco-Soviet pact lost much of its value to the U.S.S.R. The Bolshevik leaders perceived that the day would come when French troops would be shut out of central Europe by a line of German fortifications along the Reich's western border. That would leave the German Army free to push on toward the Soviet Union.

Soviet diplomacy was set to work, therefore, to build up a system of protective security that would unite the small states of central Europe against the Reich. Soviet diplomatic strategists had never lost sight of the fact that if Germany could be successfully encircled the Reich would be more amenable to a deal with the U.S.S.R. But primarily the Kremlin was thinking just now in terms of stopping Hitler's march to the East before it reached the Soviet's borders. Had not Hitler openly talked about a conquest of Soviet territory? Was not Hitler holding the Ukrainian, General Skoropadsky, as a possible puppet ruler for a German-controlled Ukraine? Was there not in Berlin a shadow government of anti-Soviet Ukrainians ready to follow German troops into their homeland? Was not the anti-Soviet fanatic, Alfred Rosenberg, continuously advocating a Nazi attack on the U.S.S.R.?

But it was no simple matter for Stalin to forge this ring of steel around the Reich. Soviet diplomacy found that it was impossible to make the little nations in the path of Hitler's conquest sink their petty feuds and unite against the common enemy. The Eastern Locarno plan had failed. The hatred of each small country for its neighbors was more vindictive than its fear of the Third Reich. Hungarian hated Czech; Czech hated Pole; Pole hated Russian; Lithuanian hated Pole; Hungarian hated Roumanian; Slovak hated Hungarian. Irreconcilable minorities of Hungarians, Ukrainians, Germans, Bulgars, Lithuanians, Poles and other peoples raised a din that drowned the voices raised in the interests of tolerance and reason. Small wonder that the suspicions and hatreds which ruled central Europe played into the hands of the totalitarian aggressors.

Dr Tibor Eckhardt, leader of the Small Farmers' Party in the Hungarian Parliament, told the writer that in 1937 he got in touch with Prime Minister Hodza of Czecho-Slovakia with a plan for a three-power pact. Inasmuch as Hodza was a Slovak, Dr Eckhardt thought he might be more conciliatory than President Beneš, a Czech. Eckhardt had in mind a defensive alliance of Czecho-Slovakia, Hungary and Austria. "If we three nations do not unite," Eckhardt said he warned the prime minister, "Austria will fall before a Nazi attack, Czecho-Slovakia will be next, and perhaps we in Hungary will be third."

Hodza would not hear of such a thing. "We would be fools," he objected, according to Eckhardt, "to enter an arrangement in which you Hungarians and Austrians would have two votes and we Czecho-Slovaks only one."

Hodza, of course, may have a different version of the story. But in any case the incident gives a clue as to why collective security failed and the small nations have gone down one by one before Brown, Black and Red aggressors.

In March 1938 Hitler's troops marched into Austria and annexed that state to the Third Reich. This act of aggression was consummated while France was having one of her "customary parliamentary crises," the Duce was away skiing and London was entertaining Joachim von Ribbentrop. And it should be pointed out that these diversions were not confined entirely to the capitalist powers. The Soviet was having its own particular kind of distraction. A sensational trial was taking place in Moscow. Bukharin, Yagoda, Rykov and other former Red leaders were being prosecuted for high treason.

With Austria crossed off his agenda Hitler could now start in earnest the drive to destroy Czecho-Slovakia. The annexation of Austria, like the remilitarization of the Rhineland, was only one part of Hitler's program. Each of these steps prepared the way for the one to follow.

Nearly two years before, President Beneš had expressed to me his conviction that Czecho-Slovakia was safe from Nazi aggression. "We have a strong, well-equipped army," he told me, "we are bound by mutual-assistance pacts to France and the Soviet Union; we are a member of the Little Entente and the League of Nations. Moreover, we have the friendship of Great Britain and all peace-loving nations." True, on September 11, 1935, Sir Samuel Hoare, British secretary of foreign affairs, had declared at Geneva that His Majesty's Government followed a consistent policy in favor of "steady and collective resistance to any and all acts of unprovoked aggression." That seemed to promise support for Czecho-Slovakia.

But by May 1938, in spite of the brave words spoken in London, Paris and Geneva, the record of aggression was highly ominous. Ethiopia and Austria had disappeared. Spain was the battleground of rival imperialisms and hostile ideologies. Japan was driving deep into China. And the Third Reich was preparing to destroy Czecho-Slovakia. The Czechs meanwhile maintained an optimistic attitude and claimed that they considered their position impregnable.

But one of Czecho-Slovakia's great dangers was inherent

in her isolation. Nearly all her border line touched hostile territory: Germany, Hungary and Poland. Only the short boundary with Roumania could be called friendly. Her friends were distant; her foes were near. The Little Entente, so important in Czech calculations, was effective only against Hungary.

Two years previously a Roumanian official close to King Carol assured me that the Czech claim for Little Entente support was a "gigantic bluff." Would the Czechs come to the aid of the Roumanians, he asked, if the Soviet Union invaded the Roumanian province of Bessarabia? Of course not. And would the Czechs go to war with Italy if the Duce attacked Yugoslavia? Certainly not. Nor would Roumania allow the Red Army to pass through Roumanian territory on the way to aid Czecho-Slovakia. Why not? Because King Carol knew well enough that if the Red Army entered Roumania it would not leave.

In Yugoslavia the prime minister, Dr Milan Stoyadinovitch, gave me his opinion that Czecho-Slovakia's willingness to listen to Soviet advice could only bring trouble down upon President Beneš and his countrymen.

Yet the Czechs were apparently making their plans on the basis of help from the Red Army. Neutral military observers in Prague reported to their home governments that the rail line from Roumania to Bohemia was of dubious value and passed through the long, vulnerable corridor of Ruthenia and Slovakia. It could easily be bombed from Poland or Hungary; perhaps even from the Reich. And if the Red Army attempted to pass through Poland on the way to Czecho-Slovakia, the Poles would unquestionably resist. Such a conflict would not only shield the Reich from Russia; it would present Hitler with a Polish ally.

On the week end of May 21, 1938, the world became

aware of dramatic movement in the heart of central
Europe. Czecho-Slovakia was mobilizing. Prague charged
that this move was a defensive measure to stop a contemplated sudden Nazi attack. Thousands of Czecho-Slovak
soldiers took up their positions behind their "little Maginot
Line" along the German frontier. Czecho-Slovakia would
fight.

In Berlin the Nazi leadership loudly protested that the
German Army had made no hostile move against Czecho-
Slovakia. They denied that there was any German Army
concentration near the Czech border. These Nazi claims
were received with extreme skepticism abroad. Editorials
in the French, British and American press praised the
Czechs for their courage and prompt measures for defense.
All a country had to do, some of these editorials explained,
was to take resolute action against the Nazis. And Hitler's
bluff could be successfully called. For several weeks to
come the Czech mobilization of May twenty-first was a
matter of intense satisfaction to all who opposed the Nazi
drive against central Europe's "island of democracy."

But the consequences of this affair were to be significant.
Neutral military observers in Germany reported to their
home governments that there was no unusual military
activity in the Reich during the week end of May twenty-
first. Some of these foreign military officers traveled long
distances along the German-Czech frontier without finding
anything to excite their suspicions. And some neutral observers in Prague reported to their home governments that
the Czechs had mobilized on the warning of the Soviet
Legation. They believed that the Czechs had credulously
swallowed the Bolshevik bait—hook, line and sinker.

It is not possible for us to sift the truth of these charges
and countercharges. Few neutral observers doubted that

Germany would seize an opportunity to attack Czecho-Slovakia. But most of them doubted that the Reich had completed its preparations for such a serious coup. Yet most of them assumed that the Czechs had been genuinely alarmed when they mobilized.

Further light was shed on this situation by Hanson W. Baldwin, able military writer of the New York *Times*. In the issue of July 31, 1938, he wrote: "Observers who are acquainted with the organization and policy of the German army also point out that during the Czechoslovak-German crisis, it was reported, although never confirmed, that German troops had been massed on the Czechoslovak frontier. Such massing of troops, it is said, is contrary to all German strategic principles. German troops in an attack on a hostile state, it is believed, would probably not be massed on the frontier, but would move, with little or no warning to the enemy, from their garrisons and barracks toward, and into, the enemy country, concentrating as they moved."

In London and Paris the suspicion spread that the Czechs had either staged the May twenty-first show or knew little about German military tactics or had been taken in completely by Soviet agents. As time went on, suspicions mounted that the Bolsheviks were at the bottom of the affair. And, rightly or wrongly, some influential men in these capitals became convinced that Moscow was attempting to hasten a clash between the Reich and Czecho-Slovakia, a conflict that would bring France into action against Germany. This increasing suspicion of the Kremlin's motives and tactics was part of the background of the approaching September crisis and the "peace of Munich." And it helped create an excuse for the sellout of the Czechs that was on the way.

By the end of August no one could any longer doubt that Hitler was determined to dismember Czecho-Slovakia. Nazi propaganda shrieked that Prague had become the central European headquarters of the Third International; the Czechs were "warmongers"; the Czechs were "massacring" Germans in Bohemia. Poles and Hungarians took up the Nazi cry against the Czechs. Warsaw demanded the district of Teschen. Budapest demanded the return of lands which had once belonged to Hungary. Hitler was making full use of his Polish and Hungarian dupes against the Czechs.

At the radio the Fuehrer was railing at the "liar" by the name of Beneš. Goering was broadcasting his contempt for the Czechs. "We know who is backing those ridiculous dwarfs in Prague," shouted the Number Two Nazi. "It is Moscow!"

Near-panic seized London and Paris. Men were feverishly digging air-raid shelters in London parks. People were rushing to leave the British and French capitals. And Comrade Litvinov was expressing the sympathy of the Soviet Union for the Czechs "in the terrible hour of their trial."

Moscow, the instigator of enmities, was by this time clamoring loudly for a firm stand against Nazi Germany. The Kremlin, patron of capitalistic confusion, demanded that Britain and France back up the hard-pressed Czechs. But little definite word came out of Moscow about the Soviet Union's plans to aid the defense of Czecho-Slovakia. True, the U.S.S.R. did notify Poland that if the Poles invaded Czecho-Slovakia Moscow would not look on with indifference. However, not only did the Soviet fail to mobilize; Marshal Voroshilov was away on a trip in the Siberian Far Eastern provinces.

But more and more Englishmen and Frenchmen came to fear that Moscow was promoting war over Czecho-Slovakia. This war was to involve western Europe in a suicidal struggle that could benefit only Bolshevism. And would the U.S.S.R. come into the conflict? At the Quai d'Orsay and at Downing Street there was suspicion that the Kremlin would refuse to enter the war on the ground that its troops had no access to the scene of fighting.

Moreover, the purges in Russia which had taken such a heavy toll of human life among the high Soviet military further undermined French and British confidence in the Red Army. How, asked many officials in Paris and London, could a military force fight efficiently which had just slaughtered a high percentage of its ablest officers?

Even the prospect of Bolshevik aid posed a dilemma for the Western democracies. If the Soviet should come to the support of the Czechs, would not Russian help for the Franco-British-Czech cause alienate many peoples who are anti-Soviet in their policies? Italy, Japan, Hungary, Spain, Portugal, Yugoslavia, Roumania, Poland, Switzerland and Finland would not look with favor on a coalition that included the U.S.S.R.

On the eve of the Munich conference the political leaders in the Western democracies concluded that it would be a hazardous move to bring the Soviet Union into the discussions. Chamberlain and his colleagues and the Bonnet faction in France were determined to avoid any chance that Stalin might torpedo the Munich parley. Accordingly, the U.S.S.R. was barred from the deliberations.

It was an ironic gesture that the fate of Czecho-Slovakia should be settled without the Soviet, Czecho-Slovakia's ally. Not only did the U.S.S.R. have pacts with France and Czecho-Slovakia; it was also a member of the League of Nations. Yet Fascist Italy, Germany's Axis partner was represented at Munich by its Duce. Stalin was publicly snubbed by the Western democracies. Hitler's "bloodless victory" at Munich was a great triumph for the Berlin-Rome Axis. For one day Mussolini's four-power coalition was a reality. And the Italian premier was one of the four arbiters of the destiny of Europe.

Moscow was bitter. Britain and France were the objects of her resentment. She apparently felt hardly any animus toward the two Fascist states. For the Soviet hierarchy realized that it was part of the Fascintern's (Fascist International's) game to fight the Comintern. After all, these two ideological imperialisms were arrayed against each other. But the democratic nations were supposed to be in the alignment with the U.S.S.R. Georgi Dimitrov, secretary-general of the Third International, issued in *Pravda* a caustic denunciation of the "policy of warlike agreement between the Fascist aggressors and the imperialist cliques of England and France."

The Munich conference which bought "peace in our time" with Czecho-Slovakia was another turning point in the history of Soviet imperialism. For here ended the Kremlin's strategy of co-operation with the Western democracies and the League of Nations. What was the use, Stalinists asked, of making agreements with allies who would betray you at the first crucial moment? The Munich conference was a definite defeat for Litvinov; it was an event that sharply deflated the prestige of the commissar of foreign affairs in the eyes of the Kremlin oligarchy. It was the beginning of his fall.

Litvinov's boast that "the Soviet Government takes pride in the fact that it has invariably pursued the principles set forth by the League of Nations" could not hide his defeat. Nor could his demands that the League invoke Article XVI, bravely and "without hesitation," conceal his humiliation. This last-ditch foe of Nazi Germany had been betrayed by his Western democratic colleagues whom he personally sought as allies against his enemies, the Nazis. Munich was a catastrophe for the Czechs and for Maxim Maximovitch Litvinov.

CHAPTER XIV

After Munich

The "Peace of Munich" was a great triumph for Adolf Hitler. It was a victory for the "young nations" (Germany and Italy) in their struggle with the "imperial democracies." With the dismemberment of Czecho-Slovakia and the consequent destruction of its military power the way was opened down the Danube for the *Drang nach Osten.* All southeastern Europe now appeared to be within the Fuehrer's grasp.

German prestige rose higher than ever since the war. The Balkan nations hastened to make their peace with the Fascist conquerors. Poland and Hungary greedily grabbed their loot from the prostrate Czech state. But Germany and Italy drew a line of demarcation past which the Magyars dared not go. Significantly enough, the fate of Ruthenia (the easternmost province of the doomed Czecho-Slovak republic, inhabited by about a half-million Carpatho-Ukrainians) was held in the balance.

Hungary clamored for this poverty-stricken, mountainous area in which the Magyars were few. But Hitler seemed to be toying with the plan of making this small region the

"Piedmont" of a Greater Ukraine. No doubt its strategic potentialities have been overrated by foreign writers. But the fact remains that Ruthenia has considerable strategic value. Not only was it a connecting link between Slovakia and Roumania; it lay between Hungary and Poland. In German hands it could prove a weapon against Poland, Hungary or Roumania. Most important of all, it might become the rallying point of the millions of Ukrainians scattered throughout a large area: Roumania, Poland, Hungary—and even in Russia.

One of the consequences of the Munich settlement was that France and Britain lost standing all over the Continent. The prestige of the Western democracies sank to a new low. Foreign ministers privately asked of their colleagues what value had a pact signed with a France which had gone back on its solemn pledge to the Czechs? What value could be placed on the British friendship which might bring a Runciman mission to your country? The Czechs were bitter against the Western democracies. Thousands of Czech and Slovak legionnaires returned their French and British decorations and service medals.

A little later on King Zog of Albania was to voice an appraisal of the British and French prime ministers that was shared by many other Europeans. Said the Albanian: "There are in Europe two madmen who are disturbing the entire world—Hitler and Mussolini. There are in Europe two damn fools who sleep—Chamberlain and Daladier."

As for the Soviet, the Munich debacle compelled the Kremlinites to review the situation in which they found themselves. The Czechs, a democratic people who believed in capitalism, had been betrayed by the British and French. What might happen if a similar crisis involved a Communist nation? And might not the frightened Western democracies try to buy safety for themselves by bribing Hitler to move eastward against the Soviet Union? Once again the fear of a coalition of capitalist states worried Stalin and his fellow Bolsheviks.

There was reason enough for the Kremlin's fear of "capitalist encirclement." The British Tories and the French Rightists were hostile to the U.S.S.R. Hitler had long invited Western support for an invasion of the Soviet Union. Moreover, the Russians and Japanese were arrayed in battle formation along their common borders in the Far East. Poland might be brought into an anti-Russian line-up. Indeed, all the border countries from the Arctic to the Golden Horn might be bribed or bludgeoned into joining the anti-Soviet alliance. The plotters of world revolution were afraid that they might fall victims to a world revolution promoted by their capitalist and Fascist enemies. The latter might steal the Bolsheviks' thunder.

There was no point in Stalin's making new advances to the Western democracies. Not only would French and British pledges be worthless, according to the Kremlin; diplomatic efforts to implement the Franco-Soviet pact might goad the Nazis into an early offensive against the U.S.S.R. Better try to reach a modus vivendi with the Nazis. Perhaps the Germans could be deflected from their path to the East and guided southward, or—even better— toward the West.

But Hitler was flushed with the Munich triumph. The victor over the Czechs was in no mood to listen to conciliatory offers from the Czechs' ally. He had no need for Stalin's support. The intelligence services of the Baltic States reported to their respective governments that the Red Army and the Reichswehr chiefs were urging upon their respective political bosses the necessity of a truce between Nazism and Bolshevism. Some of the Nazi hierarchy may have been receptive to the Soviet peace feelers. But the Fuehrer was not yet in any mood to grasp Stalin's proffered hand.

After Munich the Nazis prepared to move against Poland. To be sure, Hitler had signed a nonaggression pact with the Poles. Besides, Poland had made it possible for him to destroy Czecho-Slovakia. But gratitude is not one of Hitler's outstanding characteristics. Too, the master strategist could hardly help despising so shortsighted a nation as Poland. The Poles, he felt, should have had the vision to realize that their small Czech foe might have been turned into a valuable ally. And they should have been wise enough to sense that Poland would need an ally when its greater enemy, the Reich, would take up arms against it.

On January 5, 1939, Colonel Beck, Polish foreign minister, paid a visit to Hitler at Berchtesgaden. Already Germans and Poles had been sparring. The Poles claimed that the Germans had been worsted in an alleged clash between Polish and German troopers in the former Czech town of Oderberg. In Warsaw they told glowing tales of the havoc which the Polish cavalrymen, swinging their long sabers, had wrought on the Germans. In Polish regions along the Reich's frontier, moreover, there had been some rioting against the German minority.

In Poland the Germans were becoming bolder and were already boasting about the "*Tag*" when the Nazis would march in and "redeem" the lost provinces now held by the Poles. Young Germans in Poland wore white socks as a badge of their German nationality and their devotion to National Socialism. Many of them were beaten by Polish nationalists. From Berlin came angry anti-Polish growls. Dr Goebbels' propaganda machine had substituted anti-

Polish sound effects for the outdated anti-Czech broad-casts. The anti-Polish public-relations campaign was going full blast. "Germans in Poland Maltreated!" screamed the *Westdeutsche Beobachter's* headlines. "Brutal Acts by Mob—German Property Destroyed." The *Deutsche Allgemeine Zeitung* headlined: "Acts of Terror in Eastern Upper Silesia —Polish Bands Rage Against German Property."

Apparently the Fuehrer expected to issue orders to Colonel Beck and see them obeyed. According to Beck's report Hitler breathed fiery hatred of Bolshevism and the Soviet Union. Poland, it appears, was invited to join the Reich in a campaign against the U.S.S.R. But Poland was also scheduled to do some other things: she was to comply with Hitler's plans for German penetration of the Corridor. Beck, it seems certain, declined to enter into any kind of negotiations looking toward a revision of the Polish fron-tiers in favor of Germany.

Following the Beck visit to Berchtesgaden German prop-aganda against Poland increased in violence. The Nazis still believed that they could bluff the Poles into making concessions. In Poland, however, a powerful spirit of nationalism was sweeping the country. "We are not Czechs!" shouted the Poles. In their defiance the Poles began to lose touch with reality. Their vaunted "ferocious realism" in international relations now began to give way to utter unrealism. The Poles had defeated the Teutonic Knights at Tannenberg in 1410. They had turned back the Turkish hosts at Vienna in 1683. Was not the Polish cavalry the best in the world? The Polish public soon came to believe that Poland was more than a match for the Reich. "We are not Czechs!" was the boast that resounded from the northern tip of the Polish Corridor to the Car-pathians.

Moscow followed carefully every move in the match between the Reich and Poland. For this rising feud between
Berlin and Warsaw promised to accomplish what Stalin's
army and diplomacy had not been able to do—destroy
Poland. Not only did the Nazi-Polish quarrel dissipate
the danger of a German-Polish drive against the Soviet
Ukraine; it engendered the Russian hope that Nazi aggression might be turned against the Poles. It must be kept in
mind that the Bolsheviks, no less than their Tsarist predecessors, hated Poland. Stalin now secretly threw his support
to Hitler as a spur to the Nazis to bear down hard on
Poland.

By early March the Germans were preparing to invade
the rump state of Czecho-Slovakia and move into Prague.
Berlin and Moscow had not, however, come to terms.
The Kremlin was striving hard to placate the Nazis. It
was at the same time attempting to keep its lines open to
Geneva, Paris and London. For Stalin was too shrewd to
burn his bridges behind him. If he failed to make a deal
with Hitler, he would attempt to make the most advan-
tageous arrangement possible with the "decadent" West.
Opportunism was the leitmotif of the Kremlin in the early
months of 1939.

On the evening of March tenth an event of enormous
importance took place in Moscow. The setting was the
meeting of the All Union Congress of Soviets. Joseph Stalin
addressed the gathering. What he said carried the quin-
tessence of significance. It was a blunt speech. We can
judge what was in the Soviet dictator's mind from some of
the points stressed in his address.

Attacking the Western democracies, Stalin said: "They
let her (Germany) have Austria despite Austria's independence, they ceded the Sudeten region, they left Czecho-

Slovakia to her own fate, thereby violating all and every obligation and then began to lie vociferously in the press about the 'weakness of the Russian army,' about 'demoralization of the Russian air force,' about 'riots' in the Soviet Union, urging the Germans on to march further east, promising them easy pickings and prompting them: 'You start a war against the Bolsheviks and then everything will proceed nicely.' It must be admitted that this also looks like egging on, like encouraging the aggressor."

Referring to the question of Germany's interest in Ruthenia as the base of a Greater Ukraine, Stalin proceeded: "The fuss raised by the British, French and North American press about the Soviet Ukraine is characteristic. The gentlemen of this press grew hoarse shouting that the Germans were marching on Soviet Ukraine, that they now had in their hands so-called Carpathian Ukraine with a population of some 700,000 and that not later than this spring the Germans would annex Soviet Ukraine with a population of 30,000,000 to so-called Carpathian Ukraine."

The Red tsar sardonically continued: "It looks as if the object of this suspicious fuss was to raise the ire of the Soviet Union against Germany, to poison the atmosphere and provoke a conflict without any visible grounds for it."

The U.S.S.R., Stalin told his audience, would not act as a "cat's-paw" for anybody. The Soviet Union would not pull anybody's chestnuts out of the fire. His words were aimed directly at the Western democracies.

Two nights later Stalin's attack on France and Britain was followed up by Dmitry Z. Manuilsky, a member of the Executive Committee of the Third International. Addressing the All Union Congress in the Kremlin, Comrade Manuilsky made these scathing charges: "The plan of the reactionary English bourgeoisie is this—sacrificing of the small nations of southeastern Europe to Fascist Germany, to direct Germany eastward—namely, against the U.S.S.R.; to attempt by such counterrevolutionary war to retard the further successes of socialism and the victory of Communism in the U.S.S.R.; to bribe Germany from her imperialistic designs on English colonies."

But that was not all. Pursuing his attack on the Western democracies, Manuilsky continued: "At the same time the English reactionaries wish to pull the teeth of German imperialism by means of the U.S.S.R., to weaken Germany for many years and to retain for English imperialism a dominant position in Europe."

According to Stalin and his stooge the British were attempting to provoke a war between the Reich and the Soviet. By implication the Bolsheviks practically cleared Germany of any complicity in this intrigue. It was the English and their hirelings of the press who were trying to stir up a war over the Ukraine. It hardly seemed possible that this was the same Stalin who only a few years back had warned other nations, the Reich among them, to "keep their swinish snouts out of the Soviet potato patch!"

Moscow was beginning to agree with Berlin that London had become the *Weltlügenzentral* (world lies' center). Stalin and Hitler were obviously moving a little closer together in their common hatred of the British Empire.

In the realm of ideology Stalin could agree with Hitler about the absurdity of individual liberty. Bolsheviks could understand and applaud the statement made by Reich press chief, Dr Otto Dietrich, before a student audience at Berlin University: "There is no freedom of the individual. There is only freedom of peoples, nations or races, for these are the only material and historical realities through which the life of the individual exists."

General Clausewitz, the Prussian military writer, said that war is diplomacy carried on by other means. Hitler and Stalin have reversed this assertion. For these dictators diplomacy is merely war carried on by other means. Each of them understands the technique of the other. Each has copied from the totalitarian methods he has seen the other use. Both hate and despise the democratic nations. Each of them feared any situation that might work to the advantage of his democratic enemies. Here, then, were powerful intangible factors working for a rapprochement between these alleged ideological foes.

Stalin's speech of March tenth prepared the way for the next act in the now fast-moving melodrama of aggression and power politics.

CHAPTER XV

Litvinov Falls

One had better be a poor fisherman than meddle with the governing of men.—DANTON.

BY THE MIDDLE OF MARCH the "Aggrandizer of the Reich" found himself irresistibly pushed onward by the political and economic compulsions he had created inside Germany. The dynamics of National Socialism made a standstill policy impossible. The Nazis could advance, they could retreat, but they could not stay long in one position. It is doubtful that the Fuehrer could have tempered the speed and destructiveness of his vast politico-economic-military dynamo even if he had wished to do so.

On March fifteenth Hitler's field-gray troops clumped along the roads leading to Prague. That night the historic Hradcany was occupied by Nazi soldiers. The following day the Reich moved to establish its protectorate over Slovakia. Europe reeled under Nazi Germany's hammer blows. A week later Hitler forced Lithuania to cede the Memel territory to the Reich.

At last Britain and France became alarmed into taking action to stop the Nazi steam roller before it crushed its next prospective victim, Poland. On March thirty-first Prime Minister Chamberlain told a cheering House of Commons that the British Government saw "no justification for the substitution of force or threats of force for the method of negotiation."

At two fifty-two that afternoon Mr Chamberlain made this momentous pronouncement: "As the House is aware, certain consultations are now proceeding with other governments. In order to make perfectly clear the position of His Majesty's Government in the meantime before those consultations are concluded, I now have to inform the House that during that period, in the event of any action which clearly threatened Polish independence, and which the Polish Government accordingly considered it vital to resist with their national forces, His Majesty's Government would feel themselves bound at once to lend the Polish Government all support in their power. They have given the Polish Government an assurance to this effect."

Poland at last had a definite British pledge of support. And Mr Chamberlain went on to announce that the French Government had "authorized" him to say that they took the same position.

Almost immediately, to be sure, there sounded a note of hedging. An editorial in the influential *Times* of London, which so often reflects the views of the British Government, stated that the pledge to Warsaw did not "bind Britain to defend every inch of the present frontiers of Poland." It intimated that the undertaking might exclude such former German territories as Danzig, the Corridor and Upper Silesia. But on April first a semiofficial communiqué reinforced in still stronger terms the prime minister's pledge to Poland before the House of Commons.

On that same day Hitler spoke at Wilhelmshaven. There

he denounced "encirclement," threatened to break the Anglo-German naval accord and warned his foes that the world "will defend itself against the most severe Bolshevistic threat that exists."

Berlin feared that the Western democracies were now in earnest. Dr Goebbels' propaganda machine poured out its attacks on the "decadent" states, the "satiated" nations, the "organized terrorism of the world plutocratic clique." The world was warned of the "warmongers" in control of the "imperial democracies."

Meanwhile Stalin could look on with deep satisfaction. The threat of a democratic-Nazi coalition against the Soviet was for the moment, at least, minimized. By the same token the Kremlin's enemies were quarreling among themselves, a development that could redound only to the profit of the U.S.S.R.

Almost imperceptibly the Reich began to court the Soviet. Insulting references to the Soviet leadership no longer appeared in Nazi speeches. Dr Goebbels' propaganda even began to make friendly references to the U.S.S.R. Some of Hitler's colleagues cautiously insinuated that the Reich and the Soviet were being attacked by the same "war incendiaries"—the Western democracies.

On Monday April third there was in London a parliamentary debate of unusual importance. Winston Churchill took the floor. Said this leading foe of "appeasement": "The conquest of the Ukraine by Nazi Germany, upon which such covetous eyes have been avowedly set, would be a direct assault upon the life of the Soviet State. Then again in the Far East, the aggression of Japan upon China has brought Japan at this moment into close grips with the Eastern Russian power. No one can say that there is not a solid identity of interest between the Western democracies and Soviet Russia, and we must do nothing to obstruct the natural play of that identity of interest."

Mr Churchill's was an astounding statement. It betrayed his colossal misunderstanding of Soviet policies, especially the feeling of the Kremlin oligarchy toward the British Empire.

But Mr Churchill had more to say. "Roumania, Poland and the Baltic States all feel easier," he explained, "because this great mass of Russia is friendly behind them and lies there in a broad support."

Had Mr Churchill taken the trouble to talk with the ministers of Finland, Latvia and Estonia he could undoubtedly have saved himself from making so preposterous a statement. The Baltic States certainly did not at any time "feel easier" because Russia was near them. Nor, for that matter, did Roumania and Poland. On the contrary, these countries, especially the small Baltic States, lived in constant dread of any shift in European power politics that would give the U.S.S.R. a free hand to pounce on them.

Mr David Lloyd George was not to be left out of the debate. Regarding the problem of helping Poland he had this to say: "If we are going in without the help of Russia we are walking into a trap. It is the only country whose armies can get there. She is the only country whose air fleet can match the German's—some people say it is better."

As for the Russian Army, Mr Lloyd George continued: "I do not say it is now a perfect army but it is an army of 18,000,000 trained men, and of the bravest in the world."

Referring to the British guarantee of Poland: "I cannot understand," said he, "why, before committing ourselves to this tremendous enterprise, we did not secure beforehand the adhesion of Russia. . . . I ask the Government to take immediate steps to secure the adhesion of Russia in a fraternity, an alliance, an agreement, a pact, it does not matter what it is called, so long as it is an understanding to stand together against the aggressor. Apart from that we have undertaken a frightful gamble, a very risky gamble. With Russia you have overwhelming forces which Germany with her inferior army cannot stand up against."

Both Churchill and Lloyd George appeared to assume that the Soviet Union would be delighted to join Britain in an effort to save Poland. That this assumption was utterly illogical did not seem to occur to either of these speakers. No one appears to have asked either speaker why the U.S.S.R. should go to war to save its traditional hated enemy, Poland. These parliamentary speeches raised false hopes in the democracies and helped to confuse the world public.

Mr Anthony Eden contributed his bit to the debate. "Four years ago, when my right honorable friend the Chancellor of the Exchequer was Foreign Secretary, I went to Moscow, and at the conclusion of that visit a communiqué was issued, the terms of which I venture to recall to the House because they are not inappropriate as the basis of our relations at the present time. The communiqué stated: 'There is at present no conflict of interests between the British and Soviet Governments on any of the main issues of international policy.' "

The pronouncements of Messrs Churchill, Lloyd George and Eden give weight to the belief held by political observers in the Baltic States that it was these leaders who forced Mr Chamberlain and his supporters into seeking an Anglo-Russian alliance. Whether the Chamberlain-Hoare-Simon clique was right or wrong in their policies toward the Soviet, they were at least consistent in their suspicions of Moscow. They and influential Frenchmen like Bonnet

and Laval believed that the Soviet was constantly maneu-
vering to promote a war among the capitalist nations upon
whose ruins Moscow would spread Bolshevism.

Now that Britain had given Poland a "blank check"
guarantee, Downing Street began to perceive the serious-
ness of the situation. London was now no longer a free
agent. Warsaw could, if it chose, precipitate a crisis that
would automatically draw the British into war. Obviously
John Bull needed support.

As further steps in the campaign to stop Hitler, Britain
and France offered support to Roumania, Turkey and
Greece. When Russia joined this coalition there would be
seven nations arrayed against Nazi aggression. Already in
London this alignment was being called the "democratic
front." Someone pointed out, however, that this was hardly
a correct name for an alliance that would include one out-
right dictatorship, four quasi-dictatorships and only two
democracies. So the name was changed to the "peace
front."

During April Britain began to woo the Kremlin in
earnest. How the tables had been turned in scarcely seven
months! The previous September the Franco-British had
barred the U.S.S.R. from Munich. Now Chamberlain and
Daladier were compelled by the speeding force of events to
seek a pact with the men whom they had snubbed, the men
whom they had attempted to bar from the councils of
Europe.

Again the lack of logic in British and French policies
toward the Soviet was apparent. At Munich they had all
but destroyed the prestige of Litvinov, their last-ditch anti-
Nazi friend in the Soviet Government. Now they were asking him to build the collective security system which they
had spurned a few months previously.

Moreover, the precipitate British and French guarantees of Poland and Roumania had played into Stalin's hands. With delight the Kremlin realized that the Western democracies were holding the bag. For now the shortest road from the Reich to the Ukraine was barred to Hitler by Britain and France. The Soviet could still fight the Germans if the Nazis reached the border of the Ukraine. But long before the Reich's troops could reach this boundary of the U.S.S.R. they would be at war not only with the Poles but also with the two great Western powers. And the Soviet Union would not be obliged to take part in the fray.

Now came obvious advances from the Third Reich to Stalin. In his speech on April twenty-eighth Hitler made no attack on the U.S.S.R. No longer did he hold up the Soviet Union as "world enemy number one," the world Carthage that must be destroyed.

The German press occasionally contained discreet hints that the Reich and the Soviet were not, after all, irreconcilable enemies. The *Westdeutsche Beobachter* explained it this way: "National Socialism does not war against a State because that State has a different content from our own . . . the anti-Comintern Pact does not strike primarily at the State but, as the Pact itself says, at Bolshevism when it reaches out beyond Russian borders."

According to this Nazi organ it would be possible for the German Reich and the Soviet Union to maintain normal relations with each other. "That is the German viewpoint and it also appears favorable to the Kremlin. . . . There is nothing to prevent us respecting the territory of the Soviet Union and trading with it. Economic relations with the Soviet Union already have been useful. That they are not very good at present does not affect our general view. . . . Soviet territory is too gigantic to be ignored on the map."

Just what were the exact Anglo-French proposals to the
Soviet we do not know. This question seems likely to remain in dispute for a long time to come. But in some of the
central European chancelleries it was reported that the
Western democracies made an offer along this line: France
and Britain would protect Belgium, the Netherlands and
Switzerland, because they could easily reach those countries. But the Western powers could not offer immediate
and effective aid to Poland and Roumania. Therefore the
Soviet Union, whose borders abut both those east-
European states, should adopt the same protective policy
toward them that the Franco-British would toward the
little countries of western Europe. Thus if Hitler attacked
Poland, the Soviet would be obligated to stop him, while
the French and British held the West.

But Stalin would have none of this. And why should he?
France and Britain had guaranteed the safety of the Poles
and Roumanians. The Bolsheviks had no intention of re-
lieving them of their self-imposed responsibility.

One of the first stumbling blocks encountered by the
Franco-British in their quest for a Soviet alliance was the
question of the Baltic States. These little countries distrusted both the Reich and the Soviet. They wanted
guarantees from neither side. They abhorred the role of
pawns in power politics. They wanted to be let alone. But
they were not destined to remain undisturbed. Their
strategic position, their foodstuffs, raw materials and man
power precluded any possibility that they could escape the
effects of the conflict now threatening Europe.

Moscow argued that a Franco-British-Soviet guarantee
confined to Poland and Roumania would merely block
these two avenues to Nazi conquest and turn Hitler's
troops northeastward along the Baltic into Lithuania,

Latvia and Estonia toward Leningrad. Litvinov maintained that this gap in the collective security system actually invited Nazi aggression. Unprotected by the great powers, he contended, the Baltic States would furnish Hitler with more "bloodless victories." These three Baltic countries and Finland must be guaranteed, the Kremlin demanded, or the U.S.S.R. could not join the Western democracies in a defensive pact.

But the Baltic States had no desire to accept such guarantees from anybody. They read in the arguments of the Kremlin Stalin's intention of interfering with their internal affairs. If the Soviet guaranteed these countries, Moscow might send troops into their territory on the pretext that it was protecting their independence. Just as Hitler had invaded Austria and Czecho-Slovakia to "restore order" and destroy "Bolshevism," Stalin might invade the Baltic States on the pretext that he had to "restore order" and exterminate "Fascism." The Baltic nations bitterly denounced Moscow's efforts to drag them into the collective security system. Finns, Letts and Estonians all had suffered from Bolshevik invasions. They had all known what it was to have their countrysides looted by Red troops and their people killed in desperate fights to drive back the Russian invaders.

Moreover, the Baltic countries resented the alleged indifference manifested toward them by some British and French newspapers. At Tallinn an official of the Estonian Government showed me a feature article in a leading Paris journal which bluntly advocated a Franco-British-Soviet guarantee of the Baltic States, whether those little countries liked it or not. "We Estonians shall not soon forget that," he remarked resentfully.

But as April dragged toward its close the projected

"peace front" still lacked its seventh member. The Soviet held out for its own terms. Despite optimistic reports in London that the alliance "will be signed before the week is out," the days and weeks passed without any definite conclusion of the negotiations in sight. Some observers in the Western capitals began to suspect that, after all, Moscow might not be so eager to enter the Franco-British alignment as Mr Churchill and his friends had assumed.

But for all this, any mention of the possibility that the Reich and the Soviet might come to terms was laughed off derisively. The British and American publics had long been schooled in the premise that the hostility between the Nazis and Bolsheviks was irreconcilable. The denunciations and scatological epithets bandied back and forth between the Nazis and Bolsheviks had been taken at their face value by the Western publics.

Had not Hitler referred to the Soviet leadership as the "bloodstained scum of humanity," a "band of bloodsoaked criminals," a pack of "bloodhounds"?

In 1937 Herr Hitler had assured German workers that: "You will never see me clinking glasses or rubbing shoulders with Bolshevists. It is out of the question that we could accept help from a Bolshevist state. Those who accept help from the Soviet Union are doomed."

And there was the Fuehrer's boast at the 1937 Nuremberg Party Congress: "If the whole of the world around us were to be set ablaze the National Socialist State would stand firm as platinum amidst the Bolshevist conflagration."

The Bolsheviks had matched every Nazi outburst of anti-Soviet vituperation. Premier Molotov had referred to the National Socialist leaders as "modern cannibals." The Moscow radio repeatedly recounted the alleged extra-marital adventures of Dr Goebbels. And had not Soviet news organs mentioned the Nazis in terms which could not be reproduced in British or American publications that had to pass through the mails? True.

But well-informed Letts, Estonians and Finns had long discounted the Berlin-Moscow billingsgate as stage play. These Baltic observers regarded the verbal barrage of the Brown and Red dictatorships as camouflage for the real policies of these totalitarian regimes. In Riga, Tallinn and Helsinki the role of Litvinov was a far more trustworthy indication of the true relationship between Berlin and Moscow.

The Baltic capitals had watched Maxim Maximovitch's humiliation at the hands of the Western democracies at Munich. They had seen his attempts to make the League of Nations a powerful Russian weapon fail in the first real test. They knew that the Nazi hierarchs hated the Soviet commissar of foreign affairs. In Nazi eyes Litvinov was guilty of two heinous crimes: he favored a collective security system to stop Fascist aggression, and he was a Jew.

As the weeks of spring passed the Baltic chancelleries watched Litvinov. He was the key to the Russian riddle. If he could hold his post, they decided, then perhaps the Soviet might march with the Western democracies. But if Litvinov should fall, then Stalin was at least moving into a neutral position. He might, indeed, be preparing to cast his lot with the Nazis.

But few were the people in London and Paris who troubled themselves about Litvinov. Britons and Frenchmen assumed that the delaying tactics of the U.S.S.R. were only bluff. Some people in the Western democracies actually talked as if a word from Britain and France could send Hitler marching against the Soviet Union. This was the complacent state of mind in the Western world on the night of May second.

The following day a dramatic announcement was made in Moscow. Maxim Maximovitch Litvinov was relieved of his post. Premier Molotov would succeed him. Only the most naïve people in the Western world accepted the excuse that poor health necessitated Litvinov's retirement. The implacable foe of Nazi Germany would no longer have a voice in the Soviet's foreign policies. What would Molotov's attitude be toward the Reich and the Western democracies?

CHAPTER XVI

Stalin Vis-à-Vis Hitler

THE SIGNIFICANCE of Litvinov's fall is now clear. He could no longer serve Stalin's purpose; his usefulness to the Red tsar was over. Now that serious negotiations with Hitler were about to start, Litvinov was a liability to Soviet diplomacy.

At this point the calculating Stalin had a great advantage over his myopic enemies abroad. He was not thinking merely in terms of staving off an attack on the U.S.S.R. The capitalist world had conveniently taken that load off his mind. If that "other world" was preparing to commit suicide, there was no reason why the Kremlin should not encourage the process.

According to the information from Russia that was arriving in the Baltic capitals, Andrei Zhdanov, the Leningrad party boss, was using his influence to further a Nazi-Soviet deal. Zhdanov was the successor of the late Sergei Kirov as number-one friend of Stalin. He was chairman of the Committee on Foreign Relations of the Supreme Soviet. He was heir apparent of the Kremlin throne.

Premier Molotov, too, according to Baltic States information, favored an understanding with the Nazis. In

March 1940 the Soviet celebrated the premier's fiftieth birthday. The celebration was the occasion for an article by the vice-commissar of foreign affairs, S. A. Lozovsky, in which he declared that since 1931 "Molotov in successive speeches emphasized that the Anglo-French imperialists were preparing for war against the Soviet Union."

It would be preposterous to assume, however, that either Molotov or Zhdanov was pro-German. They were only pro-Soviet. Their suspicions of the Western democracies did not mean that they favored any policy which would help the Reich at the expense of the Soviet Union. Both these Bolsheviks favored a deal with the Nazis that would place German technical skill, industrial experience and administrative efficiency at the disposal of the U.S.S.R.

It has been a common assumption in the Western countries that Stalin, Molotov, Zhdanov and their colleagues know little about the world outside Russia. This is hardly true. These men certainly know far more about the Western democracies than the people in the democracies know about Russia.

Humorless, plodding Molotov and hustling, ambitious, scowling, hard-boiled Zhdanov fill important roles in the Soviet regime. Each has long been a trusted confidant of Stalin. Molotov plays the part of the faithful henchman who carries out orders. Lenin was reported to have referred to Molotov as "the best filing clerk in the Soviet Union." Zhdanov is a plotter and a man of action. Whenever the Red dictator has wanted to bully some small neighbor one of these Kremlin hierarchs has emitted the necessary growls.

An example: in 1936 Finland and Estonia incurred the displeasure of the U.S.S.R. For their benefit Zhdanov uttered this warning in a speech before the All Union

Congress of Soviets: "We in Leningrad are sitting at one of the windows looking abroad. Around us are a number of small countries which dream of big adventures or allow big adventures to be manipulated on their small territories. We are not afraid of little countries, of course. But if they do not mind their own business, we may be compelled to open the window a little wider, and it will be just too bad for them if we are forced to call the Red Army into defensive action."

The words came from the throat of Zhdanov, but everybody in the Baltic lands which had been threatened knew that they expressed the angry warning of Stalin.

Klementi Voroshilov, then chief of the Red Army, has been another important member of the Kremlin oligarchy. Although he is not supposed to have wielded a decisive influence on Stalin's political conduct, it seems safe to assume that his position gave him an opportunity to have some influence in Kremlin councils. And even though Stalin is the absolute dictator, there are times when he must ask for information, perhaps even suggestions, from his satraps. Like Zhdanov and Molotov, Voroshilov is a Bolshevik with only one loyalty. But his Reichswehr contacts have given him some conception of German military power. For that reason, if for no other, he might have been expected to look with favor upon any plan that would avoid an armed clash between the armies of the Reich and the Soviet.

In May 1940 Voroshilov was succeeded as war commissar by Semyon Timoshenko. The latter was almost unknown before Stalin elevated him to the post of chief of the Red Army.

Some observers have fastened upon Zhdanov the responsibility for Litvinov's fall. This seems too facile an explanation. It may well be that the Leningrad party leader urged upon Stalin the suggestion that Litvinov be ousted. But, as we have already pointed out, Stalin would keep Litvinov as foreign commissar only as long as the Red dictator needed a man of Litvinov's talents, only so long as the Geneva stage play was necessary for the Kremlin's program, only as long as it was Moscow's purpose to isolate Germany.

When Stalin started his maneuvers to play the Anglo-French forces against Germany in the spring of 1939, he needed Molotov. He was the man to make the play in Moscow. He had no preference as between Nazism and democracy. Litvinov hated Nazism. Molotov would perhaps prefer to join Hitler against Chamberlain because he believed that the Reich would be a more dangerous enemy for the Soviet.

As Stalin watched Europe's war preparations he may well have recalled the situation in ancient Greece when Athens and Sparta were preparing to destroy each other. He may have decided that if the Franco-British (Athenians) and the Germans (Spartans) fought each other, only the Macedonians (Bolsheviks) could ultimately profit. His diplomacy was, therefore, pointed toward making the Athens-Sparta collision a certainty.

But while Stalin was busily making sure that his enemies would cut each other's throats he was ceaselessly striving to ensure the protection of his own diplomatic and military position. To this end he proposed to the Western democracies that France and Britain guarantee not only the Soviet's western border but its Far Eastern one as well. If Japan invaded any of the Soviet domains the Western democracies would be obligated to come to the aid of the U.S.S.R. London and Paris did not respond with enthusiasm to this suggestion. Negotiations dragged on.

This was the situation on May 31, 1939. On that day Comrade Molotov made an address before the Supreme Soviet. The British and French were supposed to listen. "While guaranteeing themselves (the Western democracies) from direct attack by aggressors by pacts of mutual assistance between themselves and Poland," said the Kremlin spokesman, "and while trying to secure for themselves the assistance of the U.S.S.R. in the event of attack by an aggressor on Poland and Roumania, the British and French left open the question whether the U.S.S.R. in its turn might count on their assistance in the event of its being directly attacked by aggressors. . . . Thus the position was one of inequality for the U.S.S.R. . . .

"But we must remember Comrade Stalin's precept: 'To be cautious and not to allow our country to be drawn into conflicts by warmongers who are accustomed to have others pull chestnuts out of the fire for them!'"

As if these admonitions were not enough, Molotov voiced this thinly veiled intimation of possible co-operation with the Reich: "While conducting negotiations with Great Britain and France we by no means consider it necessary to renounce business relations with countries like Germany and Italy."

But the Molotov speech was not taken seriously in the Western democracies. So sold were the British and French on the theory that the Soviet had no other place to go for allies that many officials in London and Paris shrugged off the Molotov warning as "more Bolshevik bluff." Yet, as they know now, Stalin was at that time being courted by Hitler. The Fuehrer was bidding recklessly for Soviet support.

To rate Stalin as a desperate man looking abroad for friends in the early summer of 1939 was nonsense. Nine months before, it is true, the Soviet was an outcast, a pariah barred from the council tables of Munich. But by June 1939 the Germans and their Franco-British enemies together had lifted Stalin into the driver's seat in the race toward war. And this Asiatic despot who had not hesitated to condemn to death millions of his helpless fellow countrymen now looked ahead to a Europe in shambles.

According to the best information available in the capitals of the border countries and in Moscow itself, this is the situation as it looked from the vantage point of the Kremlin. In peace time Bolshevik propaganda made little progress. It was becoming increasingly clear that a well-governed, fairly prosperous nation with a strong middle class offered no encouragement to Communism. But that same country, weakened by war and its attendant sufferings and losses, would provide fertile soil for Bolshevik propaganda. Despair was the most valuable ally of Bolshevism. And nothing could bring on despair more completely than the destruction wrought by a great war.

No Soviet leader could doubt that the Third Reich was a far greater menace to the U.S.S.R. than were the Western democracies. Not only was the Reich close at hand, but for years the Nazis had waged a terrific propaganda war against the Soviet Union. Hitler had intrigued to form a coalition against Russia. And even though the Kremlinites undoubtedly realized that Hitler's fulminations against Bolshevism were largely meant for home consumption and for the extreme Right in capitalist countries, they were a factor to be considered.

Hitler's anti-Soviet diatribe at the 1936 Nuremberg Party Congress had been closely studied in the Kremlin. On that occasion the Fuehrer made his often-quoted statement: "If I had the Urals, with their incalculable store of treasures in raw materials, Siberia, with its vast forests, and the Ukraine, with its tremendous wheat fields, Germany and the National Socialist leadership would swim in plenty." Squadrons of war planes roared overhead. "Let Russia carry the five-pointed red star, the Soviet national emblem," the Fuehrer shouted. "We will conquer in the sign of the swastika!"

The British, French and American publics had jumped at the conclusion that the Reich was about to march against the U.S.S.R. The Fuehrer would take a gambler's chance to wrest the mentioned riches from the Bolsheviks. But that was not the construction put upon Hitler's words by the well-informed chancelleries in the Baltic States. It might be, they decided, that the Fuehrer himself was not sure of the methods he would use to win his Russian objectives. Inasmuch as the Kremlin may well have interpreted the Nuremberg speech as the Baltic capitals did, it may be worth while to examine the reasoning in Riga, Tallinn and Helsinki.

In the Baltic capitals it was noted that Hitler spoke of the Urals. These mountains are a thousand miles east of East Prussia. And the forests of Siberia are even more distant from Germany. Did Hitler believe that the Reich could swallow all European Russia and Siberia to boot? Hardly. Yet the Nuremberg outburst linked the Urals and Siberia with the Ukraine.

The Baltic observers appraised the Fuehrer's words in this way. Germany was woefully short of raw materials. If she had the minerals, timber and grain of the Soviet Union she would "swim in plenty." It seemed to the border-capital observers that Hitler hoped to gain access to the Urals and Siberia by some method other than armed invasion.

Hitler's words were interpreted as the expression of a hope for an eventual understanding with the U.S.S.R. This understanding would give the industrial Reich an opportunity to exploit the Soviet's riches and "swim in plenty." Simultaneously Russia would become a gigantic market for Germany's finished products. This was the interpretation put on Hitler's much-discussed words by Baltic States observers. Quite possibly it may also have been the conclusion reached by Stalin and his satrapy.

The anti-Comintern was a source of friction between Berlin and Moscow. That association of Fascist nations was aimed against the U.S.S.R. Its promoters openly claimed that it was. It was started officially on November 25, 1936, when Von Ribbentrop signed for Germany and Mushakoji for Japan. The supplementary protocol contained this sentence: "The competent authorities of both high contracting parties will, within the framework of existing laws, take strict measures against those who, at home or abroad, directly or indirectly, are active in the service of the Communist International or lend a helping hand to its disruptive work."

Less than a year later Italy joined the Reich and Japan in the anti-Comintern pact (Fascintern). Here was to be the start of a vast anti-Soviet coalition. Italy's adhesion to the pact was attended by a fanfare of propaganda and bombast. But the Fascintern never made a great deal of headway. It received support from Manchukuo, Hungary and Franco Spain, but the Western democracies and most of the smaller powers remained aloof. And it is only part of the record to mention that it never struck terror into the Kremlin. For the realistic Bolsheviks recognized it for what it really was: a gigantic bluff and an instrument of blackmail. But not necessarily a tool to blackmail the U.S.S.R.

Indeed, it was used more against the Western democracies than against the Soviet Union.

On more than one occasion Litvinov had warned the British and French that the so-called anti-Comintern pact was actually a threat to their security. The three leading "have-not" states, he said, were challenging the imperial possessions of the "have" nations.

Spain was another point of conflict between the Soviet and the Reich. On the Iberian Peninsula the anti-Comintern forces clashed with Stalin's outposts at the western end of the Mediterranean. The Kremlin saw in the Spanish turmoil an opportunity to win important advantages without taking large risks. If the Communists could dominate the Spanish Government, Stalin's U.S.S.R. would have an ally at the gateway of the Atlantic. But win or lose, the Soviet stood to gain. For here was indeed an ideal chance to start the "second imperialist world war."

Hence it was that on the fields of Spain "volunteers" from the Soviet Union waged fierce ideological struggles with "volunteers" from the Reich and from Italy. Spanish Communist delegates were received enthusiastically in Moscow. Soviet ships carrying munitions to Loyalist Spain were torpedoed by "pirate" submarines operating in the Mediterranean. Russian planes were used by the Loyalists; German and Italian planes served the Insurgents. Russian tanks, German artillery and Italian infantry destroyed Spanish property and killed off Spanish youth. Spanish Stalinists and Trotzkyists fought each other in Barcelona and other Spanish cities.

But here again crops up one of the ironies inherent in Communist-Fascist conflicts. We might expect the Soviet hierarchy to hold a grudge against the Nazis for German aid rendered to Franco. Yet the Soviet wrath was directed mainly against Popular Front France and Tory Britain for the so-called "nonintervention" policy followed by the Western democracies. Indeed, Soviet spokesmen were probably more bitter against Premier Léon Blum and his Socialist and Radical supporters than toward the Nazi fighters who invaded Spain and battled against Moscow's policies there.

The Kremlin oligarchy came to believe, rightly or wrongly, that Chamberlain Britain and Blum France were more friendly to a Fascist Spain than a Socialist Spain. Even the French Front Populaire gave little effective support to the Spanish Loyalists. And when Litvinov lashed out before the League of Nations against the German-Italian intervention in Spain, he received strangely little help from the representatives of the Western democracies. This apparent collusion aroused angry denunciation of the British and French by Soviet spokesmen. And it left a record of smoldering resentment against what the Bolsheviks declared was democratic complicity in the destruction of Loyalist Spain.

On February 20, 1938, Herr Hitler had made a blistering attack on the Soviet Union before the German Reichstag. On that occasion he shouted: "With one country alone we have scorned to enter relations. That State is Soviet Russia."

But by the spring of 1939 the Fuehrer's military advisers had informed him that it would be foolhardy for the Reich to attempt a campaign that might pit the German Army against a coalition of the Soviet Union, Poland and the Western democracies. Hitler must, they urged, prevent an alliance between the Russians and the Franco British. He must smash the wall of encirclement that Germany's enemies were trying to build around her.

Under these conditions a German bid for a deal with Russia became inevitable. It seems probable that Hitler's psychopathic personality, his mysticism and personal prejudices actually postponed a natural rapprochement with the U.S.S.R. Indeed, if the Fuehrer had listened to his army chiefs and the leaders of German industry, there would have been no feud with the Weimar Republic's Rapallo partner.

Without advertising the fact to the world Hitler's emissaries negotiated with the Kremlin. The German press threw out hints of Nazi overtures to the U.S.S.R. by asserting "that the Soviets are not disposed to serve as Britain's valets in the European east." In the Baltic capitals the chancelleries suspected that there was Nazi-Soviet bargaining in progress. But no one could find out for certain just what was going on. The Kremlin and the Wilhelmstrasse guarded their secret carefully.

Well advertised to the world, however, was the trip of Mr William Strang, the special envoy sent from the British Foreign Office to reinforce the efforts of the British ambassador in Moscow, Sir William Seeds. The mid-June arrival of Strang in Moscow was heralded by the British as the final move in the negotiation of an alliance between the U.S.S.R. and the Western democracies. But foreign wits in the Soviet capital dubbed the Strang mission the *"Strang nach Osten."*

Some observers in Moscow questioned the wisdom of the British Government in sending to the Kremlin a representative whose standing was less than cabinet rank. They expressed the fear that Strang's comparatively minor position would offend the Soviet hierarchy. Back in London some critics blamed the prime minister for not sending Lord Halifax to Moscow.

But there were those observers who wondered if Mr Chamberlain's choice of Strang indicated the prime minister's doubts that a pact could be arranged between London and Moscow. There were even charges (ill founded, it seems certain) that the prime minister sent Strang to Moscow as a move to sabotage any prospect of an Anglo-Russian alliance. The British public was quite at ease about the whole affair; it assumed that the optimistic reports issued from government quarters were the prelude to the pact with the U.S.S.R. which nearly everybody now wanted.

There certainly was point to the criticism of the British action in sending to Moscow a negotiator who did not have cabinet rank. But the continued failure of British efforts to sign up the Soviets apparently did not rest with Strang. It was probably true that Stalin resented an envoy whose status was lower than the foreign secretary's. The arrival of Lord Halifax might have made the Bolsheviks feel a trifle less resentful toward Britain. But certainly not sufficiently to influence the final results of the conversations.

Stalin is far too hard-boiled and realistic a ruler to permit trifles like the rank of a foreign emissary to sway his judgment on so important a subject. His decision was being made on the basis of factors that had nothing to do with personalities. His reasoning was in line with the *Realpolitik* directives of Soviet imperialism.

Machiavelli wrote: "A prince ought to take care never to make an alliance with one more powerful than himself for the purpose of attacking others . . . because if he conquers, you are at his discretion." Why then should the Red dictator follow a course that seems to have run counter to this advice?

In the Machiavelli tradition Stalin appears to have

reasoned along these lines: If the U.S.S.R. joined the Western democracies in the "peace front," there probably would be no war in the near future. If war should come, however, the Soviet would be in the post of danger. Russia might be pitted against the German Army in a struggle that would benefit the hated Western democracies. And Stalin certainly did not share Lloyd George's optimism of the purged Red Army's chances against the efficient, mechanized Reichswehr. If war were postponed, the British and French might come to terms with Germany. Then the Reich would be free to turn its whole strength eastward against Russia.

Moreover, as Walter Lippmann pointed out in the New York *Herald Tribune* of April 20, 1940: "Stalin did not join the Franco-British alliance because he believed, correctly enough, that Russia would receive the brunt of the attack, and because he feared, not without some justification, that the Western powers might be tempted to let the war become an anti-Communist crusade."

On the other hand, if Stalin came to terms with Hitler he could probably stay out of war if he chose to do so. The ensuing conflict would involve the principal nations in that "other world" which Stalin was resolved to destroy. Furthermore, according to what appears to be the best information available, the Soviet dictator knew that Britain and France could not afford to stand by while Hitler overran Poland. They would have to fight, unless someone would be obliging enough to do their fighting for them.

A Soviet pact with Hitler would undoubtedly spur the Fuehrer to attack Poland immediately. Thus a Nazi-Soviet entente would not only start the war that Stalin was trying to promote; it would likely spare the Soviet from involvement. The war would embroil four of his enemies at one time. For the Bolsheviks were too well informed to share the Hitler-Von Ribbentrop belief that a Berlin-Moscow deal would scare the British and French into standing by while the Nazis destroyed Poland.

By now the sands in the hourglass of peace were running low.

CHAPTER XVII

The Soviet and Poland

Whoever possesses the mouth of the Vistula and the city of Danzig will be more the master of Poland than the King who rules there.—FREDERICK THE GREAT.

IN CENTRAL EUROPE a favorite story is the tale about the book on the elephant. According to one version, a man from each of several nations wrote on the subject.

The sporting Englishman called his volume "Elephants I Have Hunted in the Jungles of India." The Frenchman named his "The Amours of the Elephant." The mystic Russian used the title "The Elephant: Is There Such a Creature?" The thoroughgoing German wrote "The Elephant: His Psychology, His Anatomy, His Habits, His Possibilities—An Introduction to a Study of the Animal in Six Volumes." The Pole called his book "The Elephant and the Polish Question."

There has been a Polish question almost as long as there has been a Poland. The geography of Poland accounts to some extent for this situation. For centuries the Poles were the bulwark of the civilized West against the barbaric East. On countless occasions they turned back the westward surges of Mongols, Tartars, Turks, Russians and other invaders. Poland has been called the most eastern of Western nations. It has long been a battlefield of Germans and Slavs. Its people have a fiery patriotism that has pulled them through many a period of defeat. It has kept alive the spirit of Polish nationalism which not even a century and a half under alien masters could diminish.

The peace settlements which brought the first World War officially to an end gave Poland nearly all the lands in which there were Polish majorities. The Poles also received large territories in which there were few Poles and many non-Poles. Millions of minorities—Ukrainians, White Russians, Germans, Lithuanians, Roumanians—came under Polish rule. And there were three million Jews destined to live in a country whose policies toward national and religious minorities were far from enlightened.

From the birth of the new Poland all intelligent Poles realized that their country occupied a post of danger. On the West was a perennial enemy, sullen and dissatisfied Germany. On the East was a traditional foe, Russia. Of the two large enemy neighbors, many Poles considered Russia the greater menace to the existence of Poland. For this Russia was no longer a Tsarist empire interested in promoting Pan-Slavic imperialism. It had become a Communist state whose oligarchy not only wanted Polish territory but hoped to replace the present government with a Soviet regime. Tsarist imperialism had been replaced by Soviet imperialism.

In the Russo-Polish War of 1920 the Red Army reached the outskirts of Warsaw before it was turned back by the embattled Poles. Just as the Bolshevik leaders looked to the day when they might incorporate Poland within the U.S.S.R., some Polish nationalists dreamed of the time when the boundaries of 1772 might be redrawn at the expense of Russia. The Treaty of Riga between the Soviet and Poland, signed on March 18, 1921, did not bring about a genuine peace. It did not pave the way for a rapprochement between Moscow and Warsaw; it merely brought to an official close the period of active warfare. The settlement at Riga provided nothing more than an armed truce between two ancient antagonists.

But Poland's bad relations were by no means confined to Germany and Russia. Poles and Czechs quarreled. Poland seized the Vilna district from Lithuania in the fall of 1920. For the following seventeen and a half years the Polish-Lithuanian frontier was closed. No train crossed it; no mail passed over it; no telegraph or telephone wires spanned it. Even the border with Latvia was hardly a friendly frontier, because many Letts believed that Poland had designs on the important Lettish railroad-junction town of Dvinsk (Dunaburg) (Daugavpils).

Perhaps the only boundary that the Poles could call a friendly one was their border along northern Roumania. Poles and Roumanians entered a mutual-assistance pact against their common enemy, the U.S.S.R. But neither Warsaw nor Bucharest put a great deal of faith in this pact.

Poland was probably more frightened than any other nation by the first Rapallo agreement reached by Moscow and Berlin. This fear was never completely dissipated, though at times the Poles became confident of their ability to play Germany and Russia against each other. When France invaded the German Ruhr in 1923, some Poles indiscreetly talked about a Polish invasion of East Prussia. Now was the time, they said, to settle accounts with the Reich and take not only Danzig but also East Prussia.

Russia, it is said, dashed cold water on these Polish ambitions by threatening to mobilize against Poland if any Polish troops crossed the German frontier.

It was nearly a decade later before Moscow and Warsaw entered a nonaggression pact. This treaty was signed in July 1932 at Moscow. Krestinsky signed for the Soviet Patek for Poland. The following year the U.S.S.R. negotiated at London treaties on the Definition of the Aggressor with Afghanistan, Estonia, Finland, Iran, Latvia, Poland, Roumania and Turkey. An exact definition of an "aggressor" state was written. Any nation which invaded the territory of another country was automatically an aggressor. The pacts specifically forbade the invasion of another country "with or without a declaration of war." It sounded well. Litvinov took pride in this triumph of the Soviet's peace policies.

When the Nazis came to power in Germany the Poles were confronted with an avowed enemy, which openly announced its intentions of recovering the Polish Corridor, Danzig and Upper Silesia. During 1933 relations between the Reich and Poland were dangerously strained. Then in January 1934 Poland and Germany signed a ten-year nonaggression pact. Each party recognized the existing frontiers and promised to refrain from any attempts to change these frontiers by force. Hitler dropped his "bleeding borders" campaign against Poland.

For Hitler the Polish pact was a great diplomatic success. It relieved him from the immediate danger of Polish interference with his rearmament policy. And it was a step toward the remilitarization of the Rhineland. The latter, as we have said, was in turn a step toward the invasion of Austria, Czecho-Slovakia and Poland. Thus the pact with

Germany was in a sense the alpha and omega of Polish independence.

But even though the Poles had nonaggression pacts with both their great totalitarian neighbors, there could be little serenity of mind in Warsaw. For the Poles did not trust either the Germans or the Russians. Moreover, Poland believed herself a great power, a key power with her own territorial ambitions. Poland's foreign policy was extremely bold. Its fundamental purpose was to play Moscow and Berlin against each other. The foreign minister, Colonel Josef Beck, followed a foreign policy which his admirers described as "ferocious realism." It provided a magnificent display of diplomatic legerdemain as long as it worked.

In 1935, 1936, 1937 and 1938 I found Warsaw an excellent place in which to obtain information about European politics. Poland was involved in deep intrigues; her support was being sought by both Germans and French. Marshal Goering was a frequent visitor to Poland, coming to hunt an elusive lynx that lived in the forest of Bilowieza. On each visit the Number Two Nazi managed to have a little chat with at least one high Polish official.

Colonel Beck was on bad personal terms with the French and Czechs. He was suspected of double-dealing by Paris and Prague; he was cordially hated in Kovno; he was violently disliked in Moscow. Berlin pretended to admire his clever diplomacy. Goering and other Nazis flattered him and catered to his vanity.

During the Czech crisis in late August 1938 I had a long discussion with Beck's *chef de cabinet,* Count Lubienski. Urbane, highly intelligent and well informed, he was a most interesting man to talk with. He spoke off the record about the German-Czech crisis and made an accurate forecast of what was going to happen. It seems obvious that Beck and Lubienski knew the German plans. Poland was playing ball with the Reich in order to get her share of the Czech loot. For there was no doubt in Beck's mind that Czecho-Slovakia was approaching the end of her days.

Ten months later when I returned to Poland I found it about the worst place on the Continent in which to obtain information. True, the Poles talked. They talked more than ever. But it was no longer sensible talk. It was fantasy. From everybody one heard the same thing: Poland could easily defeat Germany. The Poles had their chests out. They had a guarantee from Britain. Most important of all, they had their army, a far better army, they claimed, than the Reich's.

In Gdynia, in Warsaw, in trains, in restaurants, in the Foreign Ministry, in people's homes, in business offices, you heard the same refrain: "We have had conscription for twenty years, the Germans for only four years; we have the best cavalry in the world; we have more trained officers than the Germans; we have allies, the Germans have none; we have money and we can borrow more; the Germans are bankrupt; we have raw materials and we cannot be blockaded; the Reich would immediately be shut off from outside supplies; we beat the Germans at Tannenberg, and we can do it again."

Many Poles told you: "Hitler says he needs *Lebensraum;* well, we have our *Lebensraum.* And East Prussia and Danzig are part of it."

Only four weeks before the German invasion of Poland John Gunther and I were having lunch at the home of a neutral military attaché in Warsaw. Mr Gunther was extremely skeptical about the ability of the Poles to resist the Germans for long. "How long do you think the Poles can hold out against the Germans, Major?" Mr Gunther asked.

"Hold out against the Germans!" exclaimed our host. "Why, the Poles are supremely confident that they can beat the Germans without any help. Polish officers even talk about capturing Koenigsberg and Berlin a few days after war starts."

Had the Poles suddenly lost touch with reality? Was Beck, too, swept away by fantasies? Foreign observers were asking these questions.

In Tallinn a few days previously I had received an answer that seems at least plausible. It must be remembered that partly because Estonia and Poland had no common frontier (the Estonians, therefore, did not fear Polish aggression), the Estonian Foreign Ministry often looked to Warsaw for guidance. The Estonians, like the Poles, feared the U.S.S.R. Consequently the Estonians kept in touch with Colonel Beck.

During this visit to Tallinn, the last week of July 1939, a neutral diplomat repeated to me some things the Estonian foreign minister, Karl Selter, had recently told him about Poland, especially about his friend Colonel Beck. Said Selter: "Colonel Beck is under no illusions about the situation. Goering has told him that Hitler is not bluffing, that von Ribbentrop is urging immediate war against Poland. Goering has advised Beck to permit Danzig to go to Germany and allow the Reich a corridor through the Corridor.

"Colonel Beck knows that if Poland does not make these concessions Hitler will attack. And he knows that the Polish Army will not be able to resist long against the

German Army. Furthermore, he knows that the British fleet cannot come into the Baltic to Gdynia, and he knows that it will take the French Army a long time to smash its way through the West Wall. In the meantime, he realizes, Poland will be overrun by the Germans, and perhaps by the Russians. He puts no faith in British promises that the Russians will help Poland. He says that if the Russians come into Poland, they will not leave."

"Then why does not Beck come to terms with Hitler?" the neutral diplomat asked.

"Because public opinion in Poland has run away with him," Selter replied. "Beck has tried to obtain the help of Marshal Smigly Rydz, but without success. If Beck takes a strong stand, he will immediately be put out of office. He will be accused of selling out to the Nazis. British and French influence is very strong in Warsaw now. And the Polish public expects an easy victory over Germany. Beck dares not tell them the truth. He would be branded as a traitor and be accused of undermining Polish morale and helping Hitler. That is Beck's dilemma."

Karl Selter's diagnosis of the Polish situation seems to have been supported by all available facts. Beck's foreign policy had been brilliant in many respects. He had played Germans against French, Hungarians against Czechs, Germans against Czechs, Germans against Lithuanians, Russians against Germans, French against Germans. His particular brand of diplomacy needed a free hand. By the summer of 1939 possibly Beck knew that he had come to the point where it was essential to placate the Reich by a territorial concession. But there was no one in Poland (Pilsudski had been dead four years) strong enough to tell the Polish people the unpalatable truth. It seems clear that Beck had made intrigues both with the Nazis and against the Nazis. Now he found himself caught in the trap which he had unwittingly helped build.

Meantime Britain and France had been trying to force the Poles into accepting promises of Russian assistance. British and French officials did not seem to understand that the Poles would as soon be invaded by the Germans as "saved" by Russian troops. On several occasions the Poles had turned down Hitler's invitation to join the Reich in an adventure against Russia. That would have permitted Nazi forces to cross Poland. The Poles would have none of that. Nor would they consider allowing the Russians to come in. That way, too, led to disaster.

The Warsaw newspaper, *Express Poranny*, which often served as a mouthpiece for the Polish Foreign Ministry, had hinted that Poland could not accept Russian military help for "geographical-political reasons."

This influential journal went on to say that the Red Army would become an extremely powerful influence in certain European countries "after a long European war." "Many countries," it declared, "instead of enjoying victory, would have to face revolution." Those words may prove to have been prophetic.

But in August 1939 the Polish public and nearly all the government officials were in no mood to accept words of caution. French military experts claim that when they advised Marshal Smigly Rydz to withdraw his troops from the immediate frontier this logical suggestion went unheeded. Why take such precautions against so weak an army as the German? Friendly foreign military men urged the Poles to form defense lines many miles behind their borders that would make use of the country's topographical layout. The French assert that they urged the Poles to dig in behind the Vistula-Narew river line and to take advantage of canals and rivers in western Poland. But this advice, too, went unheeded. "We are not Czechs!" came the chorus of Polish voices.

All of this must have provided welcome news for Stalin. The Poles were willing to go to war with Germany. The chance that the Poles might concede some territory to Hitler was receding. The deadlock made war inevitable. The Kremlin hierarchy must have known that the Polish Army could not stand up long against the new German military machine.

Unwittingly Poles and Germans were playing into Stalin's hands. The fantastic Polish overconfidence was an enormous advantage to the Germans; it made Moscow's role of war provocateur all the easier. And it helped prepare the way for the Fourth Partition of Poland.

CHAPTER XVIII

Nazi Hierarchs and Moscow

I will conduct you into the most fertile plains in the world. Rich provinces, great cities, will be in your power; there you will find honor, glory and wealth.—NAPOLEON to his troops.

Talk about humanitarianism and morals is simply disgusting to us.—PROPAGANDA MINISTER GOEBBELS.

THE HAZARDS OF WAR, the possibilities of bomb plots and the terrific strain under which he lives make Hitler's life span abnormally uncertain. Indeed, some of the best-informed neutral observers in Germany believe that the Fuehrer rushed his program of foreign aggression because of a presentiment of early death. Hitler has investigated the lives of his ancestors, according to these neutrals, and he has found that most of his forebears died at a comparatively early age. It is rather generally known, moreover, that he thinks a malignant condition of his throat has set in.

But even if the Fuehrer were a normal man who lived a conventional life, the question of succession would naturally arise. Who would succeed him? What would be the attitude of his successor toward the Soviet? And what do his advisers urge him to do about his Russian association? The answers to these questions may be of extraordinary importance for Europe, even for the world.

For several years Marshal Hermann Wilhelm Goering has been regarded as the Number Two Nazi. And last September first, on the day that Nazi troops invaded Poland, the Fuehrer publicly named Goering as his successor. "Should anything happen to me in this fight," Hitler told the Reichstag, "my first successor shall be party member Goering."

Famous war ace who commanded the celebrated "Richthofen Circus," one time dope addict, adventurer, veteran of the abortive "Beer Hall Putsch," Goering has risen with Hitler to the top of the German Government. Anecdotes about the ponderous chief of the German air force are legion. There has been a tendency in some circles in England to portray him as a jolly fat boy. Actually Goering is no hail fellow well met. He is a ruthless despot, a cruel, hard-driving executive, an extraordinarily ambitious man who has made a tremendous success out of his membership in the Nazi party.

Goering does not enjoy being twitted about the profits which Nazism has brought him. Usually reliable quarters in Berlin relate an incident which high-lights the marshal's sensitiveness. Someone had accused Julius Streicher of living far more luxuriously than his salary would permit. "Oh well, everybody is doing it," replied the anti-Semite. "Look at Goering. Do you think he can afford to live so lavishly on his salary?" When this was relayed to the Number Two Nazi he roared with anger and ordered his gunmen to go out and shoot Streicher on sight. Only the personal intervention of Hitler saved the anti-Semitic publicist from Goering's wrath.

Some observers picture Goering as a bitter foe of the Soviet Union. This belief seems to be based on the fact that his gunmen shot down General and Frau von Schleicher in their home during the Blood Purge of June 30, 1934. Inasmuch as Von Schleicher was known as a strong advocate of a Russo-German alliance, it has been assumed by some people that Goering had him killed for that reason. I think that is not correct. The Von Schleicher murder, in my opinion, had nothing to do with the general's attitude toward Russia.

Hitler had gone down to Bavaria to superintend the killing of the notorious Captain Roehm. Goering was left in Berlin to conduct the purge there. He went about this bloody work in a thoroughly businesslike way. Dozens of S.A. leaders were quickly shot down on Goering's orders. Von Schleicher, a former chancellor, had been under suspicion of plotting to get rid of Hitler. He may have been involved in a conspiracy with Captain Roehm against the Fuehrer. Probably Hitler or Goering saw in Von Schleicher a dangerous rival. Hence the general's liquidation. It certainly had nothing to do with his former relations with the Red Army. The shooting of Frau von Schleicher was an act of savagery.

As a military man Goering certainly favored the contacts between the Reichswehr and the Red Army. He would like to see Germany obtain Russia's raw materials and, if possible, get control of the Soviet's man power. He would have no scruples against using the Bolsheviks to destroy the French and British. But we can be fairly certain that Goering would balk at any plan which contemplated the destruction of Europe through the Bolshevization of Germany. Some of Goering's intraparty enemies talk grimly of turning the Reich over to Stalin. The prospect surely does not appeal to the ponderous marshal. He would probably favor it only in the event that all was lost for the Nazis.

Goering wants to win, not lose. He wants a strong Germany, possibly a restored monarchy, with himself cast in the role of the new kaiser. When Goering married the actress Emmy Sonnemann someone asked Goebbels why the marshal married her. Goebbels, a bitter enemy of Goering, is said to have explained the marriage in these words: "Goering wants to found a dynasty. So he married Emmy to legitimize their offspring and make the first boy eligible to be Crown Prince."

Unlike some of his fellow Nazis Goering is not a National Bolshevik. Nor does he, like his Fuehrer, live in a murky, nightmare world of whispering voices, persecutions and mysticism. The marshal is a thoroughly human individual. He likes good living, gay uniforms, the companionship of women, hunting and the joy of the kill. He would not be happy in the drab, proletarian atmosphere of the U.S.S.R.

Inside the Nazi party Goering leads what might be called the Right Wing. His principal enemies—von Ribbentrop, Goebbels, Himmler, the so-called "wild men"—are in the Left Wing. They are the men who have on every occasion been willing to gamble with the Reich's existence. Some of them are National Bolsheviks. The "wild men" urged the remilitarization of the Rhineland, the seizure of Austria, the invasion of Czecho-Slovakia and the attack on Poland. Goering has advocated a more conservative course. Sir Nevile Henderson, last British ambassador to Germany, reported to his government that during the Polish crisis Goering was against war. Sir Nevile stated: "I think . . . that Field Marshal Goering would have preferred a peaceful solution. . . ." During a speech at

Sleaford, Lincolnshire, on January 25, 1940, the ambassador told his audience: "You can think what you like about Goering. He may be a blackguard, but he's not a dirty blackguard."

Across the Channel, in France, they remember Goering's words to Pierre Laval, spoken at the funeral of Marshal Pilsudski. On that occasion, as we have mentioned at the beginning of Chapter XIII, Fuehrer Number Two warned the French foreign minister that both France and Germany would be endangered by Russian Bolshevism in the event of a Franco-German war.

It seems reasonable to conclude that Goering favors military co-operation with the Soviet, that he would use the Bolsheviks whenever there was an advantage for the Reich, that he would exploit Russian natural resources to the limit. It is conceivable that he might head a crusade against the U.S.S.R., but only if he believed that it would help build a vast German empire. He would not join such a cause just to rid the world of Bolshevism or to play the game of the Western democracies.

The Number Three Nazi, Rudolph Hess, has not made his attitude toward the Soviet Union clear. It may be that he has no definite feeling about the U.S.S.R. In the intra-party feuds he has avoided taking a position with Goering against the "wild men" or with the latter against the marshal. He is the perfect party henchman to the Fuehrer. His work deals in the main with party matters. If he should rise to the position of Fuehrer, he may well adapt his Russian policies to the desires of the Reichswehr chiefs.

A man occupying a key place in Nazi-Soviet relations is the minister of foreign affairs, Joachim von Ribbentrop. "Ribbi" is the supreme example of an opportunist, a man on the make. That he has ability of a certain kind, few will

deny. His weakness is inherent in the fact that he sometimes overestimates his ability and overplays his hand.
His egotism often stands him in good stead, no doubt, but
it also causes him to make egregious errors.

Astute, cynical, hard boiled, the Nazi foreign minister is
a gambler in international politics. His own career pro-
vides a picture of his attitude toward world affairs. He has
taken advantage of the breaks; he has never scrupled to
change sides. He married his employer's daughter; he
changed from a Liberal to a Reactionary when he sensed
that Germany was forsaking the democratic way. He had
the good fortune to bring Hitler and von Papen together
at a crucial moment for the Nazis, when the Fuehrer was
making a bid for the chancellorship in January 1933.
"Ribbi" decided that he had picked a winner in Hitler
and proceeded to make the most of his opportunities.

As for von Ribbentrop's attitude toward the Soviet
Union, let us look at the record. In the early years of the
Nazi regime he was a bombastic foe of the U.S.S.R. On
every possible occasion he lectured the democratic countries about the dangers of Communism. He was busy
drawing up international coalitions aimed at Moscow.

In October 1936, when he arrived at Victoria Station,
London, arrayed in the brown uniform of a Nazi Storm
Trooper, he had this to say to his official welcomers: "The
Fuehrer is convinced that the only real danger for Europe
and the British Empire is the spread of Communism—that
most terrible of all diseases—terrible because people only
realize the danger when it is too late! Closer collaboration
between our two countries in this sense is not only important, but in my opinion a vital necessity!"

A month later "Ribbi" flew back to Berlin and signed
the anti-Comintern pact for Germany. As the "father"

of this anti-Soviet alignment of the Reich and Japan, he took pride in this move to isolate the U.S.S.R. The following year von Ribbentrop brought Italy into the Fascintern.

When the Reichswehr chiefs and Goering urged Hitler to proceed cautiously about invading Austria, von Ribbentrop called for full speed ahead. He won. A few months later, when Goering opposed an early showdown with the Western democracies over Czecho-Slovakia, "Ribbi" said the French and British would not fight. The Fuehrer followed his advice. The foreign minister won again. Next von Ribbentrop turned his attention to Poland, but the Poles refused to give ground. The foreign minister and his fellow "wild men" urged Hitler to strike at Poland. The French and British would not move, "Ribbi" assured the Fuehrer. This time von Ribbentrop was wrong, dead wrong.

But in the meantime he had made his deal with Stalin. The same man who, less than three years previously, had called Bolshevism "that most terrible of all diseases" was now entering a compact with it. He had changed sides. Here was an outstanding example of von Ribbentrop's insincerity, his barefaced opportunism.

That Stalin does not trust "Ribbi" goes without saying. It may be countered that Stalin would not trust Goering or Hess or the Reichswehr chiefs. True. Neither would the French nor British trust any of them very far. But the point is that no one would trust von Ribbentrop in the slightest. A power politician's rating for truth and trustworthiness is low enough. But "Ribbi's" rating is even lower than the average. And that is saying a good deal.

The "Unofficial Foreign Minister" of the Reich is Dr Alfred Rosenberg. A native of Tallinn, at the time of his birth a city of Tsarist Russia, Rosenberg's background is rather obscure. He and his friends claim that he is a Baltic German. His enemies charge that during the first World War he was in the Russian service against the Reich. In the early postwar era he came to Munich, where he fell into the company of Hitler. From the beginning he exerted an important influence upon the Fuehrer.

Rosenberg's overwhelming interest was foreign affairs. And his bête noire was the Soviet Union. He has been a fanatic in his hatred of the Bolsheviki. Again, his enemies say that he is not a German but a White Russian. The so-called "Rosenberg plan" called for a German drive against the U.S.S.R. He would have had the Nazis drop all schemes for conquering the West and concentrate their total energies upon the effort to invade, smash and exploit the empire ruled by Communism.

Rosenberg's influence upon Nazi foreign policies has been considerable. Perhaps his most influential post has been the leadership of the foreign affairs section of the Nazi party. But some of his other jobs have been important too. His position as editor of Hitler's own newspaper, the *Voelkischer Beobachter*, has given him no little influence upon German policies. He holds the rank of Official Philosopher and Prophet Laureate of the Third Reich.

Some conception of the Rosenberg mentality may be gained from his prediction in the *Voelkischer Beobachter* that when Hitler came to power, "Jewish bodies will hang from every telegraph pole from Munich to Berlin." Tolerance is not one of Editor Rosenberg's characteristics.

Rosenberg is extremely unpopular in the party and owes his position to the Fuehrer's friendship. Goering, in particular, hates Rosenberg. And his anti-Soviet policies continually clashed with those of the army chiefs who favored co-operation with the U.S.S.R.

What was Rosenberg's attitude toward the Nazi-Soviet deal of 1939? We do not know. If the "Unofficial Foreign Minister" opposed the pact, we did not hear about it. In view of his past bitter hatred of Bolshevism it is difficult to believe that he came around to the point where he could support a deal with Moscow. Yet he would hardly dare to oppose a policy that Hitler blessed. The chances are that Rosenberg hates the Soviet as intensely as ever but, by force of circumstances, is compelled to keep quiet about it. If at some future time a break between Berlin and Moscow seems possible, Dr Rosenberg may once more come into his own as a last-ditch foe of the Kremlin.

Heinrich Himmler is one of the most important figures in the Reich because he controls the dreaded *Gestapo* and the ruthless *Schutzstaffel* (elite guard). Unimpressive looking, with a receding chin, he wields a powerful influence in the Third Reich. A few neutral observers claim that Himmler is even more powerful than Goering. For myself, I doubt it. But there is no question that the *Gestapo* chieftain is one of the strongest members of the Nazi hierarchy. His dossiers contain unpleasant facts about nearly all of his Nazi colleagues. He and Goering are on bad terms, and it is said that on various occasions the doughty marshal has discovered with dismay that some member of his household was a plant of Himmler. As one of the "wild men," Himmler has favored great gambles in foreign policy. No doubt he supported the Nazi-Soviet deal. On the other hand, he might just as easily have backed an attack on the U.S.S.R. Like his friend von Ribbentrop, the enigmatic Himmler probably favors an opportunistic policy toward the Soviet Union.

For several years people who did not understand the inside workings of Nazi affairs talked about Joseph Goebbels as a possible successor to Hitler. Such speculations were, of course, preposterous. Not only is the Minister of Propaganda and Public Enlightenment one of the most hated men in Germany, but he has no personal machine. He has no faithful band of retainers such as the praetorian guards commanded by Goering and Himmler. Whereas the anecdotes told about Goering are usually good natured, the Goebbels stories nearly always have a sting. The marshal is Goebbels' principal enemy, though there are many others. Goering is said to refer contemptuously to Goebbels as "that dwarf!" A neutral diplomat in Berlin once predicted to me that if anything happened to Hitler, Goering would have the propaganda minister shot. "Indeed," my friend added, "I do not believe that Hermann Goering would even wait for sunrise to do it."

But as long as Goebbels retains his position as propaganda minister he is a power in Germany and in the Nazi party. He is considered a National Bolshevik. In his venomous hatred of the Jews he perhaps even outdoes Rosenberg. In the past the Goebbels propaganda offensive against the Soviet Union has been unceasing in its continuity, unsurpassed in its violence, often unequaled in its imaginativeness.

Take Herr Dr Goebbels' speech at the Nuremberg Party Congress in September 1937. Attacking the Jews as the destroyers of the world, he charged that Bolshevism was the instrument of the Jewish attack on civilization. He assured his audience that the Jewish race is "the enemy of the world, the destroyer of civilizations, the parasite among the nations, the son of chaos and the incarnation of evil, the germ of decomposition, the plastic demon of the decay of humanity." To the propaganda minister Jews and Bolsheviks were synonymous.

When the Moscow radio blared forth some especially vile story of Goebbels' private life he declared that it was, of course, a Jewish plot. Jewish guilt did not excuse the Bolsheviks, according to the minister; it merely explained the reason for the attack. There could be no peace in the world until that pesthole, the U.S.S.R., should be purged of Bolshevism.

But in the late winter of 1939 the German press dropped its attacks on Moscow. Nazi propaganda—hence Goebbels—even began to speak respectfully of the former Red pariahs. Before long we found the Reich warning the Kremlin against the nefarious plots of the "imperial plutocracies." The propaganda ground was being prepared for the Berlin-Moscow deal.

What can we assume regarding Dr Goebbels' attitude toward the U.S.S.R.? The propaganda minister is, like so many of his Nazi colleagues, an opportunist as regards the Soviet Union. His hatred of Bolshevism is intense when it suits the purpose of the Fuehrer to fight the Kremlin. But the Herr Doktor can be just as co-operative toward Moscow as his Leader desires when it is essential to cultivate the good will of the Communists. Goebbels' past is a plain picture of his future policies toward the Soviet.

So much for the Nazi key figures who are in the limelight. Every American newspaper reader knows about them. But there is still another keyman in the Reich who is unknown to the American public. He is General Karl Haushofer. He works quietly behind the scenes, but his labors are tremendously important. Indeed, what he does may be more important than the work of the others, except possibly Goering.

For Haushofer directs the Geo-Political Institute. It is located in Munich. The function of this foundation is to

solve problems in the field of what the Nazis call geo-
politics, the integration of geography with political science.
In the geo-political concept of the state, social and human
factors transcend in importance economic, military and
political values. I have seen some examples of the geo-
political maps—weird specimens of lines, graphs and
contours. But they make sense to the Nazi mind.

The master of geo-political science, General Haushofer,
wields perhaps a decisive influence on Hitler. For the
general heads an institution which Dr Edmund A. Walsh
calls the Fuehrer's own "brain trust." A large staff of
experts works constantly in geo-political research. Every
bit of their output receives careful attention from Hitler.
But because the institute operates in comparative secrecy
the world knows little about it. What comes out of its
studies may well have a vital bearing on the Fuehrer's
policies toward the Soviet Union. We may assume that
General Haushofer's graphs charted the Berlin-Moscow
pact.

CHAPTER XIX

The Soviet Union, 1939

O<small>N A SUMMER EVENING</small> we left our Leningrad hotel and strolled over to the Neva. There was a light rain; the English mining engineer called it a "Scotch mist." As we walked along the bank of the river the great buildings and palaces on the other side loomed indistinctly through the mist. The Soviet cruiser Kirov rode darkly at anchor out in the stream. The broad river, the buildings and the whole scene looked somberly impressive. The lights gave just enough illumination to outline dimly the city's architecture, the river, the ships and the trees.

Every few minutes the young man from New York would stop and stare ahead of him. It was his first visit to the Soviet Union; it was his first night in the land of Lenin and Stalin. "Isn't it wonderful what they have done?" he kept repeating.

The aged Australian, who knew Russia, had a Russian wife and was rather friendly to the Bolsheviks, finally spoke up. "Whom do you mean by they?"

The young man from New York replied: "Why, I mean the Communists."

"Well, what have they done that is so wonderful?" pursued the Australian.

The young man from New York stood still in shocked surprise. Then he pointed at a vast edifice which loomed faintly ahead through the mist and gathering fog. "Look at that great building. They have been creating a new Russia and they are going to create a new world."

"Great Caesar, man!" exclaimed the Australian. "That building at which you are pointing was erected in the time of Catherine II. If you will come back along this street in the morning, you will find that the Bolos haven't even put a coat of paint on anything in this vicinity."

The young man from New York gasped. Then he stepped back a pace and looked severely at the three of us. "I think that I understand you now," he said. "You are Fascists."

A week later the young man from New York could have pointed out some real Communist achievements in the U.S.S.R. But on this first evening he was being carried away by the enthusiasm which he had brought into the country with him. All that he saw confirmed his belief that the Bolsheviks had created Utopia. He was ready to give them credit for everything. Apparently in his conception pre-Bolshevik Russia was a barren waste which had no schools, railroads, museums or modern buildings of any kind.

On the other hand, one met foreigners who denied that the Bolsheviks had ever created anything worth while. Every backward feature of the U.S.S.R. was the fault of the Communists. All the ignorance and poverty inherited from Tsarist days had been brought on by Bolshevism.

Somewhere between these two extremes lay the Russia of 1939. It could boast of great new hydroelectric projects, canals, steel mills, vast housing construction, recently completed modern highways and double-tracked rail lines. The old rural Muscovy was gone; a semi-industrialized state had taken its place. True, the springless, horse-drawn wagon was still the standard peasant means of transport, but the automobile—even the airplane—had become commonplace.

To the visitor who knew Russia in the early twenties a sign of amelioration was the fact that there were now no *bezprizorni* (wild, homeless children). Millions of these wretched waifs used to roam the countryside and infest the cities of the U.S.S.R. They were dangerous little scavengers who stole, carried disease and occasionally committed murder. They were an appalling, tragic heritage of the mortality among Russian parents occasioned by the World War, the civil conflicts, the famine and plagues of typhus. Now there was no sign of them. The Soviet officials had gathered them into institutions and made citizens of them.

There was progress to be noted along many lines. Unless one knew Russia in the past, however, there would be no means of comparison. For that reason the first visit to the U.S.S.R. hardly enables the foreigner to make a fair appraisal. The probability is that he will not compare the Soviet Union of the present with the Russia of the past, but that he will compare it with some other country or with what he thinks it was when the Bolsheviks came to power. In either case his appraisal is almost certain to be wrong.

Certainly no unbiased foreigner could deny that in many physical respects the Russia of 1939 showed striking progress. Morally and spiritually there was retrogression. But few foreign visitors paid much attention to the effects of Soviet materialism on the Russian people. It was either the wretched village or the "Potemkin" housing project that caught the foreigner's eye. The wretched village was there before the Bolsheviks came to power; the Bolsheviks could claim the model-housing project as their own accomplishment. They could point to much material progress of that nature.

Yet it seems to the writer that three neighboring countries to the west—Finland, Estonia and Latvia—undoubtedly have made more material progress than has the U.S.S.R. And these small nations have achieved it without regimentation, persecution, wars on religion, wholesale murder of dissenting minorities and the stifling of all individualism. They have preserved the human values.

Everywhere in the U.S.S.R. the visitor meets the paradox that is Russia. Take, for example, the new Moscow subway. It is really a beautiful project. Clean, well ventilated and lighted, the train comes quietly into the station. One boards it without being pushed and mauled in a collision of inrushing passengers and outpouring passengers. Escalators work smoothly. The Moscow subway is a sight to see.

But when the passenger comes out of the station into Sverdlovsk Square he sees a long line of people waiting for a bus. He sees another queue waiting to board a trolley. When the bus and trolley arrive they are jammed so full that passengers cling to the outside.

"Why is it that the subway is not crowded?" the visitor asks a foreigner long resident in Moscow. "The bus and trolley are jammed past capacity."

"The bus and the trolley go where people have to go," replies the man who knows his Moscow. "The subway does not."

During the summer of 1939 Moscow's Hotel Metropol

was crowded with foreign visitors. The Soviet custom of mixing the sexes caused more than one conventional traveler embarrassment. In the middle of the night you might be awakened by the management with the word that a visitor had arrived and had been given space in your room. The roommate often proved to be someone of the opposite sex.

At nearly all hours of the day and night the great dining room was crowded. British and American Communists thronged about the tables and talked, talked, talked. French Communists were quartered at the Hotel National. Other visitors wer put up at the Savoy and the New Moscow. In the Metropol lobby there was a newsstand where one could buy Russian newspapers and one foreign sheet, the *Daily Worker* (London Communist journal).

Stalin once referred to Moscow as "the quiet, stick-in-the-mud, true-to-the-Romanovs old capital." In the seventeen years during which I had known Moscow it had changed from an overgrown Russian village to a city of nearly four million people. By 1939 many of its picturesque features were gone. No longer did one see a colorful variety of costumes on the streets; in their place was a universal drabness of shabbily dressed people clothed in semi-Western garb. In place of the brooding solitude which hung over Moscow in the early postwar era, the din of radio loud-speakers roared at you from every direction. Propaganda! Never-ceasing propaganda!

A few years ago one could go to a Moscow restaurant and find real Muscovite food and entertainment. Russian singers had fine voices; the instrumentalists played well. Progress has turned restaurants into places of bedlam where so-called "jazz bands" blare American swing.

In many respects the atmosphere of Soviet Moscow has

changed. A few years ago the holder of a Communist party membership was a privileged individual. He did not have to fear the "Red terror." He was part of the powerful, ruthless, ruling minority. The non-Communists were suspect; they were hunted down by the OGPU; they were mercilessly purged. Now the tables are turned. It is the Communist party member who is suspect. He lives under fear of liquidation on the charge that he is a Trotzkyist or a "diversionist."

In the summer of 1939 the foreign colony in Moscow was enjoying a story that illustrated the new role of the non-Party man. A Russian living on the third floor of an apartment house was awakened at three in the morning by an ominous rap on his door. On opening it he was confronted by four men wearing overcoats and gray caps. Recognizing them as OGPU agents, he said: "You don't want me. I don't belong to the Party. The member of the Party lives in this same room on the floor above." He closed the door, went back to bed and listened to the OGPU gunmen tramping up the stairs to arrest the unfortunate Communist in the room above.

Under the Bolshevik dispensation, as we saw earlier, there is little contact between Russians and foreigners. This often leads the foreigners to share information that they obtain. A military attaché told me the following incident: "A few days ago I had a hunch about the Red Army's staff work. I passed it along to Colonel A. Three days later Major B. came in to see me and gave me some news that seemed to confirm my hunch. At first I felt like congratulating myself. Then I asked him where he had heard the news. He mentioned Colonel C. I inquired of Colonel C. where he heard it; he said Colonel A. had told him. When I contacted Colonel A. and asked where he had heard it he replied: 'Why, you told me that yourself!' So when it was run down it was, after all, my own hunch. That's the way we work here in Moscow."

Several of the officers of the American Embassy rented a *datcha* (summer house) in the country a few miles outside the Soviet capital. On Sundays and holidays not only Americans but other members of the foreign colony gathered there. One Saturday afternoon when I went out with Spencer Williams and Major Frank Hayne we found a pleasant party gathered under the birch trees. The Bohlens, the Chipmans, the wife of the Greek minister, the Chinese military attaché and other foreigners were enjoying tea. Some guests, more athletically inclined, were playing tennis.

Suddenly loud booing sounded through an open gate in the board fence. Several Russian youths were bawling *"boorzhooey"* (bourgeois) at us. A servant came quickly and closed the gate. The group under the birch trees laughed, but everyone realized that the boys' demonstration had some significance; it signified fundamental Russian hostility toward foreigners.

A little later two young men in riding clothes joined us. Major Hayne introduced me to them. The two strangers were keenly interested in what I had seen a month before in Danzig. They asked a number of searching questions and appeared to agree with me about the situation. I answered the queries cautiously because I did not know what their nationality was or their business. When they left I inquired of Major Hayne who they were. "The chap in the black sweater is the First Secretary of the French Embassy," he replied. "The one wearing the red sweater is the Second Secretary of the German Embassy."

Early that evening, when we were having a buffet supper

inside the *datcha*, the two young embassy secretaries arrived. "We are leaving tomorrow morning for Rostov on our vacation," said the Frenchman.

"Anyone else going?" someone inquired.

"No, just the two of us," said the German. "We are using my automobile."

"That will be a hard nut for the OGPU to crack," spoke up Spencer Williams. "No Russian will ever believe that you two fellows are just making this trip for your vacation. They'll attach some deep, sinister meaning to it. And it would be interesting to know what kind of a plot the OGPU will discover."

In view of the Franco-British efforts to bring the Soviet Union into the "peace front," every major government was deeply interested in the actual economic potentialities of the U.S.S.R. An enormous amount of nonsense had been written about this subject. Some accounts pictured Russia as overflowing with practically every essential natural resource except rubber. Other stories portrayed the country as poverty stricken, with only poor and insufficient raw materials. Every embassy in Moscow was striving to furnish its home government with authentic data on this important question. Needless to say, the Kremlin's attitude was not making the task a simple one.

A neutral diplomat permitted me to read his report and to make some notes from it. He reported that the Soviet Union could export large quantities of the following: manganese, magnesite, potash, apatite, phosphate rock and asbestos. According to his analysis the following products could not be exported in large quantities without "serious injury to the national economy": iron ore, chromite, sulphur, mercury, mica, zinc, coal, cotton and petroleum.

His report stated that the Soviet must import "either entirely or in considerable part from foreign sources" the following: copper, lead, nickel, tin, tungsten, molybdenum, antimony, genuine rubber, wool and aluminum. The Soviet Union must, he wrote, obtain "ten essential raw materials abroad."

But there was a political angle to this situation, he explained to his government. If the Kremlin believed that a political gain was to be made by exporting, it would not hesitate to do so at the expense of cutting down on food for the Russians and depriving domestic manufacturing of all but necessary war materials. To substantiate this statement he referred to a speech made by Mikoyan, Peoples' Commissar for Foreign Trade, at the XVIII Party Congress, on March 15, 1939. On that occasion Mikoyan made the noteworthy statement that Soviet trade "depends directly upon political relations."

This brings us to the question of the viewpoint of the Russian masses toward their privations and low standard of living. How do Ivan and Marusha like their dinner of black bread, cabbage, cucumbers and bad tea? The answer is quite simple. They like it very much, because they have no standard of comparison. They have never known anything better. Indeed, what they have to eat today is much better in quantity and quality than their fare a few years ago. Moreover, these young people are constantly told by Soviet propaganda that they are fortunate, that in capitalistic America people are starving. Those poor Americans! How fortunate I am, thinks Ivan, as he chews his cucumber and sips his glass of steaming tea.

In Russian industry there has been a slowdown. The tempo of the early period of the five-year plans was so feverish that it could not be maintained indefinitely.

Workmen tired of the continued drive for faster and still faster production. Too, the Russian, not long off the soil, soon lost his initial interest in machinery and efficiency. He was prone to fall back into his old careless attitude toward work. Often his indifference led to serious accidents, to costly deterioration of machinery. When that happened his boss was shot on the charge of "wrecking" or "Trotzkyism." But, most important of all, the Russian workman used the slowdown method to register his protest against the burdens inherent in the frantic pace of Soviet industrialization. The slowdown had an important bearing not only upon Russian industrial progress but also upon the Soviet's military potential.

We find this editorial complaint in *Pravda:* "Goods are rotting because there is nobody to take care of effective distribution. The Ministry of Chemical Industry is utilizing only about forty per cent of crude rubber in the process of making rubber, because nobody is interested in improving production despite repeated government orders."

The military power of the U.S.S.R. was a never-ending source of conversation in Moscow's foreign colony. "Probably nobody but the Nazis really knows the strength of the Red Army," one military attaché remarked to me.

"You can't shoot eighty per cent of your high officers, as Stalin has done, and expect to have an efficient army," another military observer pointed out. "And what about the system of military commissars?" said another. "You can't have efficiency if your army officers have to get permission from a politician every time they want to give an order."

"The Russians are weakest where the Germans are strongest," remarked the first attaché. "I mean their staff. In the old days, when a lot of infantry went out and fought other infantry, staff work was not so important. But today, when you must co-ordinate your infantry, cavalry, artillery, tank corps, aviation and service of supply, an efficient staff is essential. I think that the Russian staff must be poor, to say the least. We all know the German staff is top-notch."

"But if the Germans ever get control of the Russian Army," said the second attaché, "and use Reichswehr staff officers, look out!"

Of course the favorite topic of conversation among the foreigners in Moscow during the summer of 1939 was the possibility of a British-French-Russian alliance. But these people knew no more about it than similar people in other capitals. Indeed, the foreign colony in Moscow eagerly listened to any scraps of information about Stalin's foreign policy that was brought in from the Baltic capitals. They pieced these together with rumors which were supposed to have leaked out of the British and French embassies. English newspapers privately received in the Soviet capital crackled with optimistic forecasts of a quick agreement between London and Moscow.

But the ancient, multi-spired Kremlin—mysterious, in-scrutable—maintained its air of whispering secrecy. When the great doors of the Spasski Gate swung open and the guards stepped to one side a limousine would speed out into Red Square. Passers-by could not see the occupants of the car. The curtains were drawn. The anonymity of the passenger was guarded. Was it Mr Strang? Was it the German ambassador, Herr von der Schulenberg? The public had no way of knowing. And OGPU agents discouraged any tendency on the part of Russians or foreigners to loiter about the entrance to the Kremlin. Legend has it that these thick, storied walls entomb the bodies of young women buried alive in their gloomy depths. Somewhere inside this acropolis of Moscow Joseph Stalin lives and works.

Toward the end of July, when I was taking leave of the Soviet Union, the mystery of Russia's role in the forthcoming European melodrama had not been solved. As my train crossed the border on its way from Leningrad to Tallinn I counted four separate lines of trenches and barbed wire on the Estonian side. They brought to mind Mr Churchill's statement in Parliament the previous April that "the Baltic States all feel easier because this great mass of Russia is friendly behind them and lies there in broad support." I wondered if the khaki-clad young Estonian soldiers standing guard behind their barbed wire knew about that "friendly" Russia and its "broad support."

The last town on the Soviet side of the frontier is Kingisepp, named after an Estonian Communist. Its thatched roofs, weeds, dusty streets, barefoot women and general squalor made it a primitive, ramshackle Utopia indeed. The train moved on slowly for a few miles and stopped at Narva, the first town on the Estonian side.

How sharply Narva contrasted with Kingisepp! Its well-built houses, charming gardens, neat yards, clean streets and friendly, progressive-looking people made it seem like another world from the one I had just left. And so it was. For Estonia was a tiny bit of that "other world" of capitalism which Bolshevism is avowedly planning to destroy.

In Tallinn, the beautiful capital of this little northern republic, the government was extremely uneasy. My friends here told me that they were certain an important deal was being made at their expense in Moscow. Would the French and British outbid the Germans? The Estonians frankly distrusted both sides—the Germans and the Franco British. They wanted to be let alone to live their own lives. But they were too realistic to believe that they would be. They suspected that their small country was a pawn shunted about on the chessboard of power politics.

I took the boat from Tallinn and went across the Gulf of Finland to Helsinki. There I found my Finnish friends apprehensive and rather bitter. They, too, suspected that a deal was being made at their expense in Moscow. Every informed Finn realized that his country's security was based on rivalry between the Reich and the Soviet. If these two great dictatorships ever came together, the Finns would suffer. For then their country would come within the sphere of either Germany or Russia. Some Finns frankly voiced their forebodings that a deal had already been reached between the Reich and the Soviet. And they feared that the approaching European war would make Stalin the master of Europe.

CHAPTER XX

Nazi-Soviet Deal

Who sups with the devil must have a long spoon.—IRISH PROVERB.

In order that he might rob a neighbor whom he had promised to defend, black men fought on the coast of Coromandel, and red men scalped each other by the Great Lakes of North America.—MACAULEY on Frederick the Great.

THE ANNOUNCEMENT of the Nazi-Soviet deal exploded like a bombshell in a tense Europe. The impossible had happened. Those "implacable enemies"—Hitler and Stalin—were about to sign a Second Rapallo. The following day, August twenty-second, London, Paris and other European capitals were in a state of confusion.

I happened to arrive in Belgrade that morning. At the Yugoslav Foreign Ministry a harassed official said to me: "Yesterday we had a foreign policy; today we do not know what to do. For the moment we have no international policies."

Von Ribbentrop was flying to Moscow. The Soviet press was heralding the Russo-German agreement as a "peace step." Bewildered diplomats in the rest of Europe were attempting to get their bearings. For the moment the Kremlin's motives came into question. But only momentarily.

Not even the signature of the pact between Berlin and Moscow on August twenty-fourth could shake the faith of multitudes of Soviet admirers in the Western democracies. They still believed in the Kremlin's professed loyalty to peace, collective security and democracy. The pact bound each party not to associate "with any grouping of powers which directly or indirectly is aimed at the other party." Moreover, each signatory pledged itself not to resort to any act of force against the other.

This was clear language and it bound the Reich and the Soviet to explicit pledges respecting each other. But, in spite of that, wishful thinking was far from dead in London and Paris. In the Western capitals many influential people steadfastly maintained that the Kremlin was true to its idealistic claims voiced on so many occasions at Geneva. Just wait, said these people, and you will see that Stalin is double-crossing Hitler. The Soviets will keep the Nazis waiting for ratification of this pact until it is so late in the season that Germany cannot make war on Poland this year. The Soviets are, therefore, really serving the cause of peace.

In the Baltic capitals there was no sentimentality about Soviet intentions. Letts, Estonians and Finns knew what Stalin was doing. All along they had watched the straws in the wind which diplomats and intelligence officers of Britain and France should have noted.

When, for example, I talked with Nazi officials in the so-called Free City of Danzig during the first half of July I could not help but be impressed by their confident air. When I mentioned the prospects of an alliance between the Soviet and the Western democracies they could scarcely hide their contempt for the Franco-British-Russian conversations then being held in Moscow. One Danzig official showed me a scatological cartoon depicting the British lion in a most compromising and humiliating position with respect to the Russian bear. It was ophidian Julius Streicher's conception of art. But it served to demonstrate Nazi indifference toward the attempt of the Western democracies to enlist Soviet support.

Far more important, however, was a story I heard in Riga, Helsinki and Moscow that may have had some basis of fact. In each of these capitals the details were different, but the foundation of the report was in all cases the same.

According to this story, when the Strang mission went to Moscow Molotov received a call from the German ambassador, von der Schulenberg. Hitler's representative presented a box which contained a present for Stalin. According to the neutral sources in Moscow, the box contained photostatic copies of correspondence between British and German officials. In the communications the British had urged upon Hitler the necessity of driving eastward at the expense of Russia. Chamberlain, so it was said, had attempted to provoke a Nazi-Soviet war.

In Helsinki and Riga they told me a different version. They related that during the Hitler-Chamberlain conversations before and during the Munich conference hidden dictographs had recorded the British prime minister's anti-Soviet statements. British Ambassador Henderson's alleged anti-Soviet remarks to von Ribbentrop were said to have been added to the evidence. From the dictograph recordings the Nazis had made records for the master of the Kremlin. These were presented to Stalin at the psychological moment.

I cannot, of course, tell whether these stories had any

truth, but they were certainly in line with Nazi tactics. When it comes to the double cross, Hitler and his tacticians are indeed hard to beat.

After von Ribbentrop had signed the Russo-German pact in Moscow Europe did not have long to wait for the next chapter in the European Iliad. One week later the Soviets disillusioned many of their friends in the West by ratifying the pact through the unanimous vote of the Supreme Soviet. Undoubtedly the wily Joseph Stalin foresaw the immediate consequences of the ratification. And without question he meant it as a go-ahead signal for his dictator partner.

The following morning German troops poured across the Polish frontier. Nazi airplanes bombarded Krakow, Warsaw and other Polish cities. German tanks and motorized columns smashed the Polish forces in their path.

Standing before his puppet Reichstag, Hitler thundered: "I will lead you to victory, and if not to victory then to my own death. For I shall not live in defeat." Since five forty-five that morning, he announced, the German Army had been "returning the Polish fire." It was, he said, "counter-attack with pursuit." The war was on.

Two days later Britain and France were at war with Germany. Stalin's strategy had succeeded. The "second imperialist war" that he had planned and dreamed was a reality. No longer need he fear an attack from that "other world." The old bogey of an anti-Soviet coalition of British, French and Germans was banished. No longer need he decry "the brutal fury with which the imperialist robbers of the whole world would have hurled themselves against Soviet Russia." He could sit tight, let the combatants destroy one another and emerge the winner of the conflict.

Only a few months back the U.S.S.R. still remained isolated from the consequences of Munich. Today each of the opposing sides was bidding for Soviet support. Hitler was now at Stalin's mercy. For if the Soviet should shut off supplies to the Nazis and come into the conflict on the side of the Western democracies, Germany would be in the desperate position of a besieged army that is compelled to wage war against major opponents on two fronts. As for the British and French, they realized that if Hitler could obtain full-fledged Soviet economic support the Nazis might be able to stave off the Allied blockade indefinitely. The Germans might be able to wage a long war.

Apparently Stalin's plans were simple in their purpose. He would furnish Hitler with just enough raw materials to keep the war going but not enough help to enable the Nazis to win. Stalin's plans obviously called for a long, grueling encounter, a war that would bankrupt the participants and prepare the way for economic collapse, chaos and social revolution.

In the Western democracies, however, many of the Kremlin's fanatical supporters still maintained that at the proper time Stalin would enter the war against Germany. The Red tsar, they said, was only waiting for the right time to intervene against the Poland-invading Nazis. The myth that the Soviet would fight to save democracy was dying hard.

On September fourteenth a carefully timed article appeared in *Pravda* attacking Poland for the ill-treatment of minorities. The article began by "analyzing the internal causes of Poland's military defeat."

"All reports on the situation in Poland," *Pravda* continued, "show that disorganization of the entire Polish state machine is constantly increasing and that the Polish state proved so impotent and inefficient that it began to crumble with the first military setbacks." Why did this happen?

"These causes are in the first place rooted in the inner weakness and contradictions of the Polish state," the Soviet organ explained. It is a "multi-national state." Forty per cent of the inhabitants are not Poles. Eleven million are Ukrainians and White Russians.

Then came the most ominous sentence in the article: "The national policies of the ruling circles in Poland have been characterized by the suppression and the oppression of national minorities, particularly of the Ukrainians and White Russians."

The Soviet Government could not stand aside and ignore the "fate of its blood brothers, the Ukrainians and White Russians, who . . . now have been abandoned entirely to their fate." The signal for the Russian invasion of Poland had been given.

Three days later Red troops crossed the Polish frontier. At the same time the Kremlin informed the Polish ambassador in Moscow that this action was taken "to protect its own interests and to protect the White Russian and Ukrainian minorities." The U.S.S.R. continued to be neutral, the Kremlin announced. And Comrade Molotov promised that the Bolsheviks would "free the Polish people from war."

The following statements are taken from the Russian official communiqué which heralded the Russian invasion of Poland: "On the morning of September 17th troops of the Workers' and Peasants' Red Army crossed the western frontier along the whole line from the River Zapadnaya Dvina (Soviet-Latvian border) to the River Dniester (Soviet-Roumanian border).

"Throwing back a weak advance of units and reserves of the Polish Army, Soviet troops by the evening of September 17th reached the following points . . .

"Soviet aircraft brought down seven Polish fighters and forced three heavy bombers to land. The machines' crews have been detained. The population everywhere is greeting the Red Army with jubilation." Here was Moscow's official admission that the Red Army carried out armed aggression against Poland.

In Britain and France newspapers carried the heartening news that when Russian troops entered southeastern Poland they told the Poles: "We have come to fight the Germans." Perhaps, after all, the Soviets were marching into Poland to give battle to the Nazis. In London and Paris there were still people who argued that Moscow was moving into Poland to assist the Western democracies.

The Red troops probably acted on the assumption that it would cost them fewer lives to deceive the Poles into believing that the Russians were arriving to fight the Germans. It was sardonic strategy, Asiatic in its cunning. While the Germans were losing thousands of lives in their invasion of Poland their Soviet partners advanced with few casualties.

Three days after the Russian invasion of Poland the commander-in-chief of the German Army, Colonel General Walther von Brauchitsch, issued this order of the day to his troops: "Soldiers! The Polish Army is annihilated. The operations against Poland are thus concluded."

The Kremlin had shrewdly waited until the Germans had made Polish defeat inevitable. Then the Red Army was in on the kill. The Soviet risk was nominal. And its troops moved into Polish territory to share in the Fourth Partition of Poland. Poland's nonaggression pacts with her two totalitarian neighbors proved to be scraps of paper.

And what did the members of the British Parliament think about the Russian invasion of Poland? Britain and France had guaranteed Polish independence; less than three weeks before they had gone to war with Germany in Poland's defense. Consistency would seem to demand that they defend Poland against the Russian invader as well.

But on September twentieth Prime Minister Chamberlain told the House of Commons: "It is still too early to pronounce any final verdict on the motives or consequences of the Russian action. For the unhappy victim of this cynical attack the result has been a tragedy of the grimmest character."

Sir Archibald Sinclair, Liberal party leader, had this to say: "The fact that Russia is advancing in the south and taking up positions which cover the whole frontier between Poland and Roumania, the fact that she is using for the purpose upwards of 100 divisions—rather a large quantity of troops if all they were employed upon was to clean up the remnants of the Polish forces—all these facts must be rather ominous from the standpoint of the German Army."

Mr Boothby, a Conservative and reputedly a close friend of Mr Churchill, contributed these words: "I am thankful that two days at least have been allowed to elapse between the invasion of Poland by Soviet Russia and any acrimonious debate in the House; and I think that on the whole the press of this country, with one or two exceptions, have treated that event extremely well and with the reticence which, in my opinion, it called for. I think that any hasty judgment on that particular action would be most ill advised from the point of view of our national interests."

Elucidating his point, Mr Boothby went on to explain: "After all, what effect has the action taken by Russian troops during the last three days had? It has pushed the German frontier with Russia considerably westward of where it would have been had the Russians taken no action at all."

And finally Mr Boothby revealed a thought that was probably shared by many of his colleagues: "I hope and believe that one day we shall get the support of Soviet Russia."

It was obvious that the hope of Russian military support still hovered on the horizon for many people in Britain and France. Stalin still remained in their eyes a valuable ally who had only temporarily gone wrong. Presently he would see the error of his ways and reform.

Leon Trotzky was more realistic than the leaders of the Western democracies. In a scathing attack upon Stalin, launched from Mexico City, the former commissar of the Red Army denounced the Soviet invasion of Poland as a criminal and ignoble act that was carried out under the orders of the "jackal of the Kremlin."

In the course of his statement Trotzky declared: "It is now evident that, during the last few years when the Comintern has been conducting a noisy campaign for an alliance of the democracies against Fascism, the Kremlin has been working toward a military accord with Hitler against the democratic interests. Even complete idiots must now realize that this was the goal of Moscow."

He continued: "When the French and British military missions were discussing with Voroshilov the most effective way of defending Poland, Voroshilov and members of the German General Staff were discussing the most practical method of repartitioning Poland."

It is a curious fact, however, that no matter what the U.S.S.R. might do it could count upon finding defenders among the leaders in the democratic countries. Men who bitterly denounced the "appeasement" of Hitler led the campaign to "appease" Stalin.

Once the Red Army had occupied more than half of Poland, Stalin was ready to turn his attention in other directions. Other peoples needed Soviet "protection." Other "oppressed minorities" called for the "glorious Red Army" to "free them from war." They clamored to be "liberated."

Without loss of time Stalin invited Karl Selter, the Estonian foreign minister, to visit the Soviet capital. At the same time the Kremlin announced that the Russian steamer Metalist had been sunk off the Estonian coast. Soviet complaints against Estonia regarding the escape of a Polish submarine interned at Tallinn also were highlighted. Minister Selter recognized the signs of a frame-up. His visit to Moscow was brief. On September twenty-eighth the Kremlin triumphantly announced "mutual assistance" and "trade agreement" treaties between the U.S.S.R. and Estonia.

When Mr Selter returned to Tallinn his little country had really become a protectorate of the Soviet Union. The Kremlin now had the right to garrison large bodies of troops on Estonian territory, to build naval bases and air fields. No longer could Estonia veto any demand from Moscow. Its actual independence was gone. A progressive little state, which was practically free from unemployment, had succumbed to the Soviet imperialists. Yet there was almost no protest from abroad.

On October first the Kremlin "invited" Latvia to send a delegation to Moscow to discuss problems pending between the two neighbors. The Letts quickly met the fate of the Estonians. They were given the privilege of housing Soviet garrisons. Red naval bases would be located in Latvia's excellent harbors, and Russian aviators would be established in air bases on Latvian territory. The Latvian port of Libau was marked out to be Russia's advanced naval station on the middle Baltic.

Anyone who knows Latvia and Estonia can understand the tragedy of this situation. Both countries dearly loved their hard-won independence. On the Liberty monument in the center of Latvia's capital there is an inscription, *"Tevzemei un Brivibai"* (For Fatherland and Liberty). It stands as a poignant message of the national feeling not only of the Letts but also of their Estonian neighbors.

The third small Baltic country, Lithuania, fared a little better in one respect. In return for virtually surrendering its independence to the Russians it received a small *quid pro quo*, the city of Vilna. This town, cut from the dismembered body of Poland, had been in dispute between Lithuanians and Poles ever since the first World War. Poland had not hesitated to use highhanded methods in her dealings with Lithuania. And the Lithuanians merely waited for the time to come when they could recover what they believed was "stolen property." Kovno had remained only their "provisional capital"; Vilna was their actual capital, they said, and the surrounding area was territory "occupied" by the Poles.

But there was a large fly in the Vilna ointment. The Soviets gave the Lithuanians only the city and the region immediately surrounding it. The economic hinterland was kept by the U.S.S.R. The consequence was that Vilna, cut off from its markets and food supplies, quickly experienced extreme hardships. This condition was made more acute by the influx of thousands of destitute refugees from Poland. The disillusioned Lithuanians soon came to realize that the gift of Vilna from the Soviets was no act of generosity; it was in keeping with Stalin's program of spreading economic chaos. It was a smart move on the part of the imperial Bolshevists.

Before the first week of October had passed Hitler opened negotiations with Latvia looking toward the removal of its German minority to the Reich. Similar negotiations were quickly started with Estonia. This program of Nazi repatriation did not augur well for the Reich. More than any other event of the early war period it indicated the dominant position now held by Stalin, the weakened position now occupied by Hitler.

Ever since the Nazis had come to power the Kremlin had anxiously watched the Reich's penetration of the German minorities in the *Zwischenland*, especially in Latvia and Estonia. For the Soviet leadership realized that if Hitler ever decided to attack Leningrad he would first occupy the Baltic States as a base for land operations against the northwestern region of the U.S.S.R. Stalin and his henchmen knew that the Germans (Balts) in the Baltic lands could provide the same pretext for Nazi action there that the German minorities in the Sudetenland had furnished for the Reich's destruction of Czecho-Slovakia.

In *Mein Kampf* Hitler wrote: "We will finally end the prewar era and pass over to the land policy (*Bodenpolitik*) of the future. And when we speak of new territory in Europe today, we can only think first of all of Russia and of the Russian border states." This clearly included the Baltic countries.

We can be sure that Hitler regarded the Balts of Estonia and Latvia as invaluable pawns on the chessboard of power politics. He would give them up only under pressure. But once he found himself at war with the Western democracies, he dared not refuse any demand from the Kremlin that meant less than life and death to the Reich. Stalin could now turn the screw tightly on the Nazi thumb. Apparently Moscow lost no time in requesting Hitler to take his Balts back home to the Reich. This was done promptly. The unfortunate Balts were repatriated. Stalin was left undisputed master of Lithuania, Latvia and Estonia.

In a few weeks of playing astute power politics he had accomplished results that had cost his Tsarist predecessors centuries of bloodshed and the expenditure of vast amounts of treasure. Peter the Great, looking down upon the Kremlin, might well applaud the Red tsar's successful march of imperialism. Stalin has praised Danton as "the greatest master of revolutionary policy yet known." If Danton were living today, he might say that of Stalin.

Meanwhile the Kremlin was entertaining another foreign visitor. He was Shukru Saracoglu, the foreign minister of Turkey. He had arrived in Moscow on September twenty-fifth to discuss important matters affecting Russo-Turkish relations. But in the person of his Turkish guest Stalin found a hard man to cajole or threaten. For the Turk was also a skillful player of power politics. What was more, he was an Oriental.

For centuries Turks and Russians had fought each other on countless battlefields. During the first World War they were ranged on opposing sides. After the conflict they found that they had much in common. Both had lost much territory; both had suffered huge economic losses; both were post-bellum outcasts. On March 16, 1921, they signed a treaty of friendship. During Turkey's war with

RUSSIA'S PATH OF EMPIRE TO THE MEDITERRANEAN.

the Greeks and the Versailles powers the Soviet gave not only moral support but actually some material aid to the Turks.

As long as a strong, friendly Turkey held the Dardanelles the U.S.S.R. could feel comparatively safe in the Black Sea area. At the Montreux conference (1936) and on other occasions the Soviets and Turks were diplomatic allies. The Kremlin strove to make Turkey a kind of concierge in charge of Russia's back door to the Mediterranean. Under this arrangement the Red Navy could leave the Black Sea but Western fleets could not enter it.

But Turkey's alignment with Britain and France in the first half of 1939 apparently caused misgivings in Moscow. The Turks no longer appeared to be dependable vassals of the Soviet Union. In the hope of heading off any further drift away from the U.S.S.R. toward the Western democracies, Stalin "invited" Saracoglu to visit the Soviet capital.

According to the best information available from diplomatic sources close to the Turkish Foreign Ministry, Stalin put approximately this proposition to his guest from Ankara: "For eighteen years Turkey and the U.S.S.R. have been on terms of close friendship. We wish to implement that friendship further. Today the aggressors and incendiaries of war are menacing all smaller nations. There is danger that aggressors will attack Turkey at the Dardanelles. We wish to make such an attack impossible. Therefore we shall send a Russian garrison to the Dardanelles to protect your territory. We shall establish air and naval bases in the region of the Sea of Marmora to defend your interests."

Saracoglu refused politely and firmly. Turkey, he pointed out, was no small Baltic state. It could defend itself against any aggressor. Furthermore, it had guarantees of support from the Western democracies. Stalin exerted pressure. The Turk remained obdurate. Three weeks passed. Then Saracoglu returned to Ankara. On October nineteenth a Tri-Partite Mutual Assistance Pact between the Franco British and the Turks was announced.

Stalin the Asiatic had met his first defeat since the war began. He was dealing now with no European Chamberlain, Daladier, Beck, Selter or Hitler. He was matching wits with an Asiatic like himself schooled in the ancient, devious ways of Oriental politics. Greek had met Greek. David had played as wily a game as Goliath.

True, the Tri-Partite treaty contained an "escape clause" which exempted Turkey from joining her allies in war against Russia. But that did not alter the fact that Turkey was joining the Western powers in an effort to prevent a German or Soviet invasion of the Balkans or the Near East. In spite of the "escape clause," Turkey had taken sides. And she was now aligned definitely against the Soviet's expansionist ambitions in southeastern Europe and Asia Minor.

Checkmated for the time being in the extreme south of Europe, Stalin quickly turned his full attention to the far north. He would achieve a compensating victory north of the Gulf of Finland. By taking advantage of Europe's preoccupation with the war, he could bring Finland under his hegemony. The Kremlin had already "invited" Finland to send a delegation to Moscow to "discuss certain political and economic questions interesting both countries."

The stage was now set for the Finnish tragedy.

CHAPTER XXI

Attack on Finland

Patriots cannot be made out of serfs.—BARON VON STEIN.
All that can be said against us is that as a nation we are too
small.—FOREIGN MINISTER TANNER of Finland.

RARELY is the background of a war etched in black and
white. Nearly always there is a considerable shading of
gray in the picture, and often it is extremely difficult for
us to know where the black of guilt and the white of inno-
cence blend into gray. Russia's attack on Finland is one
of those unusual cases where there is virtually no gray in
the picture. It is one clear case of unprovoked aggression.

As we have pointed out, the Soviets have suffered from
the phobia that the capitalist world was preparing a coalition against them. For that reason they have regarded
all their neighbors with varying degrees of suspicion. Finland has never stood in the Kremlin's good graces. From
the time of the Bolshevik intervention in Finland in 1918
and 1919 Russo-Finnish relations have not been cordial.
Finns have told me that their contacts with Moscow were
"correct." But they never claimed that these relations
were really friendly.

Soviet spokesmen have from time to time charged that the Finns were turning their country into a "war base" against the U.S.S.R. The proximity of the Finnish frontier to Leningrad has probably given the Bolsheviks the jitters whenever Russia's relations with Britain or Germany were tense. But it is difficult to believe that Stalin ever took seriously the Soviet charges that Finland was plotting adventures against the Socialist fatherland.

An outstanding characteristic of Finland was its desire to be allowed to live in peace. The Finns wanted to be let alone. They wanted to tend their neat, verdant lake-jeweled little garden of forests and small farms. It was their extreme bad fortune to be located next door to the sprawling Russian slum.

Probably more than for anything else the Bolsheviks hated the Finns because Finland was a successful business. It was a going concern. While the U.S.S.R. experienced famines, pestilence, shortages of all the necessities of life, purges, wholesale liquidation of "class enemies," the Finns continued to live in peace and prosperity. For that the Russian leadership could never forgive them.

Finland is a land of the little man. It is a country of small farmers, small merchants, small manufacturers. Nine men out of ten on the land own the acres on which they work. The tenth man hopes to own land someday. It is a nation of hard work, careful craftsmanship and honest business. Its co-operatives are among the best in the world. Because of short summers, long winters, the sterility of the soil and the severity of the climate, life in Finland has always been a struggle between man and nature. Only persevering, industrious men could wrest an existence from so hostile an environment.

An Englishman in Helsinki told me of an experience of

his up near the Arctic Circle in the neighborhood of Rovaniemi. On a winter trip he lost his wallet in the snow. Several months later, in summer, he was passing over the route which he had traveled the winter before. To his surprise he came upon his wallet nailed to a post by the road. When he took it down and opened it he found everything that was in it when he dropped it. Many people, he assured me, had passed along since he had lost the wallet. This incident, it seems to me, is characteristic of Finland.

But quite aside from striking down this successful little neighbor whose thrift and industry contrasted so sharply with his own country's backwardness, Stalin had still more compelling incentives for conquest. He wanted to round out the boundaries of Imperial Russia. He wanted to gain control of Finland's raw materials—especially her lumber and nickel. He wanted to possess her efficient manufacturing plants. He sought the strategic advantages of Finland as a possible base for invasion of Scandinavia, as a first line of defense against Western enemies who might strike at him by way of the northern Baltic.

Stalin's methods against Finland exemplify the technique of streamlined aggression as it has been developed into a science by the dictators. When he made his attack on Poland the way had been prepared by the German Army. But in the assault on Finland Stalin could claim the work as his own.

The Letts and Estonians had been compelled to surrender to the Soviets because the little Baltic countries realized that they could not obtain any help from the great Western powers, either Germany or France and Britain. Alone they could not hope to stand off the colossal Red Army. Resistance would mean annihilation. They

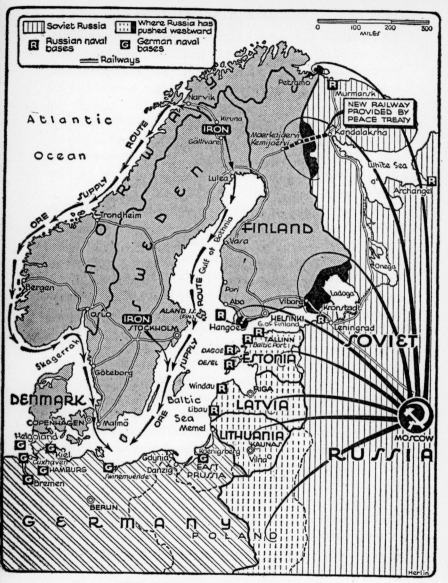

THE SOVIET PUSHES WESTWARD.

231

preferred not to fight in a suicidal cause. The Finns, however, believed that they could hold out till help came. Their army was small but excellent. Their leadership was of the highest. Their defenses had been prepared carefully for just such a day of need.

Protracted pressure from the Kremlin failed to break the will of Finland's delegation in Moscow. They would grant concessions to Stalin, but they would not surrender anything vital to their country's independence. This was the state of affairs on November twenty-ninth.

On that day the U.S.S.R. broke off diplomatic relations with Finland and ordered the Red Army and Navy to "be ready for all emergencies." Comrade Molotov took to the radio. Addressing the Soviet Union's 180,000,000 people, he told his audience that Finland's hostility "has become unbearable and the Soviet Government can no longer stand it."

The Kremlin set off a barrage of propaganda against the Finns. *Pravda* headed an article about Finland's Premier Cajander: "Buffoon in the Post of Premier." Russian newspapers railed at "Butcher Mannerheim," at the "gang of White Guard bandits" who rule Finland. Grandiose territorial ambitions were ascribed to the Finns. This nation with less than four million people was charged with a plot to annex all Russia as far as Siberia. The Finns were "bestial murderers mad with their savage dreams of a Greater Finland up to the Urals."

Stalin's great "peace crusade" was ready to start. While Red infantry moved across Finland's frontiers Red aviators bombed Helsinki and other Finnish cities. The Soviet invasion was being conducted on the model of the German thrust into Poland. It was to be another *Blitzkrieg* (lightning war). But the propaganda which accompanied it was unique. True, it was the same general plan which the Soviet had used in Mongolia, the Japanese in Manchuria and the Germans in Austria and Czecho-Slovakia. But Stalin brought it to a new state of perfection.

Of course the Red tsar was only following the precedent of all modern acts of aggression when he charged that the Finns invaded the U.S.S.R. The *Daily Worker*, New York Communist publication, for example, headlined across its front page this startling statement: "Red Army Hurls Back Invading Finnish Troops." Even then, according to the Soviet version of the war, the Red troops had not attacked Finland.

But the Moscow radio picked up a broadcast from a station in Terioki, a small town along the gulf on the Karelian Isthmus. According to the Soviet claim, a "Peoples' Democratic Government of Finland" had been established at Terioki. It was now engaged in civil war with the "White Guard bandit regime" of General Mannerheim. As a matter of fact, there has never been a radio station in the little frontier town of Terioki. But no matter. The Soviets could plead that Europe has not been meticulous about truth in the past. Why should it single out a discrepancy in Moscow's propaganda program?

Without delay the Soviet Government did a forthright thing: it recognized the "Peoples' Democratic Government of Finland" and signed a treaty with Otto Kuusinen, the head of the Terioki regime. The Moscow radio now called upon the Finns to stop fighting their "deliverers." *Pravda* called the Red Army "the hope of humanity."

Comrade Molotov bluntly told the Swedish minister to Moscow, Wilhelm Winther, that the U.S.S.R. would not deal with the Finnish Government in Helsinki. The Kremlin no longer admitted that such a government even existed. It recognized only the "Peoples' Democratic Republic of Finland" in Terioki.

A month later the first army corps of the "Finnish Peoples' Government" was organized at Terioki from deserters and so-called "volunteers." The oath administered by Aksel Antilla, the Terioki government's minister of war, was as follows: "I, a soldier of Finland's Peoples' Army, solemnly swear loyalty to my last breath to the Finnish Democratic Government headed by the true son of the Finnish people, Otto Kuusinen."

But even a world hardened by repeated crimes of aggression against little countries was not ready to swallow the Soviet version of the fighting in Finland. To its credit, the League of Nations adopted a stiff attitude toward Moscow. The Society of Geneva had allowed Japan to invade China, Italy to seize Ethiopia and Albania, Germany, Italy and Russia to intervene in Spain, Germany to gobble up Austria and Czecho-Slovakia. Yet the Soviet attack on Finland stirred up a determined protest on the shores of Lake Leman.

At the December meeting of the League the question of the attack by one member (Russia) upon another member (Finland) came up. The Finnish representative to Geneva, Rudolph Holsti, charged that the U.S.S.R. was guilty of having "attacked not only frontier positions, but also open towns of Finland, sowing death and destruction." He requested the League to "take all measures to check the aggression." He went on to quote liberally from statements made on the same spot in other times by Maxim Litvinov. These avowals of Moscow's dedication to the cause of peace rang with mockery in December 1939.

To the surprise of many observers the League took firm action. Several South American republics assumed the lead in demanding that the Soviet be expelled. From Geneva a telegram was sent to Moscow asking whether the U.S.S.R. would cease its attack upon Finland and negotiate. The Kremlin's reply was signed by Molotov.

Said the Soviet premier and foreign commissar in his dispatch to League Secretary General Avenol: "The Soviet Government thanks you, Mr President, for the kind invitation to take part in discussion of the Finnish question. At the same time the Soviet Government informs you it is not in a position to accept this invitation for the reasons given in the telegram of December 4th from the Commissariat of Foreign Affairs sent in reply to a communication from the Secretary General."

And what were the "reasons" that Comrade Molotov mentioned? On that date Molotov had asserted: "The Soviet Union is not at war with Finland and does not threaten it." Furthermore, he declined to participate in the "illegal" meeting of the Council of the League of Nations. Instead of making war on Finland, said Molotov, "the Soviet Union maintains peaceful relations with the Democratic Republic of Finland." He denounced Finland's complaint to the League as an "insult" to the pacific U.S.S.R. On December fourteenth the League of Nations expelled the Soviet Union.

"League of Nations in Hands of War Incendiaries!" read the bold type in *Izvestia*. And the *Red Star*, army organ, attacked Britain, France and America as typifying "deceit, hypocrisy and sanctimoniousness, inevitable qualities of capitalist character, like greediness and the passion for wealth."

Even Italy, usually not very squeamish about acts of international aggression, indignantly denounced the Soviet invasion of Finland. In fact, the newspaper which usually reflects the views of Foreign Minister Ciano, the *Telegrafo* of Livorno, termed Stalin's Finnish campaign "the most evident aggression in modern history."

The day after the Soviet was ousted from the League Finland's foreign minister, V. A. Tanner, broadcast an appeal to the U.S.S.R. to end its "barbarous invasion" of a small neighbor. "When I recently visited the big Agricultural Exposition in Moscow," said the Finn, "I read on the wall of one of the buildings a stirring sentence by your leader, Lenin: 'The Soviet Union does not covet one inch of the soil of other states, but will defend every inch of its own soil.'

"There is reason at this moment to save that excellent phrase from sinking into oblivion. Mr Molotov! How can you reconcile these principles, proclaimed by the Soviet Union, with your brazen attack on small, peace-loving Finland? I beg you to answer this question." But Comrade Molotov did not answer.

The Moscow radio broadcast this type of reply to all its critics: "Slaves and hirelings of capitalists and imperialistic interests have dared to abuse the glorious Red Army, which with such unselfishness has lent its help to the Democratic Finnish Republic."

Meanwhile the Red Army was encountering serious difficulties. Finland's small force fought back bravely, stubbornly and efficiently. The Red losses quickly rose to large proportions. And *Pravda* angrily denounced the Finnish tactics. "On every path and every road," one of its correspondents wrote, "every minute . . . mines burst under tanks, mines burst under heaps of manure, under hay mows—a filthy trick at every step." The Finnish soldiers were "masters of foul play." According to *Pravda*, "There is invisible danger, prepared by a vicious, barbarous hand."

But even though the Finns were winning brilliant victories, they were losing the war. Their one vital weakness was lack of man power. When a Finn fell there was no one to replace him. When a Russian was killed other Russians were sent in to take his place. When the Russians lost division after division in the Finnish snows they had only to move more men to the front. Thousands of Soviet reservists sent against the Finns in the early days of the invasion perished from bullets, cold and hunger. Once Stalin realized the formidable task upon which he had embarked, he sent first-class regular troops into the conflict.

In February the Red forces drove furiously into the Mannerheim Line. Gradually the Finns were forced to retreat. They could not spare men for counterattacks. Their excellent artillery was outranged by larger Russian guns; their pillboxes were "rocked" by the terrific Soviet barrage. The new and successful Russian tactics looked like the work of German staff officers borrowed from Hitler by Stalin.

Pravda promised its readers: "We will achieve victory over them (the 'Finnish bandits') under our great leader Stalin." This editorial went on to describe him as "a man with the heart of a scholar, the face of a workman and the appearance of a soldier."

Bringing the Western democracies into the conflict, *Pravda* charged: "Since the Anglo-French imperialists provoked a new war, they tried to drag in the Soviet by instigating the White Finnish scum to attack us!"

And in England Mr George Bernard Shaw had already asserted in an interview with the London *Daily Mail* that Leningrad could be shelled from the Finnish frontier. Finland, he said, "was being made to act by a foolish government in the interests of other powers menacing

Russia's security. No power can tolerate a frontier like that." Apparently Mr Shaw saw or chose to see no evidence of Soviet imperialism in the Finnish outrage. According to his interpretation, Russia was menaced by Finnish imperialism.

From the start of the war the Finnish military leaders knew that by themselves they could not hold out indefinitely against the prolific man power of the U.S.S.R. But they hoped, and believed, that they could stand off the invaders until help would come from the other Scandinavian countries and the Western democracies. They could not, of course, hope for any support from the Reich.

Finland was, after all, fighting the battle not only of the rest of Scandinavia; it was holding the breach for Turkey, Roumania and the Western powers. As long as the Russians were held at bay by the Finns Stalin dared not risk any adventure in the Balkans. He dared not push into Hungary; he could not offer much economic aid to Hitler. Italy, deeply interested in keeping Bolshevism out of the Balkans, had a stake in Finland's battle against the Red Army. Furthermore, if the Western democracies went to war because undemocratic Poland was invaded, they were certainly under greater obligations to save this little northern democracy. So reasoned the Finns.

But each nation which should have given direct aid to Finland waited for the others to do it. The Western democracies still toyed with the hope that Stalin could be detached from Hitler. Sweden, which gave more help to the Finns than did any other nation, dared not openly intervene. Hitler threatened to take action if the Swedes or Norwegians permitted their territories to be used as Allied bases of operations in support of Finland. And the Swedes suspected that the British and French were primarily interested in cutting off Germany from Swedish iron imports, only secondarily concerned with saving Finland.

At last, when the Finns were beaten, the British and French offered to send an expeditionary force. At best this proffered aid from the West could not reach the Finnish-Russian battle line for weeks, perhaps months. "It is the old trouble—too late!" exclaimed David Lloyd George. "Too late with Czecho-Slovakia, too late with Poland, and certainly too late with Finland. It is always too late or too little or both, and that is the road to disaster."

With her reserves gone, her Mannerheim Line battered to pieces, her cities and towns at the mercy of Soviet air raiders, the Finns could do nothing but accept Stalin's terms. And those terms were harsh. Ironically the Finns learned that the new dictates were far more severe than the ones they had turned down in November.

Finland had lost thousands of her young men; her property damage from invasion and bombings was enormous; and yet it was all in vain. Her Karelian Isthmus, her Mannerheim Line, her shore along Lake Ladoga, much of her manufacturing area, a strip of territory along the eastern border—all these were lost. Most serious of all, the Finns were compelled to surrender their defensive positions. In the future they would not be able to oppose further Soviet demands. Actually Finland became a quasi-dependency of the U.S.S.R. And part of her territory was incorporated as the twelfth republic of the expanding Union of Socialist Soviet Republics. *Pravda* could rejoice and hail the Finnish defeat as a "new triumph of the Soviet policy of peace."

In London the influential *Times* remarked that one result of the Finnish tragedy "will be renewed, strengthened determination to rid Europe of Hitlerism, author of all the

dangers to which its civilization now stands exposed." If
that sentence was called to Stalin's attention, he must have
smiled sardonically. For once more Soviet imperialism
found protection in Allied hatred of Hitler. In the convenient shadow of the swastika the Red star continued its
ascendancy.

And in Helsinki Foreign Minister Tanner broadcast
these words: "Thus our country has been left to settle its
relations with our powerful opponent alone. We have
shown the path which small nations must take in the face
of demands by dictator states. It has not been our fault
that the democratic States have either been unwilling or
unable to help us in this unequal struggle."

It was not their fault either that the Soviets were con-
summate imperialists.

CHAPTER XXII

Stalinism

There is a prince now alive (whose name it may not be proper to mention) who ever preaches the doctrines of peace and good faith; but if he ever observed either the one or the other, he would long ago have lost both his reputation and dominions.—MACHIAVELLI.

In 1924, on a summer evening, Stalin, Dzhersinsky (the late chieftain of the Cheka) and Kamenev were sitting over a bottle of wine (I know not whether it was the first bottle), chattering about various small things, when the conversation turned upon the question of what each liked most in life. I do not remember what Dzhersinsky and Kamenev (from whom I know this story) said. But Stalin declared: "The sweetest thing in life is to pick one's victim, prepare the blow carefully, take one's revenge mercilessly, and then go to sleep."—LEON TROTZKY, in *The Bulletin of the Opposition*, October, 1936.

WHAT WE SEE in Russia today is not true Communism. It is Stalinism—a combination of Marxism, Pan-Slavism, imperialism and Asiatic despotism. It might be summed up in one word—Pan-Sovietism. It is in some respects the Russian equivalent of Hitlerism. And in Germany the present regime is in some respects the German form of Stalinism. Each of these countries is controlled by a dynamic, revolutionary movement.

Stalin has been called the "Robespierre of the Russian revolution." Robespierre, according to Aulard, a contemporary French historian, was "astute, mysterious, undecipherable." That description would apply to Stalin.

Before the Nazi-Soviet deal was announced the tendency in the West was to overestimate Stalin's ability. Many people looked upon him as a superman. After his pact with Hitler the tendency in the West was to underestimate him. From one extreme Western opinion went to the other. The truth lies somewhere between these distorted estimates of the man. He is human enough to make blunders; he occasionally meets some political strategist who checkmates his plans. His method of reducing Finland is an example of the former; his unsuccessful negotiations with Foreign Minister Saracoglu are an instance of the latter. His diplomacy shows no unbroken line of triumphs. He may yet overreach himself and come a cropper.

But the fact remains, I think, that Stalin is the most astute political strategist in the Old World. His subtlety, his Asiatic cunning, his ruthlessness, his lack of moral inhibitions, his willingness to sacrifice uncounted human lives, his readiness to change front and adapt his ideology to political conditions—these factors make him not only one of the most dangerous men in the world but also one of the most successful practitioners of revolutionary *Realpolitik*.

In the foreign colony of Moscow it is widely believed that Stalin keeps a portrait of Peter the Great on his desk. Hitler believes himself to be greater than Bismarck, Frederick the Great and all other German heroes of the past.

Stalin probably does not bask in such self-adulation. He undoubtedly thinks of himself as following in the imperial footsteps of Peter and Catherine II. Peter's ruthlessness commands Stalin's respect; Peter's willingness to uproot what had been established and his enthusiasm for breaking with the past undoubtedly excite Stalin's admiration. But, most important of all, Peter pushed his frontiers westward. Stalin's Red imperialism is following the path of empire blazed by Peter.

Before the Nazi-Soviet deal Stalin was described by innumerable writers as a modest man, a proletarian of simple tastes, an unpretentious servant of the people. Was he not merely the general secretary of the Communist party? Did he not live in frugal simplicity, in almost puritanical austerity?

Stalin has never been the dynamic leader of a great popular movement. He is no great orator like Hitler nor a clever actor like Mussolini. He has not been a successful rabble rouser. Before he came to power he was not known to the masses; his name was not on every man's lips. On the contrary, for years after the Soviet revolution Stalin was virtually unknown outside the party. He had no flair for personal publicity like Trotzky. He was not an intellectual like Lenin. Nor was he a great journalist like Radek. His strength lay in his sagacity as a machine politician.

While Trotzky was receiving the plaudits of his admiring party associates for the work of creating the Red Army, Stalin was plodding along outside the limelight, building routine party organization. While Lenin was making brilliant speeches and formulating party ideology, Stalin was appointing the secretaries of party committees from the Polish border to Kamchatka. In those days Stalin's name was unknown to the Western world. But, far more important to the future master of the Kremlin, the name Stalin was known to the men who ran the party units in every district of the U.S.S.R.

Stalin was removing recalcitrant secretaries; he was doing favors; he was building his own personal machine within the party. He was gaining control of the organization. The flamboyant Trotzky might boast that he was the co-worker of Lenin; Stalin was preparing to be Lenin's successor. And the time would come when his work would bear fruit, when he would be able to thrust his brilliant—therefore hated—rival into exile and ban his name from Soviet histories and monuments.

The unit of the Communist party is the *Yacheyka* or cell. The Soviet organization is, therefore, only as strong as the collective strength of its cells. The officials from the smallest unit in the most remote village up to the bosses who run the party organizations in Moscow, Leningrad and Kharkov are of the utmost importance. On their ability and their loyalty to the party depends the life of the Soviet Government. And upon their personal loyalty rests Stalin's hold upon the party and hence upon the U.S.S.R.

It is no coincidence that the bosses of the great cities are intimate friends of Stalin. Kirov, the murdered chief of Leningrad, and Zhdanov, his successor, have been prime favorites of the tsar of the Kremlin. Sherbakov, the Moscow secretary, and Khruschchev, the Ukrainian secretary, are close allies of Stalin. Zhdanov has been sitting at Stalin's right hand at important public functions. Stalin is believed to admire Zhdanov's drive, his ruthlessness and his ambitious policies in the realm of Soviet foreign relations.

Perhaps it is the Asiatic in Stalin that causes him to pre-

fer to work in secret. He manipulates the strings from behind the scenes. He lives in a kind of hideaway within the
compound of the mysterious Kremlin, somewhere under
the forest of gilded domes and cupolas. Rarely does even
the ambassador of a great power have the privilege of
meeting him. He is inaccessible to all but the few whose
fate he desires to mold by personal contact. And more
likely than not they are not destined to be fortunate in receiving this close attention from the Soviet dictator.

After the Nazi-Soviet deal Stalin came in for a barrage
of abuse from many of his former supporters. Writers who
had once praised his modesty, the simplicity and unpre-
tentiousness of his personal life, now charged him with
vanity. They denounced him for aping Hitler. They asserted that he had suddenly changed front. He had betrayed the revolution; he had been false to his own ideals.
But they were wrong. Stalin had not changed; he had only
changed his tactics. He was still driving toward the same
goal of a new world order that would be directed from the
Kremlin.

When Stalin's sixtieth birthday was celebrated in December 1939 his enemies all over the world pointed to the
hyperbolic paeans of praise showered upon him by the
Soviet press and by countless Red orators. The Order of
Lenin was conferred on him "for his exceptional services in
organizing the Bolshevik Party, creating the Soviet state,
building a Socialist society in the Soviet Union and consolidating the friendship of the peoples of the Union."

A few years previously, when a foreign correspondent
had referred to Stalin as the successor of Lenin, the master
of the Kremlin is said to have answered: "I am only
Lenin's disciple, carrying out his teaching."

But now *Izvestia* said in an editorial: "Stalin is Lenin today. When we say Lenin we mean the Communist Party and when we say the Party we mean Stalin. Nothing in nature is more indivisible than these two concepts."

Pravda almost outdid itself in glorifying Stalin on his birthday. Five of this newspaper's six pages were taken up with a "short biography of Joseph Vissarionovitch Stalin." Issued by the Institute of Marx, Engels and Lenin, the biography lauded Stalin for practically every accomplishment in the U.S.S.R. since the passing of Lenin.

"It is difficult to conceive the giant figure of Stalin," *Pravda* said. "Since we have been working without Lenin all essential work has been done on instructions from and under the leadership of Stalin. In Stalin the Soviet people see the personification of their heroism, patriotism, hopes, aspirations and victories." Stalin is, *Pravda* told us, "the greatest man in modern times."

On the occasion of Stalin's birthday thousands of pilgrims visited the log cabin at Gori, in Georgia, the Caucasian state where Stalin, son of a shoemaker, was born. A magnificent marble-columned pavilion has been erected over the simple three-room thatched cottage. The humble little house has become a shrine for the Bolshevik faithful.

In the words of *Pravda:* "Metal workers of Detroit, shipyard workers of Sydney, woman workers of Shanghai textiles factories, sailors at Marseille, Egyptian fellaheen, Indian peasants on the banks of the Ganges—all speak of Stalin with love. He is the hope of the future for the workers and peasants of the world."

Here the reader may be reminded of Metternich's remark about himself. "My position has this peculiarity," he said, "that all eyes, all expectations are directed to precisely that point where I happen to be."

Napoleon said that Metternich "mistook intrigue for statesmanship." There are critics who feel that the master of the Kremlin "mistakes statesmanship for intrigue."

In any estimate of Stalin I believe that it would be a mistake to assume that the laudatory editorials and the pyrotechnics of adulation merely reflect a personal vanity in the man. Nor do I believe that the former divinity student is striving to deify himself, to make worship of himself a kind of ersatz religion for the Russian masses. To my mind there is a more practical reason behind this carefully directed campaign of eulogy, spoken and written.

The glorification of Stalin fits into the picture of Soviet imperialism in the same way as the campaign against religion, the extermination of the kulaks, collectivization, industrialization, the party purges and colossal propaganda offensives. It is part of the Kremlin's regimentation program. And it consolidates Stalin's authority over the heterogeneous peoples who populate the vast stretches of his empire.

Extolment of the Red dictator is one aspect of Stalinism. And Stalinism is one means of promoting the revolutionary processes which are part of the far-flung movement of Soviet imperialism.

CHAPTER XXIII

As Stalin Looks Abroad

Whoever steers a middle course betrays the revolution. He who is not with us is against us.—STALIN.

STALIN'S ATTITUDE toward the nations which compose that "other world" has many facets. Toward some governments he shows only contempt; toward other governments he manifests respect. His attitude toward the Chamberlain government in Britain, for example, was barely concealed disdain. On the other hand, his attitude toward the Mussolini regime in Italy has often been characterized by esteem for the political sagacity of the Duce. Stalin's appraisal of the Hitler dictatorship reflects both contempt and respect. The master of the Kremlin undoubtedly looks with scorn upon a government which deliberately followed a course that alienated most of the world. At the same time the Soviet chief admires the Third Reich's industrial and economic mobilization and the efficiency of its army.

The reader may well ask how we know what is in the mind of Stalin. How can we know what is going on behind the masklike face which hides his subtle mind? There is no simple answer. Stalin's policies, his attitudes, his viewpoint, are all reflected in minute detail by his henchmen. No member of the Kremlin hierarchy entertains any policy which conflicts with Stalin's. To do so would be to run the risk of being charged with "counterrevolution." No Bolshevik wants to suffer the fate of a Trotzkyist.

Germans, Turks, Letts, Estonians, Finns and other neighbors of Russia are constantly appraising Stalin's attitude toward the outside world. Their missions in Moscow have only extremely limited personal contacts with the Red dictator; they must arrive at their conclusions from what they can find out about him through his henchmen. It is a difficult process. They are continuously studying Molotov, Zhdanov, Voroshilov, Kaganovitch, Sherbakov, Timoshenko and other Soviet keymen. Their legations and secret-service operatives in the U.S.S.R. must make the most of every contact with these colleagues of Stalin. From such reports European governments reach their conclusions about the Kremlin's plans and policies. And upon the basis of these conclusions the various governments formulate their policies toward the Soviet Union.

Occasionally Stalin lifts the veil that hangs between him and the "other world." When he does so he is mercilessly frank. He leaves no doubt as to his meaning. This happened on March 10, 1939. That was the time when he announced that the Soviet would not act as a "cat's-paw" for anybody. We have already referred to this speech in Chapter XIV. He poured forth his scorn for the bourgeois world, especially for the English bourgeoisie. His audience, of course, thoroughly enjoyed his gibes at the Western democracies.

From the beginning of the Soviet regime Britain has been the bête noire of the Bolsheviks. "British spies" are proverbial. The names of Sir Paul Dukes and Sidney

Reilly have become almost legendary in these Soviet charges of British espionage in the U.S.S.R. The British intelligence service is linked with extravagant tales of spying, terrorism and sabotage. These stories attribute almost superhuman efficiency to John Bull's undercover men. But if the British intelligence service were as omnipotent as the Bolsheviks claim, why did the English not know in advance about the Nazi-Soviet deal?

From the days of active British intervention to the present, relations between Britain and the U.S.S.R. have been far from placid. The British did not recognize the Soviet Government until 1924. Even then Downing Street's attitude appeared to be motivated by the fear that Germany would monopolize the Russian market. There had been serious trouble the previous year between London and Moscow. Lord Curzon had called the Soviet notes "studied affronts." British ministers deeply resented Soviet propaganda within the Empire.

Britain broke off her relations with the U.S.S.R. in 1927 but resumed them three years later. At times the Soviet OGPU has arrested English engineers and tried them on charges of conspiracy and espionage. Anglo-Russian economic relations have been strained, frequently by Soviet suspicions that probably originated in fears of British financial, political and naval power.

Despite a certain jittery apprehension of Britain, Stalin and his colleagues have shown contempt for the Empire. It is a basic Bolshevik belief that Great Britain is a decadent nation that is slowly dying of senility. Russian Marxists, German Nazis and Italian Fascists agree that Britain and France are "tired" countries which lack the dynamism of the "young nations." Good Bolsheviks consider contemporary Britain an anachronism, a holdover

from the nineteenth century. In their opinion it has long
outlived its day. The alleged desperate attempts of British
statesmen to provoke a Russo-German war are, according
to the Kremlinites, despairing efforts to postpone the disintegration of the "moribund" Empire.

The Munich conference seemed to the Bolsheviks a public admission of Britain's surrender of her position as a
foremost world power. The Soviet oligarchy had only
scorn for Prime Minister Chamberlain's statement of
November 1, 1938, which conceded that for geographical
reasons Germany "must occupy the dominating position"
in the Danubian sector and that as a consequence Britain
entertained "no wish to block Germany out of these countries or encircle her economically." Such conciliatory
utterances are, of course, completely misunderstood in
Moscow and Berlin. They are taken as signs of weakness.

The following May Mr Chamberlain replied frankly to
his pro-Soviet critics that there was "a sort of veil or wall
between the two governments which is extremely difficult
to penetrate." The prime minister's record with respect to
Moscow may not have been exemplary by any means.
Yet it is more than doubtful whether anyone else in his
place could have dispelled the suspicions and enmity which
divided the world's greatest maritime empire from the
world's largest land empire.

On that same day Mr Lloyd George wanted to know
why an alliance had not been reached with the U.S.S.R.
"For months," he said, "we have been staring this powerful gift horse in the face."

"And have seen its false teeth!" broke in Wing Commander Archibald James, a Conservative member of the
House of Commons.

Such debates in the British Parliament, signs of democratic strength in Western eyes, undoubtedly lower British prestige in the eyes of the Kremlinites. Such things do not happen in the U.S.S.R. It must be kept constantly in mind that Stalin is an Asiatic, that he has never had any experience with Western liberalism, that he despises the philosophy of democracy.

Stalin assumes that Britain is the bulwark of bourgeois democracy in the Old World. Pan-Sovietism cannot rule the Continent as long as there is a strong Britain. To weaken and destroy Britain and obliterate British power, by one means or another, is therefore one of the principal objectives of Red imperialism.

Even though the Bolsheviks (and Nazis) believe that the British Empire is in the process of deterioration and disintegration, they realize that under anything like normal world conditions the British may be able to hold on for some time. But war would, the totalitarians believe, speed up enormously the natural process of a political, social and economic breakdown of the Empire. The Kremlin is working to accelerate the expected decomposition.

Moscow looks upon France as the less powerful of the two Western democracies. The Bolsheviks (and again the Nazis) believe that France's low birth rate spells her inevitable fall as a first-class power. But even more important in the eyes of the totalitarians is the conviction that in France there is a fatal social and economic disease at work. They point to what they claim is an increasingly deadly feud between the cities and the rural areas. The "Red suburbs" of Paris, the Bolsheviks maintain, are at war with the bourgeoisie.

The Kremlin could gather some satisfaction from the stubborn allegiance of many French Communists to the U.S.S.R. after the outbreak of the "second imperialist war." Several Red leaders went into hiding; others, notably Maurice Thorez, were accused of deserting military service. Marcel Cachin, veteran French Communist hierarch, was deprived of his seat in the French Senate. And eight former Communist deputies were deprived of their seats in the Chamber and charged with high treason. The accused were Duclos, Dutilleul, Monmoussea, Catelas, Pari, Ramette, Rigal and Tillon.

The Communist party in France was declared by the government to be dissolved on September 26, 1939. As part of the wartime anti-Communist campaign the French police seized the Red newspapers *L'Humanité* and *Ce Soir*, and action was taken against the Communist Youth Federation, the Union of Communist Students, the General Confederation of Peasant Workers, the Union of Negro Workers, the Federation of Rent Payers of the Paris Region, the Foreign Association of Russian Emigrés, the Committee on International Solidarity and Self Aid, the Association of German Political Refugees, the Association of Bulgarian Emigrés and other organizations accused of Soviet connections. During the first week of April 1940 a military tribunal imposed maximum five-year sentences upon thirty-six erstwhile Communist members of Parliament. All those pronounced guilty lost their civil rights.

Since the Stalin-Hitler pact former Premier Herriot, once an ardent advocate of Franco-Russian rapprochement, has made scathing attacks upon the Soviet Union. This leading parliamentarian charged that Germany and Russia "wish to put all free peoples in a chain gang and subjugate all the neutral nations." On February eleventh the French General Confederation of Labor, formerly friendly to the Soviet Union, published an indictment of the U.S.S.R. which included: "French labor is obliged to draw a conclusion. When Stalin's agents pretend to speak in the name of workers they lie. Hitler and Stalin are associated in the same crimes and both in the same blood."

These attacks from former friends must make disagreeable reading for the lord of the Kremlin. But he can gain some satisfaction from the loyalty of his die-hard French supporters. Deputy Florimond Blonte, for example, on trial before a military tribunal, declared that French Communists had the right to support the Nazi-Soviet pact. When asked to give his occupation Blonte replied: "I am a Deputy from Paris—and more than that I am a Deputy from the glorious St Antoine quarter." St Antoine is famous for the part it played as a center of action during the French Revolution.

As Stalin looks at Italy he sees opportunistic political action. When translations of Mussolini's writings are made for him he can understand the political implications. The *Popolo d'Italia*, the Duce's own newspaper, reaffirms the original and fundamental principles of Fascism as "corporativism, anti-democracy, anti-Bolshevism and anti-bourgeoisie." The Red dictator knows that in modern Fascist parlance "anti-Bolshevism" might well mean anything. It might be aimed at the democracies. Or, if relations between Rome and Moscow are strained, it might be aimed at the Kremlin.

Stalin's opinion of Italy's plans in the "second imperialist war" were revealed in November by the Comintern's manifesto. The Third International is the voice of Stalin; so when the Comintern said that Italy is waiting "to attack whomever is defeated to obtain a share of the loot," the words expressed the Kremlin's viewpoint.

The Kremlinites are probably not stirred by anti-Russian outbursts like *Telegrafo's:* "Russians are not men like us. They are simply human material good to be shot, deported, kicked in the rear." Hard-boiled Stalinists very likely consider such diatribes as offerings for home consumption. They have experience in that technique.

As long ago as 1933 Mussolini and Soviet Ambassador Potemkin signed a Russo-Italian treaty of friendship, non-aggression and neutrality. Inasmuch as Italy and the U.S.S.R. do not have contiguous frontiers, it is unlikely that either would directly attack the other. It is even doubtful that either would join a coalition to invade the territory of the other. But there is a possibility that Italian Fascists and Russian Bolsheviks may come to blows over some third party. They fought each other in Spain. They may do so again—this time in central Europe or the Balkans.

The *Gazzetta del Popolo* of Turin has said bluntly: "Italy will never permit the further advance of Bolshevist Russia beyond the Carpathians, in the Danube Valley, in the Balkans or toward the Mediterranean." Undoubtedly this warning was officially inspired. What Italians specifically fear is a Soviet drive into the Balkans by way of Roumania or into the Danube Basin by way of Hungary.

The Soviet newspaper *Trud* has spoken contemptuously of Italy's "tinsel strength." But it is possible that Stalin will carefully weigh Italy's attitude before he plunges into an invasion of the Balkans or Danubia.

There is little organized Marxism in Italy today. What little there is must operate underground. But the Soviets are constantly looking ahead. They have maintained that economic conditions in Italy would produce a crisis that the Duce could not surmount. And war in Italy, they have assumed in Moscow, would prepare the way for social revolution. There is furthermore, the Russians insist, a group of "Black Bolsheviks" within the Fascist party. These men may someday, Kremlinites hint, precipitate a counterrevolution which would align them with Stalin.

When Stalin looks past his Finnish frontier into Scandinavia he sees a part of Europe which formerly offered little encouragement to indigenous Communism. These bourgeois nations, with their strong middle class, good government, enlightened economic and social engineering, did not fear hostile ideological movements among their own citizens. Bolshevik propaganda made some headway, it is true, among labor organizations in Norway and Sweden. But the Soviet attack on Finland struck a heavy blow at Marxism throughout Scandinavia.

In early 1940 Nils Granevall, allegedly a former Communist, is said to have aided the police in tracking down the Bolshevik organization in Sweden. In a statement to the press he was quoted as asserting that during recent years Moscow had sent "millions of crowns" to Swedish Communists. Anti-Soviet critics in Scandinavia have long blamed Madame Kollontai, Stalin's minister to Sweden, for organizing and directing Pan-Soviet activities in the northern countries. The havoc of war in Scandinavia may create conditions that will facilitate the Kremlin's efforts to indoctrinate these little democracies with Bolshevism.

In the Danubian Basin Stalin sees a country that had a Communist regime for several months during 1919. Hungary was ruled at that time by Bela Kun and his Bolsheviks. From the extreme left Hungary swung over to the extreme right. The Magyars are one of the most nationalistic peoples in Europe. They have kept up a strong and continuous propaganda against the peace treaties. One might think, therefore, that Hungary would not be fertile soil for Communism. But there is no certainty that this is the case. For Hungary's semifeudal political, social and economic system has created conditions that once opened the door to Bolshevism and may do so again.

Hungary's great weakness and acute danger is inherent in the plight of millions of landless peasants. The "rural slums" of Hungary are recruiting grounds for subversive movements. In 1919 these propertyless peasants provided disciples for Bolshevism; in the late thirties they furnished many followers for Nazism. In both cases there was the same incentive—the hope that under a different system they could own land. Hungary's aristocracy does not seem to realize the full measure of this danger.

Then there is the problem of Hungary's strategic location. For two decades after the World War no country in Europe was more vociferously anti-Soviet. Hungary became aligned with the anti-Comintern states and for a time had no minister in Moscow. Meantime the Hungarians were raising a hue and cry about the Magyars who were compelled to live under other governments. For this they had some cause for complaint. But when Czecho-Slovakia was broken up, as we have seen, the Hungarian Army invaded Ruthenia.

The Ruthenians are Slavs, not Magyars. And the large majority of people in Ruthenia are Ruthenians (Carpatho-Russians) (Ukrainians). The Hungarian Army, vastly better equipped than the miserable Ruthenian force, attacked the *Sitch* (Ruthenian nationalist organization) and slaughtered a considerable number. Hungary acted in a far more brutal way toward the Ruthenians than Roumanians, Yugoslavs and Czechs had acted toward Magyars. But Hungary got possession of Ruthenia and at the same time obtained the common frontier with Poland that she was so anxious to get.

The sequel to this Hungarian seizure of Ruthenia is that a few months later, September 1939, when the Red Army occupied southeastern Poland, the U.S.S.R. established a common frontier with Hungary. An independent Ruthenia would have given Hungary a buffer between her territory and the Soviet Union. The Bolsheviks are now carrying on a strong propaganda campaign among the Ruthenians. In view of the latter's discontent with Magyar rule, the propaganda bids fair to make headway. Hungarians are not happy about this situation. For Stalin is now in a position where his troops are poised for a thrust into the Danube Valley when, and if, conditions make it seem a profitable venture.

South of Hungary lies Yugoslavia, a country which refused for more than two decades to have any dealings with the Soviet Union. Dynastic reasons partly account for this. The Prince Regent Paul married a Russian aristocrat. As a boy he lived in St Petersburg and had close ties with the Romanov court. But the fact remains that there is no inconsiderable sympathy for the U.S.S.R. in the Kingdom of the South Slavs. Probably it is inspired more by a feeling of Pan-Slavic solidarity than by Marxism, but the fact remains that it is there. After the start of the second World War there were some Communist demonstrations in Yugoslavia that caused the government no little uneasiness. In December 1939 there was a serious riot in the Adriatic city of Split when about two thousand workmen demonstrated and attacked the police. The Communist leader, Mile Buljanovitch, was killed in the fighting.

In Belgrade the authorities complain that many of the middle-class students have been attracted by "drawing-room Communism." Apparently reliable reports from Yugoslavia relate that during the final weeks of 1939 sixteen Yugoslav students, workers and police were killed in clashes between Communists and police. Indeed, the Belgrade police charged that they were confronted not merely by students but by trained Red terrorists.

In spite of these Communist disorders within the South Slav kingdom, there has been since early 1940 a marked rapprochement between Belgrade and Moscow. The motivation of the improved Yugoslav-Soviet relations has been provided by the menace of Italian aggression against Yugoslavia. Turkey, acting as intermediary, is believed to have brought South Slavs and Russians together. The Turks have worked to draw Soviet influence into Yugoslavia in order to form a barrier against the southward thrust of the Germans and the eastward drive of the Italians. As short-term strategy this may profit the Turks; as a longer range policy it may serve Turkey badly by bringing Russian political, economic—and perhaps military—power nearer the Dardanelles.

Just across Yugoslavia's eastern frontier lies Bulgaria, a country that is developing increasingly close relations with the Soviet Union. Here, again, Pan-Slavism plays a part. During centuries of servitude under Turkish rule the Bulgarians looked to Russia as their friend. Today both countries have certain potential enemies in common; especially Roumania, perhaps Turkey. In fact, some observers believe that Bulgaria may become an advance base for a Soviet drive toward the Golden Horn. *Pravda* justifies the close relations between Moscow and Sofia on the ground that they have in common "deep roots in the past."

Alexander Tsankoff, Fascist leader, speaking in the Bulgarian Parliament, aroused applause when he said that the U.S.S.R. was entirely justified in striking out to obtain her "living space, a space as necessary to Russia as Bulgaria's living space, Dubrudja and the Aegean outlet."

The Kingdom of Roumania occupies one of the most dangerous positions in the world. It has a long, not easily defendable frontier with the Soviet Union, a hostile Hungary on the west and a revisionist Bulgaria on the south. Its province of Bessarabia belonged for over a century to Russia. The Roumanians have strong ethnic and historical claims to the territory. But they may not be able to hold it for long. In the heyday of Litvinov's collective security campaigns at Geneva, he and the Roumanian foreign minister, Nicholas Titulescu, were on friendly terms. Frequently they were diplomatic allies. Titulescu's supporters in Roumania claimed that he would obtain from Litvinov Soviet recognition to Roumania's ownership of Bessarabia.

Furthermore, the Titulescu people argued that Russia had all the land she wanted. She had no use for Bessarabia. Just the same, Titulescu never obtained the Soviet recognition that he wanted. Litvinov always stalled him off. Certainly Stalin had no intention of handing over such a valuable Trojan horse. For economic reasons the Soviet did not need this dusty, inhospitable stretch of territory lying between the Pruth and the Dniester. But it is located near the mouth of the Danube. Every recent Russian tsar has looked covetously upon the Danube delta as a spot of great strategical value. Not only is it the Danube entrance to central Europe; it is on the road from Russia to the Dardanelles.

After the Soviet invasion of Poland a Balkan diplomat stationed in Paris told me that if the Russians moved against Bessarabia, "the Roumanians will fire six shots and retreat to the Pruth." Why fire six shots? "Because," my informant told me, "the Roumanians will fire six shots for the record. Then when the inevitable peace conference comes, the Roumanians can put in their claim that they defended Bessarabia but were driven out by superior force."

Finland's magnificent struggle against the Red Army gave the Roumanians some confidence. French, British and Turkish promises of support gave Bucharest further encouragement. And Comrade Molotov's speech before the Supreme Soviet on March twenty-ninth asserted that the Soviet Union did not plan to recover Bessarabia "by force." Nevertheless, he said that there was "no pact of nonaggression" between the U.S.S.R. and Roumania, and he called attention to the fact that Moscow has never recognized Roumanian occupancy of this disputed province. It might be pointed out that Roumania would hardly be more secure if she had a nonaggression pact with the Soviet Union, because Finland did have such a Soviet guarantee and it proved to be useless. But the danger remains that the longer the war goes on, the greater becomes the possibility that Stalin will use it as an opportunity to move into Roumania.

Turkey is a thorn in Stalin's side in more than his relations with Roumania; Turkey checkmates the Kremlin in other fields. No ruler of Russia, Red or White, can feel that his Black Sea coast is safe as long as the Dardanelles are in other hands. Nor can Stalin look with complacency upon a situation that places the safety of his vital Caucasian oil fields at the mercy of Turkish politicians. The Kremlin has worked for years to make Turkey a satellite, but all that labor appears to have been lost. In October 1939, as we have seen, the Turks joined the Western democracies in a definite alliance.

Stalin is compelled, therefore, to make the acquisition of

the Dardanelles one of the main aims of his foreign policies.
If he can control this enormously important sector, he can
keep hostile fleets out of the Black Sea. He can maintain
his shipping lines from Batum to Russian, Bulgarian and
Roumanian ports. And there is still another reason why
he would like to gain hegemony over Turkey and control
the Dardanelles. His imperialistic ambitions include some
of the countries of the Near East. Stalin, remember, is a
native of Georgia, a province on the threshold of Turkey
and Iran. Soviet agents have been operating in Iran, Iraq
and Afghanistan.

But Turkey is bound to these countries in the pact of
Saadabad. It is a nonaggression treaty, but it probably
goes farther than that. For it is well understood in the
Near East that Turkey would not stand by and permit any
other power (Russia, Italy or Germany) to attack her
friends. Indeed, Turkey probably would fight Russia if
Stalin moved against any of her neighbors. She would do
that as a measure of self-defense. And the Turks are redoubtable soldiers. No longer is their country "the Sick
Man of Europe."

That all has not been quiet in this part of the world
was indicated by an article in *Red Star* in January 1940. It
described an incident on "the southern border" when a
"subversive band" was defeated in its attempt to enter
the Soviet Union. "A carelessly broken twig betrayed the
fighter," said *Red Star*. "One of the bandits rushed to the
water. 'Thou shalt not escape, O viper!' whispered frontier guard Knovalov, and one accurate shot laid the
bandit low. Like beasts the bandits receded to an island,
firing in a disorderly manner. With accurate bullets the
border guards stopped the bandits. Thus was a band of
subversive agents liquidated."

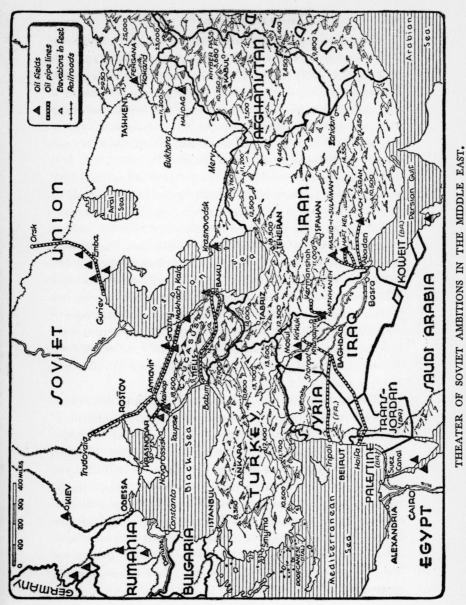

THEATER OF SOVIET AMBITIONS IN THE MIDDLE EAST.

Moscow's suspicion of British activities in the Near and Middle East was set forth in an article (May, 1940) in *Red Fleet*. This Soviet publication charged that: "England is strengthening her positions there by concentration of troops in territories and countries under British influence, through a 'purse' policy of granting loans not only to Turkey but also to Iraq, Iran and Saudi Arabia, and finally by bribing small feudal princes."

Relations between Moscow and Ankara have not been cordial since Foreign Minister Saracoglu's three weeks' sojourn at Moscow in the fall of 1939. *Izvestia* and *Communist Youth Pravda* have published articles deploring the work of "Anglo-French imperialists" in the Near East. *Izvestia* went on to say that Turkey has been "fully drawn into the orbit of Anglo-French influence." The Turks answered that their policies have not changed; they are following the undeviating line marked out by the late President Ataturk. It is Russia, they say, that has changed. And there is nothing they can do about that. They must take all measures to be on guard and wait, in their characteristically fatalistic way, for whatever may come.

Molotov has warned the Supreme Soviet that certain nations in the Black Sea area are "playing with fire." Presumably he was referring to Roumania and Turkey. Stalin can hardly gain much satisfaction from the Turkish situation, but it seems inconceivable that he will drop his attempts to bring Turkey under his control. He is dealing with a crafty, resourceful opponent, backed by the Western powers. Yet the master of the Kremlin is playing for huge imperialistic stakes in the Near East, and he is not likely soon to quit the game. His tactics may change, he may use force or diplomacy, but his goal will remain the same. It is control of the Dardanelles.

CHAPTER XXIV

Berlin-Moscow-Tokio Axis?

The democratic Western powers today play the part of an over-rich capitalist who stubbornly refuses a piece of bread to a hungry man and then screams "aggression," "assault," when the hungry man at last seizes the bread for himself.—HITLER's newspaper, the Voelkischer Beobachter.

WE HAVE DISCUSSED in earlier chapters the plans of German reactionaries—industrialists and militarists—to create a Russo-German coalition. These men hoped to exploit Russia to the profit of the Reich. But there was another element in Germany which also sought close Reich-Soviet ties. These were the Communists and the Left Wing of the Nazi party. The late ill-famed Captain Roehm and his followers have been called National Bolsheviks. They wanted to Bolshevize the Reich. And they favored close ties with the U.S.S.R.

During the closing months of 1938 there emerged still another German group which advocated a Berlin-Moscow deal. They might be called the "opportunists," or the "dynamists." Their leaders are the so-called "wild men" of the Nazi party—von Ribbentrop, Goebbels and Himmler. They have no such deep-seated principles as the former groups; they are not champions of a cause; they are gamblers.

The von Ribbentrop plan envisaged an alliance of the so-called "proletarian nations" against the "plutocracies." Why, asked the von Ribbentrop strategists, should the "have-not" countries fight each other?—a policy that only helps their common enemies, the "haves." Why should they not unite against their victims and divide the loot? Each member of the "proletarian" coalition would receive plunder at the expense of the "satiated" powers. The rich British, French and Dutch empires would be under attack from Scapa Flow to the Yellow Sea.

Five months before the Nazi-Soviet deal was announced the periodical, *Berlin-Rome-Tokio*, published under von Ribbentrop's patronage, asserted: "The world already is forming itself for life after victory over England, and this life has as a beginning and goal a new Europe with strong nations and without the English knout."

At that time the emphasis was on the anti-Comintern alignment. But von Ribbentrop was at work to bring Russia into the accord. In order to do this he was willing to risk the loss of either Italy or Japan. For in the eyes of the von Ribbentrop-Himmler-Goebbels faction the Soviet Union was more important than Italy, Japan, Spain and Hungary combined. If these nations took offense at a Reich-Soviet deal, Germany could afford to lose them providing she won the U.S.S.R. But the Nazi "wild men" saw no reason why Berlin should have to part company with any of the anti-Comintern states.

Von Ribbentrop may have had in mind the *Dreikaiserbund* of Bismarck's day, an entente of the emperors of Germany, Austria and Russia, which Disraeli is said to have termed "the Northern Conspiracy."

After all, the proposed coalition would be an aggregation of states on the march in quest of booty. Italy would reap her share in North Africa; Spain would receive Gibraltar and some of French Morocco; Russia would get Iran, Iraq, perhaps Afghanistan and a share of Turkey; Japan would be deflected from North China (where she came into conflict with the Soviet) southward toward French Indo-China and the Dutch East Indies. India would be divided among the various "proletarian" victors.

Such a coalition was to be based on *Realpolitik*. There would be no genuine friendship among the member nations. Self-interest would be the bond. Von Ribbentrop could stress the assertion that Britons and Frenchmen do not like each other. But the two countries can co-operate, because they are bound by a "community of interests." Germans and Russians, it was argued, have the same incentives for long-range co-operation. To be sure, the Nazis and Soviets are imperialists. But, von Ribbentrop replied, so are the Western democracies. Four decades earlier Britain and France had come near war at the time of the Fashoda affair. Yet they had compromised the issues at stake and saved themselves an expensive conflict.

Once Hitler was won over to the scheme, the "wild men" rushed their negotiations with Moscow. And when the Berlin-Moscow deal was at last a reality von Ribbentrop might have repeated to Stalin the question which Alexander put to Napoleon: "Why did not we two meet earlier?"

Out of the Berlin-Moscow pact has developed some economic co-operation. There has probably been more military collaboration than the world realizes. Although other countries take it for granted that the Reich and the Soviet are co-operating in the economic field, there is much dispute about the details, infinite argument regarding the scope. Those who belittle this totalitarian co-operation call attention to the shortage of food, dearth of certain raw materials and inadequate industrialization in Russia. But, most important of all, they emphasize the backward state of Russian transportation.

All these points may be well taken. At the same time the Germans may obtain enough supplies from the U.S.S.R. to eke out their local production and reserves to enable them to carry on for some time. The end of the Finnish campaign relieved the Russian railways of some stress. In December it was announced from Moscow that Reich-Soviet rail connections had been established at the following frontier towns: Augustowo, Protzken, Malkin, Brest-Litovsk, Zimiatycze, Ravarusskaya, Przemysl and Newzagorz. Because Russian railroads use the broad gage and German roads the standard gage it is necessary to unload Soviet shipments from the Russian cars and reload them into German ones.

But inasmuch as Russians and Germans are impressing Poles into labor corps, the work incidental to the transfer of shipments at the rail points is not an insuperable burden on either Nazis or Soviets. Considerable co-operation between them seems to have developed along the rail line running eastward from Krakow to Lwow, thence southward to the Roumanian border. Up to the time of this writing the Russians appear to have allowed the railroad running through this part of partitioned Poland to remain standard gage as an accommodation to the Germans. It is also reported by usually reliable sources that German police and soldiers guard the trains on their way through this section of Polish territory now incorporated in the U.S.S.R.

When the spring of 1940 came, shipments by way of the Baltic Sea from Leningrad to North German ports started. Russian railways also transported products bound for Germany to Tallinn and Riga, where they were loaded on vessels and sent to the Reich. Other Soviet loadings, notably oil and manganese, were shipped from ports on Russia's east coast of the Black Sea to Roumanian and Bulgarian harbors, where they were reshipped to the Reich. Black Sea shipments for Germany have been, however, in constant danger of interruption by British cruisers which the Turks might admit to this inland sea.

There is also an inland waterway which the Germans and Russians are developing, a canal-river system. A canal has been dug to connect Russia's Dnieper with the Bug. The canal is located not far from Brest-Litovsk of unhappy memory. From there this water course moves westward along the Bug and Vistula to Bromberg (Bydgoszcz). Here it turns northward to the Baltic near Danzig. From a point near Bromberg a canal connects the Vistula to the Netze, thus establishing a route into central Germany. If the Nazis and Soviets wish to equal their 1931 trade peak, they must increase their 1940 commerce thirteen times the 1938 total. This promises to be no easy matter.

We should, I think, take with reservations a boast that appeared last February in Marshal Goering's *Essener Nationalzeitung:* "The Russian-German trade pact is for Germany more than a victorious battle; it is the decisive victory . . . The blockade, as the strongest weapon of attack Britain has against Germany, has been destroyed by the Russian-German pact." Discounting the exaggeration, the Reich is receiving some economic support from the U.S.S.R.

Certainly the Nazis will do everything in their power to

repair Russian railways and speed up Russian mining, farming and lumbering. And we may be sure that Stalin, with a huge stake in keeping the war going, will do all that he can to feed enough products into the Reich's military economy to prevent any near-term collapse in Germany. He will do it even if it entails suffering at home.

In the so-called "cultural" (really ideological) field the Reich and the Soviet have been making rapid progress in their collaboration. Last October it was announced from Moscow that the *Voelkischer Beobachter* would be represented in the Soviet capital. This was, indeed, a startling turn of journalistic affairs. For years, under Alfred Rosenberg's direction, this publication shrieked its hatred of Russia and Bolshevism. Three other German newspapers, the *Fremdenblatt* of Hamburg, the *Neueste Nachrichten* of Leipzig and the *Nationalzeitung* of Essen, were likewise sending representatives to Moscow. In addition to these journals the D.N.B., German official news agency, also was established there. But this appears to have been only a beginning of Nazi-Soviet propaganda co-operation.

Even months after the Berlin-Moscow deal the Western world does not grasp the significance of totalitarian strategy. We are slow to understand the Nazi-Soviet technique; instead of using revolutionary propaganda and penetration as an auxiliary weapon to support their armies, they use their armies as an auxiliary weapon to promote their revolutionary offensive. Their goal is "permanent revolution."

The slogans of the two totalitarian states are so much alike and their sociopolitical philosophies are so similar that some observers believe that the two revolutions are fusing. I think it is more likely that in the end they will join when one is strong enough to take the other over.

Now each believes that it can gain control of the other. The course of the European war will decide the issue whether Moscow shall rule Berlin or whether Berlin shall dominate Moscow. But in either case it will mean a powerful revolutionary movement that is likely to grow progressively more dangerous and destructive to the Old Order in Europe and Asia.

Let us examine briefly a few examples of the similarity of Nazi and Soviet philosophy. "There is no such thing as unconditional liberty in international life." Is that a Nazi or a Soviet pronouncement? It happens to be Nazi, a line from the *Voelkischer Beobachter*. But it might just as easily have appeared in *Pravda*.

Both Nazis and Soviets constantly inveigh against "encirclement."

Hitler has boasted: "I am perhaps the only head of a state who does not even have a bank account." The Fuehrer has described the present war as a conflict between the rich nations on the one side and the poor ones on the other. The latter are waging a "great revolution," actually a "revolt against capitalism." They are destroying the "tyranny of gold." He has described it in these words: "social war between nations, in which the have-nots are fighting the haves for a new division of the world." The German New Year's proclamations were copiously interlarded with such expressions as: "international revolution," "socialistic millennium" and "young and productive nations to which belongs the future."

"Workers of all lands, unite to smash the rule of English capitalism!" That exhortation sounds as if it were taken from Marx and Engels. It might have been cited from the Communist Manifesto. Actually it was uttered on February 13, 1940, by Dr Robert Ley, head of the German Labor

Front. He continues: "You young upward striving nations of the earth, combine to annihilate the old English dragon, who blocks the treasures of the earth and withholds from you the riches of the world!" He savagely attacked "base, despicable capitalism."

A few days before, Dr Ley wrote in the *Angriff:* "Money rules the world. But National Socialism does not acknowledge the rule of money. In National Socialist Germany business, like everything else in this State, is directed by responsible State leadership. And this State leadership is wholly independent of the moneybag."

In the early days of National Socialism there was emphasis upon Germany as a nation. Today the emphasis is on revolution, a world revolution not unlike the Soviet objective. It is clear that Hitler's philosophy is approaching Stalin's more and more. Their goals, their methods, their propaganda—all show striking similarities.

For the past two years certain intelligence services working inside Germany have been reporting to their respective governments that Communists have been systematically penetrating the Nazi Gestapo, Storm Troops and Elite Guard. As to the measure of control which the Communists exercise in these organizations the reports do not agree. But it is an arresting fact that at least one foreign intelligence service advises its government that Himmler's organizations are now controlled by National Bolsheviks —that is, men who are really Communists.

It is also reported on excellent authority that the German Army hierarchy is aware of this situation but has been unable to do anything effective to stop it. Hitler has backed Himmler. And just as long as the Fuehrer supports Himmler, Communist power appears likely to increase inside the

Reich's police and extramilitary organizations. The time may come when Himmler's followers will attempt to take over control of the army itself, much as the Soviet commissars controlled the Red military.

There have also been apparently reliable reports from intelligence services that Hitler has permitted the Comintern to set up propaganda centers in Germany for campaigns against France. Renegade Frenchmen and professional revolutionists are appealing to French workmen to sabotage the republic's war efforts and to revolt against war service both at the front and in factories. Later, perhaps, the Comintern will start a serious campaign to make trouble in Britain. But for all that it would be naïve to assume that the Comintern agents do not take advantage of their residence in Germany to prepare the Reich for Stalinism.

An unpublicized minor trend on the Paris stock exchange may possibly be moving the Soviet toward greater co-operation with Germany. This is the rising price trend of prerevolution Russian securities. Until the beginning of the second World War these issues had been practically valueless. One example of this rise is to be found in Baku Industrials. In August they were quoted at sixteen francs, in December at eighty and in February at two hundred. Other Russian oil stocks have been rising correspondingly.

This quiet interest in Russian holdings undoubtedly leads the Kremlinites to suspect that if the Allies win the war Britain and France may set about on some drastic revisions of the map of Europe. And Moscow has long denounced alleged Franco-British designs upon the rich Caucasus oil preserves.

Both Nazis and Soviets have cogent motives for keeping French, British and Turkish hands off the Russian oil fields. The motives are not identical, but the object is. Reports indicate that General Todt, who built the West Wall for Hitler, has made a tour of the Russo-Turkish frontier to advise the Soviets about the construction of fortifications. Hitler has a heavy stake in this region.

According to the von Ribbentrop plan, the Soviet was to be kept out of the Balkans. The Nazis do not want the Russians at the Dardanelles, because in that situation the Soviets would be established athwart the Reich's "path of destiny." The Balkan region was to be a German sphere. Nazi strategy would encourage a Soviet drive southward into Persia and Iraq, thereby striking the British at a vulnerable spot in Britain's imperial armor. Stalin is believed to be harboring the ambition to do what no previous tsar was ever able to do: break through the line of buffer states that separates Russia from the warm waters of the Persian Gulf and the Indian Ocean. During the early months of the present war the Soviet was known to be exerting economic pressure against Iran, apparently in the effort to prepare the way for political hegemony there. In the attempt to control Iran, Stalin has the blessings of the Nazis and the opposition of the Turks and British.

The von Ribbentrop plan to forge the Nazi-Soviet axis eastward from Moscow to Tokio has met with serious difficulties. Japan's foreign minister, Hachiro Arita, did say in January 1940 that "we intend to make the strongest possible effort to adjust relations with Soviet Russia." And partial settlements have been reached between Moscow and Tokio on two troublemaking problems: the payments still due from Japan for the Chinese Eastern Railway, and a year's extension of the permission given to Japan to

fish in Russian waters. But the Soviet continued to support
the Chinese Nationalists against the Japanese, and Russian
and Japanese soldiers were still skirmishing along their
long, tortuous common frontier.

Meanwhile Japan has been making gestures toward the
Dutch East Indies which have looked suspiciously like
feeling-out processes. Perhaps Tokio wanted to know just
how much opposition she would encounter if her navy
moved down to Dutch Borneo to "restore order," "pursue
bandits" or "drive out Communism." In February the
Japanese Government announced that it had notified the
Netherlands of the abrogation of the 1933 treaty of arbi-
tration and reconciliation. This gesture appeared to be
part of the Nipponese political maneuvers in the "South
Seas." But Mr Arita hastened to reassure anyone made
uneasy by his country's policies that Japan had no intention of seizing the Dutch East Indies. She merely wanted
to "exploit" the natural resources of those islands. The
word "exploit" is, of course, open to broad interpretation
which can turn out to mean aggression.

No one can say in which direction Russo-Japanese relations may develop. Even if renewed fighting on a considerable scale started, that would prove nothing definite.
For such a conflict might be only part of the horse-trading
preliminaries used by two Asiatic powers in their negotiations. Certainly a great deal will depend upon America's
attitude toward Japan. And much will depend upon
Britain's policies toward the Mikado and her success
against Hitler.

That there may be more British "appeasement" of
Japan was intimated by Sir Robert Craigie, British ambassador to Tokio, in a speech late in March 1940. "Our
methods may, in some cases, differ," he told the British-

Japanese Society, "but both countries ultimately are striving for the same object, namely, lasting peace and preservation of our institutions from extraneous subversive influences." And just who may those "extraneous subversive influences" be? The Russians? The Chinese? Who?

In their efforts to woo the Japanese the Nazis find their so-called "Aryan superiority" theory embarrassing. But Himmler's newspaper, the *Schwarze Korps*, shows how that difficulty can be evaded. "Experience has taught us that Latin peoples, yes, even the peoples of distant Japan, are incomparably closer to us in their attitude toward life and their philosophy than our 'Germanic cousins' on the British Isles."

One of the current mysteries of the Far East centers around the lonely, remote Kamandorsky Islands off the coast of Kamchatka. Mr Hallett Abend reported from Shanghai to the New York *Times* that early in 1940 a "large group" of German naval officers visited this Soviet outpost and remained for over a month. He also reported that these islands have been heavily fortified by the Russians and that Japanese "fishing boats" which have ventured into the vicinity have dropped out of sight, never to be seen again.

Many questions naturally arise. Why are Germans and Russians fortifying these bleak islands in the North Pacific? Is it a threat to the Japanese? Or to the Allies? Or to whom? Or can it be part of the von Ribbentrop scheme to divide the Far East into two grand spheres of influence, with Russia taking the northern, Japan the southern sphere? Is it a step in the forging of a Berlin-Moscow-Tokio axis? Or is it just the opposite, preparation for an eventual armed clash between Japan and the Soviet? The answers to these questions are bound up in the superpower politics now being played on a colossal stage that stretches from the Rhine eastward to the Pacific.

The von Ribbentrop plan to forge a gigantic totalitarian axis does not stop with the Reich, the Soviet and Nippon. It takes in a fourth partner, Italy. In early March 1940 the German foreign minister went to Rome on an official visit. On the eighteenth of that month Hitler came to the Italian frontier town of Brennero for a talk with the Duce. In Berlin afterward von Ribbentrop's press aides let it be known that Italy was to be included in a German-Russian-Italian combination of "dynamic" nations that would settle the destinies of Europe. But the Duce has been forced to consider the Vatican and the House of Savoy, two powerful factors in Italy which are opposed to all association with the atheistic, regicide Soviet Union. Some arrangement may yet be forthcoming that will connect Rome and Moscow, via Berlin, under the label of an economic entente or a move to "keep peace in the Balkans."

But it can hardly be said that the U.S.S.R. is popular in Italy. This was demonstrated in reverse when Count Ciano defended Germany's position in the deal with Russia. The Italian foreign minister blamed the British and French for driving the Reich into the pact. By their efforts to win the Soviet as an ally they had "brought Russia back into the arena of international politics." Therefore, the Duce's son-in-law argued, the Allies were to blame for a development that was so unpopular among Italians.

Although a country like Italy is naturally a valuable ally for Germany, it is second rate as compared with the U.S.S.R. If Berlin ever has to choose between the friendship of Rome and Moscow, the German Army and most of the political strategists will choose the Russians. According to the von Ribbentrop plan Rome would be merely a European arm of the Berlin-Moscow coalition, just as Tokio would be an Asiatic arm. For Germany has definitely staked her effort to win the war on the strength of her relations with Russia. That fact gave Joseph Stalin the whip hand.

CHAPTER XXV

Conclusion

The war which began before all the world on May 10 is the greatest of revolutionary wars. An outworn era is crumbling to dust beneath the marching feet of the German army.—ALFRED ROSENBERG.

AT THE TIME of the 1918 Armistice Marshal Foch is said to have remarked: "Gentlemen, the war is postponed for twenty years." Every policy, every act of the Kremlin has been made on the assumption that another great war was inevitable. When it would come, Stalin was determined, he would be prepared to turn it to his advantage.

In a long article in *Bolshevik* during November 1939 Emil Yaroslavsky develops this fundamental Communist thesis. Throughout the years of so-called peace, he says, the capitalist countries did not "ripen" for Communism as quickly as the Soviets wished. But "the first imperialist war so hastened the downfall of tsarism that within eight months the Bolshevik Party was able to organize the workers, peasants and soldiers for the overthrow of capitalism and the dynasties of the Romanovs, Hapsburgs and Hohenzollerns.

"The second imperialist war has already led to the collapse of the patchwork state of Poland and intensified the centrifugal tendencies of the oppressed people of Britain, whose greatest colony, India, demands independence. It will undoubtedly further weaken imperialism and hasten its collapse . . ." Comrade Yaroslavsky exults in the approaching triumph of Sovietism. "Can there be doubt that the Bolsheviki will obtain a full victory for Communism?" he asks. "None, for they will advance under the banner by which they conquered in October 1917, led by Comrade Stalin."

Stripped of its bombast and Stalinist lip service, the Yaroslavsky article is an expression of Soviet rejoicing that the "second imperialist war" has arrived. For it will, he argues, complete the disintegration of capitalism that was carried so far in the first one. And it will duplicate in other countries the triumph of Communism that the Soviet victories scored in Russia.

At the outbreak of the war Stalin's chief concern may well have been that something would happen to precipitate an early peace. In the late days of August the European chancelleries heard whispers that the Reichswehr hierarchy would make a *Putsch* against Hitler, establish a military dictatorship and head off the war. For two days France and Britain postponed their declaration that a state of war existed with Germany. Those were crucial days. The Nazi military machine was smashing its way into Poland. The doomed Poles were crying for help. Why did the Allies wait?

The answer seems to have been General von Fritsch. The French and British knew that the former commander-in-chief of the German Army smarted under the humiliation of his demotion and resented the fact that a former lance corporal was now head of the Reich's army. In August von Fritsch had sent a special agent to France to see Daladier. The insiders in Paris and London believed that on the outbreak of war von Fritsch and his colleagues would lead an army revolt against the Nazis and that they would place Hitler in *Schutzhaft* (protective custody). An immediate attack on Germany might interfere with the von Fritsch plan. Hence the Allied delay in declaring war.

If the French and British knew about von Fritsch's plan, doubtless others did too. On the twenty-third of September it was announced that von Fritsch was killed "leading an offensive reconnaissance patrol before Warsaw." No informed person in Europe believed this. It is not army practice to send a former commander-in-chief out on a scouting patrol with a handful of soldiers. That was certainly not the fate of von Fritsch.

Perhaps he had not even left Germany. The truth is known only to Himmler's men and a few Nazi hierarchs. At any rate, the death of von Fritsch eliminated the foremost personal danger to Hitler. Moreover, the formidable threat of a move to stop the war disappeared. There was no one left to take up the counterrevolutionary role played by von Fritsch. Those who hoped for a long struggle could now breathe more freely.

In Paris, during September, the attaché of a Balkan country told me that his government knew that the Soviet OGPU was guarding Hitler against his enemies within Germany. It sounds fantastic. But power politics and revolutionary dynamics make this a fantastic world. And why would it be so strange for Stalin to take measures to protect the man who is so effectively furthering the ends of Bolshevism? Those OGPU agents may, after all, be Germans in the black uniforms of the *Schutzstaffel*. They may be acting with Himmler's connivance. They may be guarding the Fuehrer's life against Goering's men. Intrigue inside a great dictatorship is more sensational than a Hollywood plot. Witness the Moscow treason trials. Or the bomb explosion in Munich only eleven minutes after Hitler left the hall.

But once the war was under way in earnest, Stalin could rest assured that it was not likely to end abruptly. In several countries there were forces at work to prolong the conflict. Many factors precluded a surrender on either side; many factors made a compromise impossible.

The Western democracies could not accept Hitler's destruction of Poland without acknowledging his hegemony over Europe. Any patched-up peace would merely be a prelude to the next Nazi hammer stroke. The dynamics and economic compulsions of National Socialism render impossible any prolonged appeasement. For a Germany truly appeased and dedicated to the ways of peace would no longer be Nazi.

As for the Germans, surrender to the Allies was unthinkable. The Kremlinites undoubtedly listened with pleasure to reports of the talk in London and Paris about the "atomized" Reich which is to emerge from the next peace conference. They knew of the talk among influential Frenchmen, especially the army leaders, about a Germany cut into small parts, with large tracts of the Reich's present territory given to greater Polish and Czech states.

On the eve of the war a parliamentary leader of a neutral nation bordering Germany told me that he had just returned from London, where he talked with "Churchill and practically everybody." "When Hitler is defeated," he told me, "the British and French will take over the last pine tree in Germany." That sort of talk was bound to filter into the Reich and play into the hands of the Nazis. A sentence like that will be Hitler's trump card when Germans begin to manifest war weariness. He can play it to advantage with even the strongly anti-Nazi people in the Reich. For Germans, Nazi and anti-Nazi alike, do not want the fatherland broken up into small pieces.

The Kremlin oligarchs, too, can count upon German memories of the early postwar era to bolster the Reich's morale throughout a protracted conflict. Now the Nazis can tell the German people that if they surrender to the French and British the blockade will go on just as it did after the last war. And Germans would have no more to eat if they surrendered. Perhaps more than any other factor the memories of the Versailles period strengthen the non-Nazi Germans' will to resist.

Stalin could foresee, moreover, that the social and economic conditions within Germany which put Hitler in power will not be eliminated by his fall. Those conditions will be far worse at the end of a long war. And they will not be confined to Germany. If the British and French should win a complete military victory over the Reich, their real task of saving themselves from economic and social collapse will begin after the last shot is fired. Every true Bolshevik believes that the "second imperialist war" will spell the doom of the Western democracies.

In the event of a German victory, Stalin would probably not face any immediate trouble from Hitler. The Fuehrer would be absorbed in consolidating his loot from the British and French empires. And for aiding the Reich the Soviet would receive its reward in the form of a cut of the plunder in the Near and Middle East.

The Bolsheviks are more intelligent than Nazi hierarchs like Dr Robert Ley. Stalin and his colleagues do not encourage war for war's sake; they bring it on to serve their purpose. Dr Ley, on the other hand, brutally glorifies war. He calls it a "blessing of God, the eternal fount from which new generations of men are born." Ley is a nihilist, a promoter of chaos, one of the Germans who are preparing the destruction of their own fatherland along with Western civilization. Unwittingly these Nazi "wild men" are bearing out the theory that the present crisis in Europe is, in the words of Archibald MacLeish, primarily "a revolt against Western culture."

After their meeting at Tilsit Napoleon wrote to Alexander: "The work of Tilsit will regulate the destinies of the world." With far more reason Hitler could write to Stalin that their pact "will regulate the destinies of the world." But certainly not in the way that Hitler had expected. For every day that war goes on, the Soviet's economic support becomes more essential to a Reich that is being choked by the Allied blockade.

Meanwhile Stalin has used this conflict to subjugate Finland; he is spreading confusion in the belligerent nations; he encourages Germany by promises of economic aid; he keeps alive British "appeasement for Russia"; he works underground in France; he keeps the countries of the Balkans and the Near East in a state of jitters. He wages war, but a revolutionary form of war, on many fronts. He thus supplements the "civil war of the West." If it ever serves the purpose of spreading chaos and Bolshevism, he will not hesitate to come to an agreement with the British. Then he would use the British, just as he has used the Nazis, to further his own ends.

Stalin is vastly more concerned with internal conditions of the warring countries than with action along the Maginot Line or in the North Sea. The front which interests him most is the "second front," in the homes, the factories, the mines, the banks, the farms in the nations at war. He knows that rising taxes, debts, inflation, a declining standard of living, hopelessness are his allies. He knows that they can create more lasting havoc in this war than tanks and bombing planes.

Hitler cleverly turned the class struggle within Germany to his own purpose. And he transferred that conflict from within the Reich to the world stage. There he pits the Germans of all classes in a struggle against the privileged nations. Stalin plans to reap the profits of this combat from all the nations that have been drawn into it. Hitler's repeated "bloodless victories" may turn out to have been Stalin's triumphs. For the Reich today is the spearhead of world revolution.

Adolf Hitler may be the German Kerensky. The Fuehrer may be playing the same role with reference to Stalin in the Reich that Kerensky played with reference to Lenin in Russia. The longer the war goes on, the more this sinister possibility becomes a probability.

According to Dr Alfred V. Kidder of the Carnegie Institution, a plot of the course of human development seemed to show that "our present order is due for a terrific smash and that the next advance will be made by races other than those of western Europe and the United States." Stalin may prove to be the prophet of that advance.

Within the Third Reich there has developed a morbid philosophy of self-destruction which must be taken into consideration in any appraisal of the Russo-German situation. It manifests itself in strange ways. A German ship caught trying to run the Allied blockade is sent to the bottom by its own crew. The commander of the Graf Spee sinks his ship and then commits suicide. These gestures are not regarded by Nazis as acts of cowardice. On the contrary, the men who make them are given seats of honor in Walhalla. Wagnerian opera has been included in the Nazi ideological setup.

The Nazis may have distorted Wagner's philosophy. They may have utterly misunderstood the meaning of his operas. But the significant fact is that Hitler, Rosenberg and Goebbels have exploited Wagner to promulgate their own philosophy of destruction. Their hero is not the brave, chivalrous Siegfried, but the murderous, nihilistic Hagen. Suicide and destruction are powerful motivating influences of National Socialism.

By contrast, it is not destruction but construction that is the keynote of Bolshevism. Construction, that is, in their own sense of the word. And where the Nazis are desperately reckless the Bolsheviks pursue cautious policies. Their strategy is to force their enemies into risking the gambles. Stalin is not influenced by whispering voices; he does not live in a mystic's half world. Hitler is carried away by supernatural myths. He consults astrologers. Stalin, the stark materialist, cold-bloodedly charts his course whether he is planning a purge of Old Bolsheviks or the destruction of the French, German and British gladiators of his "second imperialist war."

The Nazi leaders knew that the invasion of Poland was the start of a gamble that might bring down destruction upon them and their state. They knew that their path of destiny led from one desperate tryst with fate to the next. But their revolutionary dynamics made any other course impossible. Yet if they lost they would lose all. But this win-or-lose-all realization was balanced by their conviction that even if they were destroyed they could at the same time be instruments of destruction. Hitler, von Ribbentrop, Himmler, Goebbels and their fellow Nazis hate the British and French with a consuming violence. These apostles of destruction would not hesitate to thrust a defeated Reich into the waiting arms of Stalin. They know that this war may be Germany's *Götterdämmerung* (Twilight of the Gods).

The chief of the Foreign Affairs Section of the Nazi party and Official Philosopher of the Third Reich, Dr Alfred Rosenberg, throws some light on the Nazi attitude toward the war and the possibility of German defeat. "If we lose," he told me grimly, "our defeat will drag all Europe down into the abyss with us."

Inasmuch as Germany's "Samson psychosis" may spell doom to the Reich and may ultimately destroy the present order in western Europe, it serves the Kremlin's ends. It works against a negotiated peace. It may make Stalin the eventual victor of the "second imperialist war." It threatens either to make a victorious Reich the master of Europe or to incorporate a defeated Reich in the expanding Soviet empire. It promises to answer the question as to which of the two revolutionary imperialisms will gain control of the other.

Index